A Guide

to Virginia Military Organizations in the American Revolution, 1774-1787

Compiled by E. M. Sanchez-Saavedra

HERITAGE BOOKS
2019

HERITAGE BOOKS
AN IMPRINT OF HERITAGE BOOKS, INC.

Books, CDs, and more—Worldwide

For our listing of thousands of titles see our website
at
www.HeritageBooks.com

Published 2019 by
HERITAGE BOOKS, INC.
Publishing Division
5810 Ruatan Street
Berwyn Heights, Md. 20740

Copyright © 1978 by The Library of Virginia

Republished by Heritage Books for The Library of Virginia

All rights reserved. No part of this book may be reproduced or transmitted in any form or by any means, electronic or mechanical, including photocopying, recording or by any information storage and retrieval system without written permission from the author, except for the inclusion of brief quotations in a review.

International Standard Book Number
Paperbound: 978-1-58549-652-5

 *Contents*

Preface		vii
1	The American Military Establishment	3
2	Provincial Forces, 1774-1776	7
3	The Virginia Continental Infantry	27
4	The Additional Continental Regiments, 1777-1781	73
5	Miscellaneous and Special Units and the Partizan Legions	79
6	The Continental Artillery	97
7	The Continental Light Dragoons	101
8	The Virginia State Line	109
9	The Virginia Militia, 1775-1783	137
10	The Virginia State Navy, 1775-1787	149

Appendixes

A.	Virginia Troops at Charleston, South Carolina, 1779-1780	177
B.	Virginia Troops at Yorktown, 1781	183
C.	Loyalist Organizations, 1775-1776	185
D.	A Calendar of Unit Names and Variants	189
E.	Short Titles	195

Notes 197

Index 211

 *Preface*

VIRGINIA'S role in the American Revolution was a complex one; often it was a dominant one. Her statesmen and soldiers were involved in nearly every phase of the political, social, and military upheaval which transformed a group of thirteen isolated English colonies into a unified and independent republic. A Virginian was the second commander in chief of the Continental armies (Artemas Ward was the first) and later the first president of the new nation.

Other Virginians conquered the Old Northwest, fought and won at Stony Point, fought Indians on the Ohio and in Georgia, and stormed the citadel of Quebec. Virginians tasted defeat at Charleston and Camden, suffered hunger and disease at Morristown and Valley Forge, rotted in prison hulks, and died as captives in New York City. Cannon, muskets, and powder for the Continental forces were fabricated in Virginia. Enemy armies twice invaded her, and a major British force surrendered within her borders. The names of Washington, Jefferson, Madison, Monroe, Marshall, and Mason are still venerated; those of Woodford, Lawson, Scott, Weedon, and thousands of others are lost in obscurity. Nevertheless, the future president and the nameless private each shared a common experience, and each played his own unique and vital part.

Men from the Old Dominion served in all branches and services, in those units raised under congressional authority and in those raised by the government of the commonwealth. The Continental and the state military establishments were complicated organizations, each consisting of an often confusing and sometimes bewildering array of regiments, battalions, corps, legions, detachments, and companies—some of them permanent and others temporary. The variety and multiplicity of units has been a source of difficulty and perplexity for historians who have attempted to record which units were engaged in a particular battle or campaign and to identify the units by their correct names. This confusion has often resulted in vague and inexact references to "Weedon's brigade," "Morgan's men," and "the Virginia Line." The present volume attempts to present as complete and accurate an account as possible of Virginia's military participation in the Revolution.

Even the most carefully done works on the subject have flaws and imperfections. The series of articles by C. A. Flagg and W. O. Waters of the Library of Congress, "Virginia's Soldiers in the Revolution," which appeared serially in the *Virginia Magazine of History and Biography* between 1911 and 1914, represents a landmark effort, the first serious attempt to identify the different Continental and state units from Virginia. Flagg and Waters set out to list only officers of field rank and made no effort to include anyone of lower rank than major. Even with this self-imposed limitation, their work contains gaps and discrepancies. After completing the sections on the fifteen numbered Continental regiments, they had to make revisions of their list for the 1st Virginia Regiment on the basis of material that had come to light since the original list appeared.

Another important work in this field was Hamilton J. Eckenrode's *List of the Revolutionary Soldiers of Virginia*, which appeared about the same time as Flagg and Waters's contribution. Eckenrode's work, issued in two volumes, set out to list every soldier and seaman from Virginia who had served in the Revolution, and he documented his lists with references to both manuscript and printed sources. Eckenrode's work was supplemented by John H. Gwathmey's *Historical Register of Virginians in the Revolution,* which appeared in 1938. Gwathmey listed more names than Eckenrode, but he supplied fewer references to his sources. Both Eckenrode and Gwathmey were often vague in identifying military units, and they referred to a particular officer as having "commanded in a state regiment." Gwathmey also tended to put companies on the same level as regiments. Many of his errors stem from the fact that relatively few original muster rolls were available to him.

Each unit treated in these pages has been selected because of its actual or administrative connection with the state. Three battalions of the Georgia Line, for example, were recruited almost completely in Virginia; therefore they are included, even though the officers listed were all Georgians. Units such as Armand's Partizan Legion (initially made up largely of foreign-born volunteers and raised in New York and Pennsylvania) are included because a large number of Virginians joined them or because they were credited to the Virginia Continental quota.

The units are presented according to the priority in which they stood during the Revolution: Continental infantry, artillery, cavalry; state line infantry, artillery, cavalry, militia; navy and marines. Within each section a fairly strict chronological order is observed. Thus, the section on the

Preface

provisional forces raised in 1774-1775 comes before the sections on the regiments ordered by Congress.

Many people were necessarily involved in preparing this work, both in the research and editorial processes. I wish to acknowledge the generous assistance of staff members of the following institutions and organizations: the Virginia State Library, the Virginia Historical Society, the National Archives and Records Service, the National Park Service, the Pennsylvania History and Museum Commission, Colonial Williamsburg, Inc., the William L. Clements Library, and the Company of Military Historians. In addition, the following individuals deserve special mention: Lee A. Wallace, Jr., whose personal encouragement inspired and assisted my research; Patricia P. Hickin and William H. Gaines, Jr., who supervised the early stages of the manuscript; Jon Kukla, who edited the final manuscript for publication; Thomas J. Headlee, Jr., for his valuable research assistance; Anne H. Cresap, Emily J. Williams, and Cynthia A. Miller, who performed the often thankless task of copyediting; Sherryl Johnson Hunt, who prepared the name index; Marko Zlatich and Peter F. Copeland, whose research into military uniforms uncovered many obscure manuscript sources; and my wife Susan, who had to put up with me while the work was in preparation.

E. M. SANCHEZ-SAAVEDRA

A Guide

 *The American Military Establishment*

1

THE regiment was the basic unit in the Continental army, as it had been in the English army since Cromwell's time. As will be evident in the guide sections that follow, the term *regiment* was used interchangeably with *battalion* throughout the Revolution. In September 1776 Congress established the size of the Continental army at eighty-eight battalions, fifteen of which were assigned as Virginia's quota. The fifteen numbered units that Virginia actually sent into congressional service, however, were officially designated regiments. According to established British custom, a battalion was one-half of a regiment. Since most American regiments were chronically below the prescribed strength of 680 men, the use of the word was not inaccurate.

The basic units that composed a regiment were companies, each commanded by a captain. Ten companies, each of sixty-eight men, made up a full regiment. Generally, the captains recruited their own companies and were commissioned after raising a set quota of men, usually about twenty. Because of this procedure it is possible, if one knows the captain's county of residence, to determine the area in which a given company was raised.

All the regiments or units from a given state were referred to collectively as that state's *line*, a term derived from the tactical line of battle which was still very much a part of eighteenth-century warfare. The Virginia forces in Continental service were thus designated "the Virginia Line on Continental Establishment," and the entire American army was generally known as "the Continental Line."

Virginia and several other states also raised individual state lines. These were made up of regular troops paid by the state governments for local defense, and they were distinct from the common militia. The 1st Virginia Continental Regiment and the 1st Virginia State Regiment were separate organizations, one paid by Congress and the other by the Virginia General

Assembly. There would be no reason to confuse the two if the local units had remained within the state boundaries, as specified in the legislative acts that created them; however, most of the state line regiments were called into temporary congressional service, beginning in 1777, to replace Continental units which had been captured.

In addition to their official names, many Virginia units also had unofficial designations and local nicknames. On muster rolls and in dispatches, for example, the 8th Virginia Continental Regiment also appears as "the German Regiment" and as "Muhlenburg's Regiment." In the guide sections, these local designations are listed after the official regimental names.

Virginia raised men for other branches of service besides the infantry (or foot soldiers). There were also cavalry (light dragoons) and artillery, as well as engineers (sappers and miners), artificers, riflemen, grenadiers, light infantry, and pioneers. Each branch performed specialized functions and required arms and equipment other than the infantry musket and bayonet. These branches will be dealt with under the appropriate sections of the guide.

All branches of service were bound, to a greater or lesser degree, by the strict formalities of "civilized" warfare that characterized eighteenth-century conflicts. The Revolution was a war in which Sir William Howe could lose his lapdog at Germantown and have it returned with the compliments of George Washington. It was also a war in which Burgoyne's Indian allies and Butler's Loyalist Rangers could scalp women and commit other atrocities against noncombatants. This dichotomy of the old and the new is well illustrated by the battles of Kings Mountain and Yorktown, fought a year apart. Kings Mountain exemplified the harsh guerilla warfare waged on the frontier. The techniques of camouflage, sharpshooting, and infighting used by the "over-the-mountain men" differed little from combat practices in Vietnam and elsewhere. Yet a year later, in October 1781, Washington's army besieged Cornwallis at Yorktown, using Vauban's classic seventeenth-century methods of fortification. The trenches, salients, and parallels dug by French and American sappers would not have been unfamiliar to Gustavus Adolphus or the duke of Marlborough.

Between these two extremes were the customs and tactics practiced by average American regiments. The internal organization of these units—the subject matter of the present guide—was an outgrowth of the line-of-battle concept, which in turn was based on the capabilities of the musket. This weapon, lighter than the old arquebus and heavier than modern infantry rifles, was only moderately accurate at distances over fifty yards. Both the English Brown Bess and the French Charleville muskets consisted of an iron barrel (plugged at one end), a flintlock mechanism, a ramrod, and a wooden stock that extended to within an inch or two of the muzzle. The principal differences between the two styles lay in the calibers (about .75 for the

English and .69 for the French) and in the method of attaching the barrel to the stock (pins for the English and barrel bands for the French). All infantry muskets used during the war resembled one or the other of the two styles.

Assuming that the soldier kept his powder dry and his flints sharp, he could be expected to fire his weapon from one to five times per minute under most weather conditions. To compensate for the wobbly flight of round bullets fired from smooth barrels, the line-of-battle formation evolved. This involved lining all the available soldiers in ranks, shoulder to shoulder. The manual of loading and firing was performed slowly on voice commands, enabling the entire line to fire simultaneously in volleys. Even if no soldier hit the man at whom he pointed his musket, the hail of lead from such a volley usually proved devastating to the opposing line of battle. The average engagement usually involved two or three volleys from each side, followed by a bayonet charge. Bayonets were long steel spikes, triangular in cross-section, which were fitted to the muskets by cylindrical sockets. Considering the unpredictable nature of the musket, it is not surprising that most tacticians considered the bayonet a superior weapon.

In the line of battle, as well as on parade, regiments and companies were arranged according to the seniority of their commanders. Traditionally, the right flank was the post of honor, and the eldest captain, who commanded the first company, was stationed on the right. A British custom, whereby the colonel, lieutenant colonel, and major each commanded a company, was adopted in the Virginia Continental Line after September 1778.

From 1775 to 1780 the line of battle in the American army was subject to considerable regional variation, due in part to the wide range of early drill manuals available. The Virginia troops used Harvey's *Manual Exercise As Ordered by his Brittanic Majesty in 1764* for instruction in musketry and Humphrey Bland's *Treatise of Military Discipline,* published in 1740, for battalion exercises. The same wide range of available manuals held true for the other colonies-turned-states. Massachusetts militiamen performed simplified maneuvers according to a manual by Timothy Pickering, while the Georgia battalions struggled with the *Highland Military Discipline* of 1757.

In 1779 Friedrich Wilhelm Ludolf Gerhard Augustin, baron von Steuben, the drillmaster of the Continental army, reduced this plethora of manuals into a semblance of order, added bits of the Prussian discipline, which he knew best, and created the famous "blue book," officially entitled *Regulations for the Order and Discipline of the Troops of the United States.* Von Steuben's comments on line of battle, regimental organization, and company drill (school of the soldier) are concise:

> A Company is to be formed in two ranks, at one pace distance, with the tallest men in the rear, and both ranks sized, with the shortest men of each in the centre . . . the captain to take post on the right of the first platoon, covered by a serjeant;

the lieutenant on the right of the first platoon, covered by a serjeant; the lieutenant on the right of the second platoon, also covered by a serjeant; the ensign four paces behind the centre of the company. . . .

A Regiment is to consist of eight companies, which are to be posted in the following order, from right to left.

    First Captain's
    Colonel's
    Fourth Captain's
    Major's
    Third Captain's
    Lieutenant Colonel's
    Fifth Captain's
    Second Captain's

. . . each regiment consisting of more than one hundred and sixty files [enlisted men] is to be formed in two battalions, with an interval of twenty paces between them, and one colour [flag] posted in the centre of each battalion; the colonel fifteen paces before the centre of the first battalion; the lieutenant colonel fifteen paces before the centre of the second battalion; the major fifteen paces behind the interval of the two battalions; the adjutant two paces from the major; the drum and fife-major two paces behind the centre of the first battalion; their places behind the second battalion being supplied by a drum and fife; and the other drums and fifes equally divided on the wings of each battalion.

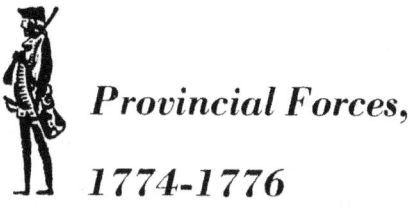

Provincial Forces, 1774-1776

2

Independent Volunteer Companies, 1774-1776

IN the fall of 1774 small numbers of well-to-do young men throughout Virginia organized themselves into companies of "gentlemen independents," ostensibly to prepare for an attack by Shawnee Indians. By the time they procured weapons, uniforms, and drill manuals, Andrew Lewis's militia regiments had defeated Chief Cornstalk at Point Pleasant and ended the immediate threat. After discovering the fun of being peacetime soldiers, however, the youths were loath to disband, so a few of the volunteers in Prince William and Norfolk counties remained mobilized.

In April 1775 Governor Dunmore infuriated the leading rebels by removing the public gunpowder in Williamsburg to safety aboard a British ship. Imitating the volunteers of 1774, young men all over the colony hastily organized vigilante companies and planned to march on the capital and recover the powder. In the midst of the oratory and "patriotick" imbibing, only one company—Patrick Henry's Hanover Gentlemen Independents— actually reached the vicinity of Williamsburg, and they turned back only after they received reimbursement for the powder. All the others returned home on the advice of George Washington, who had been asked to lead them.

Two months later the third Virginia convention created the minute service and ordered the independent companies to disband. The colony was divided into sixteen recruiting districts, each of which was expected to raise one battalion of 500 minutemen. (Because of its exposed situation, the

Eastern Shore battalion was to number 680 rank and file.) Each county was governed by a committee of safety, subordinate to the central Committee of Safety, which acted as the executive branch of the convention. The local committees were in charge of raising and equipping the minute companies.

The central Committee of Safety raised two special battalions of minutemen in May 1776 to assist in the defense of North Carolina. Although the expedition was called off, the 2d Battalion was later sent to the southwestern frontier to discourage Cherokee raiding parties. A third battalion was raised in August but disbanded in December 1776 along with the other remnants of the minute service.

The Independent Companies of Williamsburg, 1775

The Williamsburg Volunteers. A volunteer company existed in Williamsburg at least by April 1775, and perhaps as early as 1774. James Innes (later to become a member of both the Virginia Board of War and the navy board, lieutenant colonel of the 15th Virginia Regiment, and attorney general of Virginia) was chosen captain. The company failed to prevent the theft of gunpowder from the public magazine on the night of April 15, 1775. Two months later, shortly before Lord Dunmore's flight to the comparative safety of H.M.S. *Fowey,* the House of Burgesses ordered Captain Innes to mount a special guard over the magazine and its remaining contents.[1]

The Williamsburg Boys' Company. The activity of the second of Williamsburg's volunteer units, the Boys' Company, prompted this order. On June 3, 1775, a number of youths broke into the magazine to steal guns, and in doing so, set off a booby trap placed there by Lord Dunmore's secret orders to the keeper of the magazine. It consisted of a shotgun wired in such a way that opening the door pulled the trigger. Three of the boys were injured, but their companions were not deterred. Two nights later fourteen-year-old "Captain" Henry Nicholson led a second foray and succeeded in pilfering about fifty Indian trade muskets with blue-painted stocks.[2]

The Independent Company of the Town of Fredericksburg, 1775

       Captain Hugh Mercer
       1st Lieutenant George Weedon
       2d Lieutenant Alexander Spotswood
       Ensign John Willis

On April 24, 1775, a group of gentlemen volunteers met in Fredericksburg and pledged themselves to recover the powder taken from the magazine at Williamsburg. The Fredericksburg company, equipped as light cavalrymen, was joined by a number of like-minded volunteers from Fairfax and Prince William counties. As he had advised other volunteers, Colonel Washington asked these patriots to stay home.

Unlike the Hanover company, they obeyed. Hugh Mercer became colonel of the Caroline District Minute Battalion on September 12, 1775, and afterwards became colonel and brigadier general in the Continental Line. He was killed leading his troops at Princeton in January 1777. Both George Weedon and Alexander Spotswood also became brigadier generals in Continental and state service during the war. John Willis rose to a major's command in the 5th Virginia Regiment of Foot in 1779.[3]

The Independent Company of Prince William

(Independent Company of Cadets), 1774-1775

Captain William Grayson
Captain Philip Richard Francis Lee

On November 11, 1774, an independent company of cadets was organized among the gentry of Prince William County. After adopting a uniform based on one designed by George Washington in the French and Indian War, they took the King's Regulations of 1764 (also presented by Washington) as their drill manual. Washington even assisted the officers in procuring their uniforms.

The Prince William company adopted the motto Aut Liber, Aut Nullus and used it on their colors and drums. With some of the other independent companies, it took part in the abortive march on Williamsburg in April 1775 but turned back on Washington's orders.[4]

The Independent Company of Caroline, 1775

Captain William Woodford
Adjutant Thomas Davis

This company was probably organized in February or March 1775. On August 11, 1775, Purdie's *Virginia Gazette* reported that Woodford's company "went through the manual exercise, with a great variety of new and useful evolutions, at the Bowling Green in that county, before upwards of 1500 spectators, who were exceedingly pleased with the dexterity and alertness of the men, they performing only by the beat of the drum. . . ."

Later in the month Edmund Pendleton, a distinguished citizen of the county, presented the company with a "stand of colours, a drum and two fifes" to remedy the deficiencies in field music.

Presumably the company was incorporated into the Caroline District

Minute Battalion and later into the 2d Virginia Regiment of Foot. Woodford was commissioned colonel of the 2d Regiment in February 1776.[5]

The Independent Company of Albemarle, 1775

>Captain Charles Lewis, April-July 11, 1775
>1st Lieutenant George Gilmer, April-July 11, 1775
>2d Lieutenant John Marks, April-July 11, 1775
>Ensign William Wood
>Sergeants John Martin and William Terrill Lewis
>Corporals Thomas Martin, Jr., Pat[rick] Napier, David Allen, and F. W. Wills

The Independent Company of Albemarle County was organized in Charlottesville before April 29, 1775. It mustered twenty-three privates at first, and later thirty-four. Each volunteer swore to attend musters four times a year and to equip himself with gun, shot pouch, powder horn, and hunting shirt.

Under Lieutenant Gilmer the company prepared to take part in the march to Williamsburg. Colonel George Washington's circular letter telling the volunteers to remain at home reached them en route, and the men returned to Charlottesville.

On July 11 the company was organized as part of the Buckingham District Minute Battalion. Captain Lewis became lieutenant colonel of the battalion and, in 1776, colonel of the 2d Minute Battalion. Lieutenant Gilmer rejoined the Albemarle militia after serving briefly in the minutemen; Lieutenant Marks joined the 2d Virginia Regiment of Foot as a captain in late 1775.[6]

The Independent Company of Fairfax, 1774-1775

>Captain William Ramsey, 1774
>Captain James Hendricks, 1775
>1st Lieutenant Robert Hanson Harrison, 1774
>1st Lieutenant George Gilpin, 1775
>2d Lieutenant John Fitzgerald, 1775

On September 21, 1774, a committee of "Gentlemen and Freeholders" of Fairfax County met at the courthouse in Alexandria to organize the Fairfax Independent Company of "Voluntiers," which was not to exceed one hundred men.

Pinckney's *Virginia Gazette* said of them in October:

> . . . a number of gentlemen in Fairfax county, Virginia being alarmed in this time of extreme danger with the Indian enemy in

their own country, and threatened with the destruction of their civil rights and liberties, and all that is dear to British subjects and freemen, are determined to use their utmost endeavours to make themselves masters of the military exercise, and to hold themselves in readiness in case of necessity, hostile invasion, or real danger of the community, of which they are members, to defend to the utmost of their power, the legal properties of our sovereign king George the third, and the just rights and privileges of their country, their posterity and themselves, upon the principles of the British Constitution.[7]

The Fairfax Independents joined the Fredericksburg and Prince William companies in the abortive expedition to Williamsburg in April 1775 but turned back when advised by Colonel George Washington to do so.

The Independent Company of Hanover, 1774?-1775

Captain Samuel Meredith, resigned May 2, 1775
Captain Patrick Henry, May-June 1775
Lieutenant Samuel Meredith (formerly captain), May-June 1775
Ensign Parke Goodall, May-June 1775

Of all the independent companies raised in response to Dunmore's seizure of the public powder, only the Hanover Gentlemen Independents took any real action. This unit had been organized earlier by Samuel Meredith, who resigned his command in favor of Patrick Henry, whose fiery oratory had aroused the gentlemen independents for a march on the capital; Meredith served thereafter as a lieutenant.

The company got as far as Duncastle's Ordinary (now Barhamsville) in New Kent County, where they camped the night of May 3. There they were persuaded by more moderate men to stop their advance and accept payment for the lost powder. Henry and his followers returned to Hanover in triumph, and most of the members of the company were later absorbed into the minute service. Their captain went on to become the first governor of the commonwealth of Virginia.[8]

Minute Service, 1775-1776[9]

Minute Service Recruiting Districts, 1775-1776

Accomack   Accomack and Northampton counties
Amelia   Amelia, Chesterfield, and Cumberland counties

Berkeley   Berkeley, Frederick, Dunmore, and Hampshire counties
Buckingham   Buckingham, Amherst, Albemarle, and Augusta counties
Caroline   Caroline, Spotsylvania, King George, and Stafford counties
Culpeper   Culpeper, Orange, and Fauquier counties
Elizabeth City   Elizabeth City, Warwick, York, James City, Charles City, and New Kent counties and the city of Williamsburg.
Gloucester   Gloucester, Middlesex, Essex, King and Queen, and King William counties
Henrico   Henrico, Hanover, Goochland, and Louisa counties
Lancaster   Lancaster, Northumberland, Westmoreland, and Richmond counties
Mecklenburg   Mecklenburg, Lunenburg, Charlotte, Halifax, and Prince Edward counties
Pittsylvania   Pittsylvania, Fincastle, Bedford, and Botetourt counties
Prince William   Prince William, Fairfax, and Loudoun counties
Princess Anne   Princess Anne, Norfolk, Nansemond, and Isle of Wight counties and Norfolk Borough
Southampton   Southampton, Sussex, Surry, Brunswick, Prince George, and Dinwiddie counties
West Augusta   the district of West Augusta

Accomack District Battalion

(Counties of Accomack and Northampton)

Field Officers

(Names unknown)

    The Accomack District, comprising the entire Virginia Eastern Shore, was ordered by the convention to raise a regiment of 680 men, unlike the other districts, whose battalions were to number 500 men. The vulnerability of the Eastern Shore to naval attacks made a larger force desirable. Recruiters for the minute service in the district soon ran into difficulties. Burgess Southey Simpson, of Accomack, complained to the convention on November 30, 1775, that "altho' the County almost to a man are ready to embody themselves as a Militia, yet we find insuperable Difficulties in forming our companies of Minute-men. Not one is yet compleated. . . ." In the same month the Northampton committee of safety wrote to the delegates in Congress that their people "were averse to the minute service."[10]

    The Eastern Shore apparently failed to raise an actual minute battalion, since only two companies were in existence by February 1776. Meanwhile, in December 1775, the convention had repealed the portion of its July ordinance concerning the Accomack District Battalion and substituted a provision for a regular regiment (later numbered the 9th Virginia Regiment of Foot). The recruiters for the so-called Eastern Shore Regiment encountered none of the difficulties which the minute service recruiters had faced, and enlistments were sufficient to fill the regiment. (See "9th Virginia Continental Regiment.")

Companies, July 1775-February 1776
Captain John Cropper, Accomack County
Captain William Henry, Northampton County

Amelia District Battalion

(Counties of Amelia, Chesterfield, and Cumberland)

Field Officers
Colonel Archibald Cary, 1775-1776
Lieutenant Colonel (name unknown)
Major Richard James, 1775-June 1776 (transferred to 1st Battalion)
Adjutant Littleberry Mosby, July 1776
Paymaster Thomas Randolph, 1775-1776

By October 30, 1775, the Amelia Battalion had raised three full companies in Chesterfield County, one in Amelia, and one in Cumberland. That month the two Chesterfield companies were ordered to Williamsburg. Seven others were raised later. The Amelia Battalion was divided between the 1st and 2d battalions of minutemen in August 1776.

Companies, October 1775-December 1776
Captain John Markham, Chesterfield County, October 1775
Captain William Randolph, Chesterfield County, October 1775
Captain Samuel Sherwin, Amelia County, October 1775
Captain Joseph Carrington, Cumberland County, October 1775
Captain Francis Goode, Chesterfield County, November 1775
Captain Edward Carrington, Cumberland County, December 1775
Captain Ralph Faulkner, Amelia County, late 1775
Captain Lewellin Jones, Amelia County, May 1776
Captain (?) Stevens, (?) County, June 1776
Captain Charles Fleming, Cumberland County, 1776 (later commanded by Captain William Turpin)

Berkeley District Battalion

(Counties of Berkeley, Frederick, Dunmore, and Hampshire)

Although the convention ordered a minute battalion raised in the

Berkeley District, the threat of Indian attack in those counties precluded the formation of an organized minute service. Since most of the male inhabitants were already on active militia duty following Dunmore's War of 1774, the convention made no effort to enforce its orders. Several companies of regulars, mostly riflemen, were organized from the district in late 1775 and throughout 1776 and 1777. These units joined the Continental army. (See "Colonel Hugh Stephenson's Virginia and Maryland Rifle Battalion," "Colonel Daniel Morgan's Battalion of Riflemen," and "11th Virginia Continental Regiment.")

Buckingham District Battalion

(Counties of Buckingham, Amherst, Albemarle, and Augusta)

Field Officers

Colonel George Mathews, September 1775
Lieutenant Colonel Charles Lewis, September 1775 (commissioned colonel, 2d Battalion of Minutemen, May 10, 1776)
Major Daniel Gaines, September 1775
Commissary Thomas Patterson, September 1775
Paymaster Gabriel Penn, March 1776

The Buckingham District Battalion was organized in September 1775, using the old Independent Company of Albemarle as a nucleus. The battalion held its first muster near Rockfish Gap in mid-September. Enlistments in the regular service depleted the battalion, and five of its companies were merged into the 2d Minute Battalion, commanded by Colonel Charles Lewis.

Companies, September 1775-May 1776

Captain Nicholas Cabell, Amherst County, September 1775
Captain Gabriel Penn, Amherst County, September 1775
Captain Abraham Penn, Amherst County, September 1775
Captain Henry Bell, Buckingham County, September 1775
Captain Charles Moore, Buckingham County, September 1775
Captain Benjamin Harrison, Augusta County, September 1775
Captain Daniel Stephenson, Augusta County, September 1775
Captain Alex[ander] Long, Augusta County, September 1775
Captain Nicholas Lewis, Albemarle County, September 1775
Captain John Ware, Albemarle County, September 1775
Captain Roger Thompson, Albemarle County, September 1775
Captain Henry Christian, Amherst County, November 1775

Caroline District Battalion

(Counties of Caroline, Spotsylvania, King George, and Stafford)

Field Officers

Colonel Hugh Mercer, September 1775-February 1776
Colonel Richard Johnson, February 1776-September 1776
Lieutenant Colonel Mordecai Buckner, September 1775-February 1776
Lieutenant Colonel Lewis Willis, February 1776-September 1776
Major Richard Johnson, September 1775-February 1776
Major Andrew Buchanan, February 1776-September 1776
Adjutant John Francis Mercer, 1776
Quartermaster Thomas Towles, 1776
Paymaster John Taylor, March 1776
Commissary Charles Washington, 1775

Although organized in September 1775, the Caroline Battalion was not called into active service for almost a year. Very soon thereafter, in September 1776, the newly raised 3d Minute Battalion absorbed five companies from the Caroline District.

Companies, September 1775-September 1776

Captain George Stubblefield, Spotsylvania County, late 1775
Captain Andrew Buchanan, Caroline County, late 1775
Captain John Taliaferro, Caroline County, September 1775
Captain Oliver Towles, Spotsylvania County, 1775
Captain Francis Taliaferro, Spotsylvania County, 1775
Captain Walter Vowles, King George or Caroline County, 1775
Captain John Mountjoy, Stafford County, 1776
Captain Vivion Minor, Caroline County, 1776
Captain Thomas Minor, Spotsylvania County, 1775

Captain William Woodford's Caroline Independent Company of 1775 is included in the Caroline Battalion in some sources. (*See* "Independent Virginia Frontier Companies.")

Culpeper District Battalion

(Counties of Culpeper, Orange, and Fauquier)

Field Officers

Colonel Lawrence Taliaferro, 1775
Lieutenant Colonel Edward Stevens, 1775
Major Thomas Marshall, 1775
Paymasters Henry Field, John Slaughter, 1776
Surgeon (Dr.) Samuel Boyd, April 1776

The largest and best known of the minute battalions was raised in the Culpeper District. Its distinctive flag had in the center a rattlesnake coiled to strike. Below it were the words, "Don't tread on me!" at the sides, "Liberty or Death!" and at the top, "The Culpeper Minute Men." Colonel Patrick Henry, acting as commander in chief of the Virginia forces, ordered the separate minute companies in the district to rendezvous about half a mile from present-day Culpeper Court House and to form into a battalion under Lawrence Taliaferro, of Orange County; Edward Stevens, of Culpeper; and Thomas Marshall, of Fauquier. In the fall of 1775 the new battalion, numbering about 350 men, marched to Williamsburg to join the main body of Virginia troops. About 150 men under Captain Joseph Spencer were sent to Norfolk County, where they participated in the battle of Great Bridge on December 9, 1775. During the bombardment of Norfolk on New Year's Day, 1776, two of Captain Abraham Buford's men were killed.

The Culpeper Battalion was eventually composed of fourteen companies, mostly riflemen. Among its more illustrious members was future Chief Justice John Marshall, son of Thomas Marshall, battalion major, who served as a lieutenant in Captain William Taliaferro's company.[11]

Companies, 1775-1776

Captain Joseph Spencer, Orange County, October 1775
Captain James Jameson, Culpeper County, October 1775
Captain James Slaughter, Culpeper County, late 1775
Captain Elias Edmonds, Fauquier County, June-December 1776
Captain William Payne, Fauquier County, October 1775
Captain William Pickett, Fauquier County, October 1775
Captain William McClanachan, Culpeper County, October 1775
Captain Francis Triplett, Fauquier County, October 1775
Captain John Chilton, Fauquier County(?), October 1775
Captain John Blackwell, Jr., Fauquier County (?), October 1775
Captain Abraham Buford, Culpeper County, November 1775
Captain John Williams, Orange County, October 1775
Captain George Johnston, Fauquier County, October 1775
Captain James Scott, Culpeper County, late 1775

Captain John Green (Riflemen), Culpeper County, 1775 (originally a minute company, it joined the 1st Virginia Regiment in September 1775).

Elizabeth City District Battalion

(Counties of Elizabeth City, Warwick, York, James City, Charles City, New Kent, and the city of Williamsburg)

Field Officers
Colonel Champion Travis, September 11, 1775
Lieutenant Colonel Hugh Nelson, September 11, 1775
Major Samuel Harwood, September 11, 1775

By September 16, 1775, according to Dixon and Hunter's *Virginia Gazette*, a minute battalion had been formed in Elizabeth City District. Champion Travis, of Jamestown, later a commissioner of the state navy board, was chosen colonel. Several companies were added during its service on the Peninsula and around Hampton Roads.

Companies, September 1775-August 1776
Captain Robert Anderson, Williamsburg, September 1775
Captain John Cary, Elizabeth City County, September 1775
Captain Richard Cary, Warwick County, September 1775
Captain William Sheldon Sclater, York County, September 1775
Captain William Goosley, York County, September 1775
Captain John Walker, James City County, September 1775
Captain John Tyler, Charles City County, September 1775
Captain Thomas Massie, New Kent County, September 1775
Captain William Gregory, Charles City County, late 1775
Captain Andrew Anderson, New Kent County, September 1775
Captain Walter Hopkins, New Kent County, late 1775
Captain Turner Southall, Charles City County, September 1775
Captain Miles King, Elizabeth City County, March 1776
Captain (?) Nicholas, Williamsburg(?), October 1775

Gloucester District Battalion

(Counties of Gloucester, Middlesex, Essex, King and Queen, and King William)

Field Officers
Colonel (name unknown)
Lieutenant Colonel Thomas Elliott

Major (name unknown)
Adjutant William Taliaferro, late 1775-1776
Adjutant Richard Stevens, October 1776
Paymaster John Quarles
Recruiter Benjamin Temple, November 1775

Most of the companies in the Gloucester Battalion were on active duty at Gloucester Court House from late 1775 through March 1776. Several of the officers and men took part in the small skirmish at Kemp's Landing in Princess Anne County on October 19, 1775, where Captain Mathews was captured by Dunmore's troops. Other companies served at Hampton and at Point Comfort.

Companies, November 1775-December 1776

Captain William Smith, Gloucester County, late 1775
Captain Gregory Smith (formerly under Captain William Smith), March 1776
Captain Mordecai Throckmorton, Gloucester County, May 1776
Captain Drury Ragsdale, King William County, late 1775
Captain Benjamin Temple, King William County, October 1775
Captain Richard Mathews, Gloucester County, October 1775
Captain George Lyne, King and Queen County, September 1775
Captain John Sayres, Gloucester or Middlesex County, October 1775
Captain Thomas Peyton, Gloucester County, prior to May 1776
Captain Robert Cary, Gloucester County, June 1776
Captain John Thruston, Gloucester County, January 1776
Captain William Richards, King and Queen County, June 1776
Captain Philip Taliaferro, King and Queen County, June 1776
Captain Warner Lewis, Jr., Gloucester County, February 1776
Captain John Pleasants, King and Queen County, March 1776

Henrico District Battalion

(Counties of Henrico, Hanover, Goochland, and Louisa)

Field Officers

Colonel (name unknown)
Lieutenant Colonel (name unknown)
Major (name unknown)
Quartermaster Richard Anderson

The Henrico Battalion does not seem to have been well organized, although at least five companies were in service by 1776.

Companies, December 1775-December 1776
Captain Charles Dabney, Louisa County, December 1775
Captain James Dabney, Louisa County, April 1776
Captain John Winston, Hanover County, 1776
Captain William Duval, Hanover or Henrico County, March 1776
Captain Garrett Minor, Louisa County, October 1776

Lancaster District Battalion

(Counties of Lancaster, Northumberland, Westmoreland, and Richmond)

Field Officers
Colonel Thomas Jones, November 1775-early 1776
Colonel William Peachey, March 1776
Lieutenant Colonel Peter Presley Thornton
Major (name unknown)
Paymasters William Beale and John McKay
Commissary John Lawson, July 1776

In May and June 1776 nearly all minutemen from the Lancaster Battalion were called into active service to stop Lord Dunmore's forays along the shores of the Potomac and Rappahannock rivers. Three companies were stationed in Northumberland County, two in Westmoreland County, and a detachment of twenty-five men in Richmond County. After Dunmore's defeat at Gwynn's Island, the Committee of Safety discharged the Lancaster Battalion from active service.

Companies, November 1775-August 1776
Captain Richard Bernard's "upper company," Westmoreland County, November 1775. Bernard was commissioned a captain in the 5th Virginia Regiment in February 1776.
Captain William Augustine Washington, February 5, 1776 (formerly under Captain Bernard)
Captain William Tabb's "lower Company," Westmoreland County, November 1775
Captain William Lee, Lancaster(?) County, June 20, 1776
Captain William Middleton, Westmoreland County, August 1776 (formerly under Captain Tabb)
Captain John Berryman, Lancaster County, June 1776
Captain John Taylor, Lancaster County, June 1776
Captain William Nelson, Westmoreland County, 1776

Mecklenburg District Battalion

(Counties of Mecklenburg, Lunenburg, Charlotte, Halifax, and Prince Edward)

Field Officers
Colonel (name unknown)
Lieutenant Colonel (name unknown)
Major John Glenn, June 10, 1776

The Mecklenburg Battalion probably was organized during February 1776. On March 5, a "sett of colours" for the battalion was purchased from James Slate. Within three or four months after their organization, the Mecklenburg District minutemen were divided between the 1st and 2d battalions of minutemen.

Companies, February-June 1776
Captain John Ballard, Mecklenburg County, 1st Battalion Minutemen
Captain James Anderson, Mecklenburg County, 1st Battalion Minutemen
Captain John Glenn, Lunenburg County, 2d Battalion Minutemen
Captain Robert Dixon, Lunenburg County, 2d Battalion Minutemen
Captain Samuel Garland, Lunenburg County, 2d Battalion Minutemen
Captain Thomas Collier, Charlotte County, 2d Battalion Minutemen
Captain Peter Rogers, Halifax County, 2d Battalion Minutemen
Captain James Turner, Halifax County, 2d Battalion Minutemen
Captain Charles Allen, Prince Edward County, 1st Battalion Minutemen
Captain David Garland, Lunenburg County(?), June 1776

Pittsylvania District Battalion

(Counties of Pittsylvania, Fincastle, Bedford, and Botetourt)

Field Officers
Colonel (name unknown)
Lieutenant Colonel (name unknown)
Major (name unknown)

As in other frontier districts, the men of the Pittsylvania District were primarily concerned with defense against the Indians during and after Dunmore's War. Nevertheless, some companies of minutemen were raised, although no district battalion was ever fully completed. Both companies from Pittsylvania were assigned to the 2d Battalion of Minutemen in mid-1776.

Companies, April-July 1776
Captain Thomas Dillard, Pittsylvania County, April 1776
Captain Peter Perkins, Pittsylvania County, 1776
Captain Charles Lynch, Bedford County, 1776

An independent company from Botetourt, under Captain Matthew Arbuckle, served at Fort Pitt. (*See* "Independent Virginia Frontier Companies.")

Princess Anne District Battalion

(Counties of Princess Anne, Norfolk, Nansemond, and Isle of Wight and Norfolk Borough)

Field Officers
Colonel Joseph Hutchings, captured November 1775
Colonel Anthony Lawson, captured November 1775
Major (Dr.) Wright(?)
Paymaster Solomon Shepherd

Virginia's first battles of the Revolution took place in the Norfolk-Hampton area between October 1775 and January 1776. The minute companies of the Princess Anne District seem to have acted in concert with independent volunteers and the common militia in the affair at Kemp's Landing (Kempsville) in October 1775 and in the rout of the Americans by Dunmore's troops at the same place on November 14, 1775. In both encounters the combined forces were commanded by officers of the militia. In September 1776 the Princess Anne Battalion was ordered into service at Portsmouth, after having served at Petersburg and Cobham.

Companies, October 1775-December 1776
Captain William Robinson, Princess Anne County, October 1775
Captain Josiah Parker, Isle of Wight County, October 1775
Captain Thomas Bressie, Princess Anne County, February 1776
Captain Thomas Mathews, Isle of Wight County, October 1775
Captain Thomas Reynolds Walker, Princess Anne County, February 1775
Captain Willis Wills, Isle of Wight County, prior to July 1776
Captain William Hoffler, Norfolk County, prior to July 1776
Captain Samuel Carr, Norfolk County, 1776
Captain John Washington, Nansemond County, February 1776
Captain Charles Conner, Princess Anne County, February 1776
Captain James Murdagh, Nansemond County, February 1776
Captain Nicholas Faulcon, Princess Anne County, March 1776
Captain Elvington Knott, Norfolk County, March 1776

Prince William District Battalion

(Counties of Prince William, Fairfax, and Loudoun)

Field Officers

Colonel William Grayson, resigned, March 21, 1776. Became assistant secretary to General Washington, June 21, 1776.
Colonel James Hendricks. Commissioned as colonel but did not accept.
Colonel John Quarles, March 1776-?
Lieutenant Colonel (name unknown)
Major Levin Powell, 1775-1776. Commanded the battalion after March 1776.
Adjutant William Johnson
Paymaster Francis Peyton
Surgeon (Dr.) David Griffith(s)

The Prince William Battalion was formed late in 1775 and participated in the activities around Norfolk and Hampton in early 1776. In August 1776 the battalion was ordered to replace the two regular regiments stationed in that area which were sent north.

Companies, October 1775-August 1776

Captain Charles West, Loudoun County, October 1775
Captain Andrew Leitch, Prince William County, October 1775
Captain William Johnson, Prince William County, October 1775
Captain John Fitzgerald, Prince William County, January 1776
Captain William Mason, Fairfax County, January 1776
Captain Simon Triplett, Loudoun County, March(?) 1776
Captain Cuthbert Harrison, Prince William County, March 1776
Captain Henry(?) Lee, Prince William, 1776

Southampton District Battalion

(Counties of Southampton, Sussex, Surry, Brunswick, Prince George, and Dinwiddie)

Field Officers

Colonel David Mason, March 1776
Lieutenant Colonel John Ruffin, December 1775
Major (name unknown)
Paymaster Richard Bland, Jr., March 1776
Quartermaster Richard Cooke, 1775-1776
Quartermaster John Taylor, 1776

Surgeon's Mate William Ridley, 1776
Quartermaster Sergeant William Miller, 1776

On December 29, 1775, Lieutenant Colonel John Ruffin and 180 Southampton District minutemen arrived in Williamsburg to relieve regular troops on duty there. In May 1776 three companies (under captains Reeves, Mason, and Pelham) were called into active service as part of the 1st Battalion of Minutemen. On August 10, 1776, four companies were ordered to Yorktown to replace the regular troops ordered to New Jersey. On November 10, 1776, the battalion officers advertised in the *Virginia Gazette* for an adjutant, a drummer, and a fifer. This implies that the battalion was probably in existence until the minute service was abolished in December 1776.

Companies, November 1775-December 1776

Captain Henry Taylor, Southampton County, November 1775
Captain George Reeves, Sussex County, May 1776
Captain James Mason, Sussex County, prior to June 1776
Captain Peter Pelham, Brunswick County, prior to June 1776
Captain (?) Dunn, Sussex County, prior to June 1776
Captain Edward Walker, Dinwiddie County, June 1776

West Augusta District Battalion

(County of West Augusta)

The frontier district of West Augusta, including the now-defunct counties of Monongalia and Yohogania and comprising land in the present states of West Virginia, Pennsylvania, and Ohio, raised few minutemen. Large numbers of riflemen from this district, including members of Stephenson's, Morgan's, and Cresap's companies and the infamous Gibson's Lambs, enlisted in the Continental regular forces. The Fort Pitt independent frontier companies under captains Matthew Arbuckle and William McKee were also drawn from this district.

At least a portion of a minute battalion was raised by 1776. On January 23, 1776, the state treasurer paid James Brown "Six pounds-ten, for a Rifle gun furnished the West Augusta Battalion."[12]

1st Battalion of Minutemen, 1776

Field Officers
Colonel Samuel Meredith, May 10, 1776-December 10, 1776
Lieutenant Colonel John Ruffin, May 10, 1776-August 1776
Major Richard James, May 10, 1776-October 15, 1776 (promoted to lieutenant colonel)

Major Evan Shelby, August 1776 (on Cherokee expeditions)
Adjutant John Winfrey, June 1776
Adjutant John Overton, June 28, 1776-December 1776
Quartermaster William Meredith, June 28, 1776-December 1776
Surgeon (Dr.) John K. Reid (Reade), June 28, 1776
Surgeon's Mate Thomas Jenkins, July 1, 1776
Armorer Benjamin Thackston, November 1776

Companies, May-December 1776

Captain John Ballard, Mecklenburg County
Captain James Anderson, Mecklenburg County
Captain Samuel Sherwin, Amelia County
Captain Charles Dabney, Louisa County
Captain James Dabney, Louisa County
Captain John Winston, Hanover County
Captain Charles Allen, Prince Edward County
Captain James Mason, Sussex County
Captain George Reeves, Sussex County
Captain Peter Pelham, Buckingham County

2d Battalion of Minutemen, 1776

Field Officers

Colonel Charles Lewis, May 10, 1776-November 12, 1776
Lieutenant Colonel Haynes Morgan, commission dated May 10, 1776
Major John Glenn, May 10, 1776-August 1776
Adjutant William Fog, June 1776-?
Adjutant Epaphroditus Rudder, July 19, 1776-August 29, 1776
Quartermaster Robert Rakestraw, July 3, 1776-?
Surgeon (Dr.) Walker Bennett, July 3, 1776-?

Companies, May-August 1776

Captain Thomas Collier, Charlotte County
Captain Samuel Garland, Lunenburg County
Captain Robert Dixon, Lunenburg County
Captain Thomas Dillard, Pittsylvania County. (Captain Jesse Heard commanded on Cherokee expedition.)
Captain Peter Perkins, Pittsylvania County
Captain Peter Rogers, Halifax County
Captain James Turner, Halifax County
Captain Nicholas Lewis, Albemarle County
Captain Roger Thompson, Albemarle County
Captain Nicholas Cabell, Amherst County
    (merged with Gabriel Penn's company of Buckingham District)
Captain Abraham Penn, Amherst County

This battalion was active at Gwynn's Island in July 1776 and also took part in a short expedition against the Cherokees in the summer and fall of 1776. Captains Dixon, Dillard, Perkins, Lewis, and Thompson were ordered to march against the Indians. Captain Thompson's company later spent a short tour of duty guarding Highland prisoners captured aboard the H.M.S. *Oxford*.

3d Battalion of Minutemen, 1776

Field Officers

Major (Commandant) Andrew Buchanan, September 12, 1776-October 2, 1776

The first two minute battalions were raised in May 1776 to assist in the defense of North Carolina. The 3d was raised between August 6 and September 12, 1776, and was made up of five companies, all from the Caroline District. By September 25 the battalion was on duty transferring gunpowder from Hampton to Portsmouth. When the battalion was disbanded on October 2, 1776, only fourteen men were reported fit for service.

Companies, August-October 1776

Captain John Taliaferro, Caroline County
Captain Francis Taliaferro, Caroline County
Captain Vivion Minor, Caroline County
Lieutenant Walter Vowles, Caroline County
Lieutenant John Mountjoy, Caroline County

The Virginia Continental Infantry

3

1st through 15th Virginia Continental Regiments, 1775-1783

BETWEEN July 1775 and February 1776, Virginia's revolutionary conventions raised nine regiments of infantry for both local defense and eventual service in the main army under George Washington. The Continental Congress, hard-pressed for troops, took all nine regiments, leaving none for local service. By August 1776 the bulk of the Virginia Line on Continental Establishment was in Pennsylvania and New Jersey, except for the 8th Virginia Regiment, which served at the defense of Charleston, South Carolina.

In September 1776 Congress created an American army of eighty-eight battalions and set a quota for each state. Virginia's quota was fifteen, which meant that six more units had to be raised to augment the nine already in service. In October the General Assembly authorized the six additional regiments, and by early 1777 Virginia had fifteen numbered regiments in the field under Washington.

By September 1778 the three-year enlistments of the first nine regiments were about to expire. The hardships of the New Jersey campaigns and the harsh winter at Valley Forge had reduced the Virginia Line to a dangerously low level. To compensate for the attrition of manpower, a board

27

of Continental field officers met at White Plains, New York, where the army was then encamped, to reduce the fifteen Virginia regiments to a more manageable eleven. This was accomplished by combining the first eight regiments into four and by renumbering the remaining seven. Two further rearrangements of the Virginia Line took place, the first at Middlebrook, New York, in May 1779, and the second at Ramapo, New Jersey, in September. Neither of these affected the number of regiments, but both involved the transfer of a considerable number of officers from one regiment to another. The Middlebrook board also created three detachments of recruits for service in the Carolinas.

The 9th Virginia Continental Regiment (formerly the 13th) remained on garrison duty at Pittsburgh, but the balance of the Virginia Line—three numbered regiments and two of the three new detachments—marched to Charleston, South Carolina, where they were besieged and captured by Sir Henry Clinton's army in May 1780. The third detachment, commanded by Abraham Buford, was destroyed as a fighting unit in a battle near The Waxhaws in the same month.

On February 10, 1781, a fourth board of field officers met at Chesterfield Court House to create yet another arrangement of the Virginia Continentals. Since over thirteen hundred Virginians were still captives at Charleston, the Chesterfield arrangement was largely a paper transfer and was designed to establish the relative seniority of individual officers. Nevertheless, one regiment was created (the 1st Virginia Battalion) and one redesignated: the 9th Virginia Regiment (formerly the 13th) became the 7th Virginia Regiment. The 2d, 3d, 4th, 5th, 6th, and 8th regiments consisted wholly of prisoners and existed only on paper. At Yorktown the Virginia Continental infantry consisted of the 1st Virginia Battalion, composed of veterans, and Thomas Gaskins's battalion of new levies.

The Virginia Continental Line was rearranged twice more: at Cumberland Court House in May 1782 and at Winchester Barracks in January 1783. The first arrangement merely established the seniority and promotions of various officers. The second swept away the paper establishment and created one full regiment of ten companies and an auxiliary regiment of two companies. This arrangement remained in effect until July 25, 1783, when the Virginia Line was disbanded.

This chapter includes a separate section for each of the fifteen numbered Continental regiments.[1] All units that bore the same numerical designation (such as the 1st Virginia Regiment) are dealt with under the same heading, even though such units might share nothing but a number and might have been entirely different in personnel. In all cases where a given regiment was renumbered as a result of one of the rearrangements, there are cross-references to guide the reader to the section or sections dealing with that regiment under its previous and subsequent designation or designations.

1st Virginia Regiment of Foot, 1775-1783

(Also designated at various times: 1st Battalion, Virginia Forces on Provincial Establishment; 1st Virginia Battalion of Foot in the Service of the United States; 1st Virginia Regiment on Continental Establishment; 1st Virginia Battalion; and Posey's Virginia Battalion.)

Field Officers

Colonel Patrick Henry, July 1775-February 13, 1776. Resigned, February 28, 1776.
Colonel William Christian, March 18, 1776-July 1776. Resigned to lead Cherokee expedition.
Colonel Isaac Read, August 13, 1776-September 4, 1776. Died.
Colonel James Hendricks, September 27, 1777-February 10, 1778. Resigned.
Colonel Richard Parker, February 10, 1778-April 24, 1780. Mortally wounded at Charleston, South Carolina.
Colonel William Davies, February 12, 1781-January 1, 1783. Retired.
Colonel James Wood, January 1, 1783-end of war
Lieutenant Colonel William Christian, February 13, 1776-March 18, 1776
Lieutenant Colonel Francis Eppes, March 18, 1776-August 27, 1776. Wounded on Long Island.
Lieutenant Colonel John Green, March 22, 1777-January 26, 1778. Transferred.
Lieutenant Colonel Robert Ballard, January 1778-September 14, 1778
Lieutenant Colonel Burgess Ball, September 14, 1778-February 12, 1781. Captured at Charleston, May 1780.
Lieutenant Colonel Samuel Hopkins, February 12, 1781-January 1, 1783.
Lieutenant Colonel Samuel Hawes, January 1, 1783-end of war
Major Francis Eppes, February 13, 1776-March 18, 1776. Promoted to lieutenant colonel.
Major Andrew Leitch, March 18, 1776-October 1, 1776. Mortally wounded at Harlem Plains.
Major John Green, August 13, 1776-March 22, 1777. Promoted.
Major Robert Ballard, March 22, 1777-October 14, 1777. Promoted.
Major Edmund B. Dickinson, October 26, 1777-June 28, 1778. Killed at Monmouth.

Major Richard Clough Anderson, September 14, 1778-February 11, 1781. Retired.
Major Thomas Posey, February 12, 1781-September 8, 1781. Promoted to lieutenant colonel, 7th Virginia Regiment.
Major Thomas Ridley, 1781-January 1, 1783
Major David Stephenson, January 1, 1783-end of war

The 1st Virginia Continental infantry regiment was raised as a provincial or state defense unit according to an order by the third Virginia convention in Richmond on July 17, 1775. Originally it consisted of eight companies, each numbering sixty-eight enlisted men. Patrick Henry, lately of the Hanover Gentlemen Independents, was chosen as the regiment's first colonel. Colonel Henry's political abilities exceeded his military talent, and the Committee of Safety passed over his regiment in favor of William Woodford's for duty at Norfolk and Great Bridge in December 1775. Only the 7th and 8th companies were sent to Norfolk following the battle.[2]

On December 28, 1775, the Continental Congress decided that six battalions of ten companies each were necessary to defend Virginia from invasion. The Congress ordered that the battalions were to be raised and paid "upon the same terms" as the Continental forces already in camp at Cambridge, Massachusetts—in other words, the two existing Virginia regiments would be augmented by two companies each, and four more regiments of ten companies each were to be raised.

Congress resolved on Feburary 13, 1776, to issue Continental commissions to the officers of the six Virginia battalions, thus changing their commands from state to Continental units. From that date until it was disbanded in mid-1783, the 1st Virginia Regiment of Foot remained a Continental unit.

Between February and August 1776 the regiment trained in Williamsburg under the direction of Brigadier General Andrew Lewis. On August 16 Colonel Read marched his men north to join Washington's Grand Army in New Jersey. During the many reshufflings of the Continental army from 1776 to 1778, the 1st Virginia Regiment was successively part of Weedon's, Stirling's, Mercer's, and Muhlenburg's brigades.[3]

Companies, September 1775-January 1776[4]

1st Company: Captain John Green, September 6, 1775. Raised in Culpeper.
2d Company: Captain John Markham, September 16, 1775. Raised in Chesterfield (part of Amelia Minute Battalion).
3d Company: Captain John Sayres, September 18, 1775. Raised in Gloucester.
4th Company: Captain William Davies, September 30, 1775. Raised in Princess Anne.

5th Company: Captain John Fleming, October 2, 1775. Raised in Goochland.
6th Company: Captain Robert Ballard, October 7, 1775. Raised in Mecklenburg.
7th Company: Captain William Campbell, December 15, 1775. Raised in Augusta (Fincastle). Riflemen.
8th Company: Captain George Gibson, December 1775. Raised in West Augusta. Known locally as Gibson's Lambs. Riflemen.

In February 1776 two additional companies were added to the regiment to bring it up to Continental regulations.

9th Company: Captain Thomas Nelson, Jr., February 22, 1776
10th Company: Captain Edmund B. Dickinson, February 26, 1776. Raised in York or Williamsburg.

After the regiment became part of the Continental Establishment, several changes in personnel occurred. Between March 1776 and June 1778, the following captains were commissioned in the regiment:

Richard Taylor, March 5, 1776
William Cunningham, April 22, 1776
John Taylor, April 29, 1776
Goodrich Crump, June 5, 1776
William Lewis, September 4, 1776
John Moss, September 15, 1776
Charles Pelham, November 11, 1776
John Eustace, May 1777
Joseph Scott, Sr., August 9, 1777
Tarleton Payne, November 18, 1777
Callohill Minnis, November 18, 1777
Francis Boykin, 1777
Alexander Cummins, June 1778

Deaths, desertions, and the expirations of enlistments greatly reduced the regiment by the summer of 1778. A special board of field officers convened at White Plains, New York, on September 14, 1778, to arrange, or reorganize, the shattered Virginia Continental Line. The captured 9th Virginia was absorbed into the remnants of the 1st Virginia Regiment, but there still were only enough men to fill up six companies.

Companies, September 1778-June 1779
Colonel's Company: Captain-Lieutenant James Culbertson
Lieutenant Colonel's Company: Lieutenant Alexander Cummins

Major's Company: Lieutenant Joseph Scott, Jr.
4th Company: Captain William Lewis
5th Company: Captain Charles Pelham
6th Company: Captain Claiborne W. Lawson
7th Company: Captain Callohill Minnis
8th Company: Captain Tarleton Payne
9th Company: Captain Custis Kendall

Even the White Plains arrangement was not sufficient to bring the regiment up to its original strength.

Companies, June-November, 1779

1st Company: Lieutenant Colonel Burgess Ball. Personnel of this company were later combined with the companies commanded by Captain Reid of the 1st Regiment and Captain Winston of the 10th Regiment.
2d Company: Captain Charles Pelham
3d Company: Captain Nathan Reid. Personnel combined with 1st Company.
4th Company: Captain John Marks
5th Company: Captain Peter Jones
6th Company: Captain John Overton
7th Company: Captain Claiborne W. Lawson
8th Company: Captain Callohill Minnis
9th Company: Captain Custis Kendall
10th Company: Captain Holman Minnis

For service in the Carolinas, the 1st Virginia Regiment was consolidated with the 5th, 7th, 10th, and 11th Virginia regiments and assigned to General William Woodford's brigade. The entire regiment was captured when Benjamin Lincoln surrendered Charleston to Sir Henry Clinton on May 12, 1780.

1st Virginia Continental Regiment, November 1779-May 1780

Field Officers
Colonel William Russell
Lieutenant Colonel Burgess Ball
Major (name unknown)

Companies
Captain Callohill Minnis, 1st Virginia Regiment
Captain Tarleton Payne, 1st Virginia Regiment
Captain Custis Kendall, 1st Virginia Regiment

Captain Thomas Holt, 1st Virginia Regiment
Captain Holman Minnis, 1st Virginia Regiment
Captain Thomas Buckner, 5th Virginia Regiment
Captain Mayo Carrington, 5th Virginia Regiment
Captain William Moseley, 5th Virginia Regiment
Captain William Bentley, 5th Virginia Regiment
Captain William Johnston, 7th Virginia Regiment
Captain James Wright, 7th Virginia Regiment
Captain Thomas Hunt, 10th Virginia Regiment
Captain Lawrence Butler, 11th Virginia Regiment
Captain Philip Mallory, 11th Virginia Regiment

On February 12, 1781, a special board of Continental field officers at Chesterfield Court House arranged the 1st Virginia Regiment as a paper organization. The personnel who had escaped the Charleston capitulation were formed into a temporary battalion under Lieutenant Colonel Thomas Posey. (See "Posey's Virginia Battalion.")

In May 1782 a second board of field officers met at Cumberland Old Court House to arrange the paper Virginia Continental Establishment internally. Unlike the majority of the Virginia regiments, which existed only in theory after Charleston, the actual 1st and 2d regiments were reconstituted from new conscripts and the few uncaptured veterans.

On January 1, 1783, another board of Virginia Continental officers met at Winchester Barracks to consolidate the troops still in service. The 7th Virginia Regiment at Fort Pitt, the veterans of Posey's Battalion, and the contingent of recruits at Winchester were formed into two new units: one large battalion, thereafter designated the 1st, and one small regiment of two companies, which became the 2d Virginia Regiment. As officially organized by the Winchester arrangement, the 1st Virginia Regiment of 1783 included the following officers:

Colonel James Wood
Lieutenant Oliver Towles
Major David Stephenson
1st Company: Captain Henry Young
2d Company: Captain Nathan Reid
3d Company: Captain John Gillison
4th Company: Captain William Johnston
5th Company: Captain Clough Shelton
6th Company: Captain Nathaniel Pendleton
7th Company: Captain John Stith
8th Company: Captain Thomas Edmunds
9th Company: Captain Thomas Bowne
10th Company: Captain Custis Kendall

Captains Philip Sansum, Samuel Hogg, and Thomas Parker were also included in the arrangement, although they were not commanding companies. All had been lieutenants prior to 1783, and all seem to have been promoted as rewards for service.

Since most of the captains and subalterns in the official arrangement of the 1st Virginia Regiment were absent from the Winchester Barracks on other assignments (recruiting, gathering military stores, etc.), the above list differed in many respects from the roster of those actually on duty at Winchester. According to pay and subsistence accounts, the garrison there was made up of the following officers and companies:

    Colonel James Wood
    Lieutenant Colonel Samuel Hawes
    Major Samuel Finley(?)
    1st Company: Captain William Johnston
    2d Company: Captain John Stith
    3d Company: Captain Thomas Edmunds
    4th Company: Captain Abraham Kirkpatrick
    5th Company: Captain John Anderson
    6th Company: Captain James Williams
    7th Company: Captain Robert Woodson
    Artillery Company: Captain Ambrose Bohannon

Although most of the Virginia Continentals were mustered out of service in June 1783, the companies under captains Johnston, Kirkpatrick, and Bohannon remained in service until July or August of that year, when they were discharged.

2d Virginia Regiment of Foot, 1775-1783
(Also designated at various times: 2d Battalion, Virginia Forces on Provincial Establishment; 2d Virginia Battalion of Foot in the Service of the United States; 2d Virginia Regiment on Continental Establishment; 2d Virginia Detachment; 2d Virginia Battalion.)

Field Officers

Colonel William Woodford, July 1775-September 3, 1776. Resigned, but promoted to brigadier general, February 21, 1777. Captured at Charleston, South Carolina, May 1780. Died while a prisoner in New York, November 1780.

Colonel Alexander Spotswood, February 21, 1777-October 9, 1777. Resigned.

Colonel Christian Febiger, September 26, 1777-January 1, 1783. Retired.

Virginia Continental Infantry

>Lieutenant Colonel Charles Scott, July 1775-May 7, 1776. Promoted to colonel, 5th Virginia Regiment.
>Lieutenant Colonel Alexander Spotswood, August 13, 1776-February 21, 1777. Promoted to colonel.
>Lieutenant Colonel Richard Parker, February 10, 1777-February 10, 1778. Promoted to colonel, 1st Virginia Regiment.
>Lieutenant Colonel Charles Dabney, June 23, 1777-September 14, 1778. Retired after arrangement of Virginia troops.
>Lieutenant Colonel Charles Simms, September 14, 1778-December 7, 1779. Resigned.
>Lieutenant Colonel Richard Taylor, December 7, 1779-February 12, 1781. Retired.
>Lieutenant Colonel Gustavus Brown Wallace, February 12, 1781-January 1, 1783. Captured at Charleston, South Carolina, May 1780.
>Major Alexander Spotswood, July 1775-August 13, 1776. Promoted.
>Major John Markham, August 13, 1776-December 23, 1776. Promoted to lieutenant colonel, 8th Virginia Regiment.
>Major Morgan Alexander, December 23, 1776-March 22, 1777. Transferred to 8th Virginia Regiment.
>Major Ralph Faulkner, March 22, 1777-May 1778. Retired from service, September 1779.
>Major Thomas Posey, April 30, 1778-September 14, 1778. Transferred to the 7th Virginia Regiment.
>Major Thomas Massie, September 14, 1778-June 25, 1779. Resigned.
>Major Charles Pelham, June 25, 1779-February 12, 1781. Captured at Charleston, South Carolina, May 1780. Transferred to the 7th Virginia Regiment, February 1781, while still a prisoner.
>Major Smith Snead, February 12, 1781-January 1, 1783. Became major-commandant of reorganized 2d Virginia Battalion. Served to end of war.

The initial organization of the 2d Virginia Regiment in July 1775 was identical to that of the 1st Virginia Regiment. This regiment saw considerable service in the Norfolk area against British forces and loyalists under Dunmore. Colonel William Woodford, of Caroline County, became the de facto commander in chief of Virginia's forces from October through December 1775, after which time he turned over his command to Colonel Robert Howe, of North Carolina.[5]

After being taken into Continental service the regiment mustered at Suffolk and then marched north to join Washington.[6]

Companies, September 1775-January 1776

1st Company: Captain George Johns(t)on, September 21, 1775. Raised in Fairfax.

2d Company: Captain George Nicholas, September 28, 1775. Raised in Hanover.

3d Company: Captain Richard Parker, September 28, 1775. Raised in Westmoreland.

4th Company: Captain William Taliaferro, September 29, 1775. Raised in Caroline.

5th Company: Captain William Fontaine, October 21, 1775. Raised in Amelia.

6th Company: Captain Richard Kidder Meade, October 24, 1775. Raised in Southampton.

7th Company: Captain Morgan Alexander, November 27, 1775. Raised in Frederick. Riflemen.

In December 1775 three companies of sixty men each were added to the regiment.

8th Company: Captain Buller Claiborne, January 31, 1776. Raised in Prince George and Petersburg.

9th Company: Captain Samuel Hawes, February 19, 1776. Raised in Caroline.

10th Company: Captain Wood Jones, March 8, 1776. Raised in Amelia and Williamsburg.

Originally attached to Weedon's brigade, the 2d Virginia Regiment became a part of Woodford's brigade following Woodford's promotion to brigadier general. From March 1776 through the White Plains arrangement of September 1778, the following officers commanded companies in the regiment:

Captain Everard Meade, commissioned March 8, 1776
Captain Francis Taliaferro, March 1776
Captain Francis Taylor, May 8, 1776
Captain John Willis, June 15, 1776
Captain William Sanford, December 25, 1776
Captain William Taylor, December 28, 1776
Captain Marquis Calmes, January 17, 1777
Captain Peyton Harrison, March 11, 1777
Captain John Peyton Harrison, May 4, 1777
Captain Alexander Parker, June 1, 1777
Captain Philip Taliaferro, September 23, 1777
Captain Thomas Tebbs, 1777
Captain Benjamin Holmes (Hoomes), April 24, 1778
Captain James Upshaw, 1778

On September 14, 1778, the depleted 2d Virginia Regiment was consolidated with the 6th Virginia Regiment at White Plains, New York.

Companies, September 1778-Spring 1779

Colonel's Company:	Captain-Lieutenant Thomas Catlett
Lieutenant Colonel's Company:	Lieutenant Colin Cocke(?)
Major's Company:	Lieutenant Francis Cowherd(?)
4th Company:	Captain William Taylor
5th Company:	Captain Marquis Calmes
6th Company:	Captain John Peyton Harrison
7th Company:	Captain Alexander Parker
8th Company:	Captain Benjamin Taliaferro
9th Company:	Captain John Stokes

In 1779 Captain Calmes was captured by the British. Captains Valentine Harrison and Colin Cocke joined the regiment toward the end of the same year.

Late in 1779 the 2d Virginia Regiment was temporarily consolidated with the 3d and 4th Virginia regiments and sent to Charleston as part of General William Woodford's brigade. Except for a handful of men under Captain Alexander Parker, the amalgamated regiment was captured by Sir Henry Clinton's forces and kept in captivity for the rest of the war. Parker's refugees returned to Virginia and participated in the Yorktown campaign.

The 2d Virginia Regiment, although in captivity, was arranged on paper by boards of field officers meeting at Chesterfield Court House, at Cumberland Old Court House, and at Winchester, in 1781, 1782, and 1783, respectively.

Companies, 1781-1782

Captain Robert Higgins (from 8th Virginia Regiment)
Captain John Stith
Captain Alexander Parker
Captain Benjamin Taliaferro
Captain Henry Moss
Captain Isaiah Marks
Captain Colin Cocke
Captain Robert Porterfield
Captain Francis Cowherd
Captain John Jordan
Captain Beverley Stubblefield
Captain James Mabin (Maybone)

Because they were on detached service with Colonel Abraham Buford, captains Thomas Catlett and John Stokes escaped capture at Charleston, Catlett only to be killed and Stokes wounded at The Waxhaws later in the month.[7]

The final arrangement of the Virginia Line, which took place at Winchester on January 1, 1783, created a tiny regiment of two companies, which was designated the 2d Virginia Regiment. One company was composed of veterans, and the other of recruits who were serving out their enlistments "for the war."

Companies, January-September 1783
Major-Commandant   Smith Snead
Captain   Alexander Parker (veterans)
Captain   Samuel Booker (recruits)
Brevet-Captain   Thomas Parker, September 30, 1783

3d Virginia Regiment Of Foot, 1776-1782

(Also designated at various times: 3d Virginia Battalion of Foot in the Service of the United Colonies, 3d Virginia Regiment on Continental Establishment.)

Field Officers

Colonel Hugh Mercer, December 1775-June 6, 1776. Promoted to brigadier general. Mortally wounded at Princeton.

Colonel George Weedon, August 13, 1776-February 21, 1777. Promoted to brigadier general.

Colonel Thomas Marshall, February 21, 1777-February 21, 1778. Resigned. Became colonel of State Artillery Regiment.

Colonel William Heth, April 30, 1778-February 12, 1781. Taken prisoner at Charleston, South Carolina, May 1780. Paroled and retired.

Colonel Abraham Buford, February 12, 1781-January 1, 1783. Retired.

Lieutenant Colonel George Weedon, December 1775-August 13, 1776. Promoted.

Lieutenant Colonel Thomas Marshall, August 13, 1776-February 21, 1777. Promoted.

Lieutenant Colonel William Heth, April 1, 1777-April 30, 1778. Promoted.

Lieutenant Colonel Charles Fleming, June 28, 1778-September 14, 1778. Promoted to colonel, 8th Virginia Regiment.

Lieutenant Colonel Thomas Gaskins, September 14, 1778-January 1, 1783. Retired.

Lieutenant Colonel Richard Clough Anderson, honorary lieutenant colonel, 1781-1783.

Major Thomas Marshall, February 13, 1776-August 13, 1776. Promoted.

Major William Taliaferro, August 13, 1776-February 1, 1777. Promoted to colonel, 4th Virginia Regiment.

Major Charles West, February 1, 1777-July 6, 1778. Resigned.
Major John Hays, April 23, 1778-February 12, 1781. Taken prisoner at Germantown, October 1777, and remained captive until retirement.
Major James Lucas, September 14, 1778-May 15, 1779. Retired.
Major William Lewis, February 12, 1781-January 1, 1783. Prisoner of war at Charleston, South Carolina, 1780-1783.

Unlike the 1st and 2d Virginia regiments, the 3d was initially organized (on December 1, 1775) with ten companies. Because of delays in establishing points of rendezvous, the first companies were not recruited until February 1776, only a week before the regiment was taken over by Congress. By August the partially formed 3d Virginia was ordered to join the main army in New Jersey. In October Colonel Weedon was placed in temporary command of a brigade that included his own regiment, now numbering 104 officers and 611 enlisted men. After brief service under General Lord Stirling at Trenton the regiment was transferred to Woodford's brigade.[8]

Companies, February 1776-January 1777

1st Company: Captain Andrew Leitch, February 5, 1776. Raised in Prince William. (In March Leitch was promoted to major, 1st Virginia Regiment.)

2d Company: Captain John Fitzgerald, February 8, 1776. Raised in Fairfax or Prince William.

3d Company: Captain Charles West, February 9, 1776. Raised in Loudoun.

4th Company: Captain John Thornton, February 12, 1776. Raised in Culpeper. (His lieutenant was James Monroe.)

5th Company: Captain Gustavus Brown Wallace, February 20, 1776. Raised in King George.

6th Company: Captain William Washington, February 26, 1776. Raised in Westmoreland. (William, a kinsman of George Washington, later won fame as a cavalry commander under Greene.)

7th Company: Captain William McWilliams, February 1776. Raised in Spotsylvania.

8th Company: Captain Philip Richard Francis Lee, March 8, 1776. Raised in Prince William.

9th Company: Captain John Ashby, March 18, 1776. Raised in Fauquier.

10th Company: Captain Thomas Johnson, Jr., March 21, 1776. Raised in Louisa.

To replace captains who had been promoted or who were serving on detached duty, four other captains were commissioned in the regiment during 1776. In March 1776 Thomas Hutchings's Pittsylvania County company from the 6th Virginia Regiment was temporarily attached to the 3d Regiment.

> Captain John Chilton, April 29, 1776
> Captain John Peyton, June 19, 1776
> Captain David Arell, September 28, 1776
> Captain Robert Powell, Sr., October 18, 1776

The regiment sustained heavy casualties in the battles for New Jersey and Pennsylvania in 1776-1777. Captains Chilton and Lee were killed at Brandywine, Captain Washington was wounded at Long Island and Trenton, Captain Ashby at Germantown, and Captain Peyton at Brandywine. In the spring of 1777 Colonel Thomas Marshall reorganized the depleted 3d Virginia Regiment. In June 1777 he instructed Lieutenant Robert Slaughter, a recruiting officer, to enlist only able-bodied men under the age of sixty and free from suspicious principles. Each recruit was given twenty dollars, a uniform, and a promise of 100 acres of land for a three-year enlistment. British and American deserters were prohibited from joining the service, which had already suffered greatly from such persons. (Other commanders were less scrupulous than Marshall: Armand's Legion, for instance, recruited large numbers of former deserters.)[9]

Companies, January 1777-September 1778

Colonel's Company: Captain-Lieutenant John Francis Mercer (?)
Lieutenant Colonel's Company: Lieutenant Robert Beale (not the same as Robert Beall of the 13th and 9th Virginia Regiments)
Major's Company: Captain Leroy Edwards
4th Company: Captain John Chilton
5th Company: Captain John Thornton
6th Company: Captain William Washington
7th Company: Captain Reuben Briscoe
8th Company: Captain John Francis Mercer (promoted, September 1777)
9th Company: Captain Valentine Peyton
10th Company: Captain John E. Blackwell

In the White Plains arrangement of September 14, 1778, the 3d Virginia Regiment and the 5th Virginia Regiment were combined.

Companies, September 1778-February 1781

Captain Robert Powell, Sr.
Captain John Francis Mercer
Captain William Fowler (from 5th Virginia Regiment)

Captain John Anderson (from 5th Virginia Regiment)
Captain Valentine Peyton
Captain William Bentley (from 5th Virginia Regiment)
Captain David Miller, May 1, 1777
Captain Leroy Edwards, June 19, 1779
Captain Robert Beale, June 19, 1779
Captain John Henry Fitzgerald, May 10, 1780
Captain John Hawkins, May 13, 1780

In May 1779 the regiment was temporarily consolidated with the enlisted men of the 4th Virginia Regiment at Middlebrook. Later in 1779, the 3d Virginia Regiment was temporarily consolidated with the 2d and 4th Virginia regiments, designated the 2d Virginia Regiment, and sent to Charleston as part of General William Woodford's brigade. There the regiment was captured and remained in captivity for the rest of the war.

Companies (on paper), 1781-1783
Captain William Johnston
Captain Nathaniel Pendleton
Captain Thomas Edmunds
Captain John Anderson (out of captivity in January 1781)
Captain John E. Blackwell
Captain William Bentley
Captain Robert Beale
Captain James Wright
Captain Thomas Warman (prisoner since 1776)
Captain Nathan Lammé
Captain Thomas Ransdell

Captains Lammé, Bedinger, and Ransdell were not prisoners when they were arranged with the 3d Virginia Regiment, but they seem to have been acting as recruiters and in other capacities.

4th Virginia Regiment of Foot, 1776-1783

(Also designated at various times: 4th Virginia Battalion of Foot in the Service of the United States, 4th Virginia Regiment on Continental Establishment.)

Field Officers
Colonel Adam Stephen, February 13, 1776-September 4, 1776. Promoted to brigadier general.
Colonel Thomas Elliott, September 3, 1776-September 28, 1777. Resigned.

Colonel Robert Lawson, April 1, 1777-December 17, 1777. Resigned. Later brigadier general, Virginia Militia.
Colonel John Neville, September 14, 1778-January 1, 1783. Captured at Charleston, South Carolina, May 1780.
Lieutenant Colonel Isaac Read, February 13, 1776-August 13, 1776. Promoted to colonel, 1st Virginia Regiment.
Lieutenant Colonel William Taliaferro, February 21, 1777-February 1, 1778. Taken captive at Brandywine and died.
Lieutenant Colonel Thomas Gaskins, May 16, 1778-September 14, 1778. Transferred to 3d Virginia Regiment.
Lieutenant Robert Ballard, September 14, 1778-July 4, 1779. Resigned.
Lieutenant Samuel Jordan Cabell, July 4, 1779-February 12, 1781. Taken prisoner at Charleston, South Carolina, May 1780. Transferred to 7th Virginia Regiment.
Lieutenant Colonel Richard Campbell, February 12, 1781-September 8, 1781. Killed at Eutaw Springs.
Major Robert Lawson, February 13, 1776-August 13, 1776. Promoted.
Major John Sayres, August 13, 1776-January 30, 1777. Promoted to lieutenant colonel, 9th Virginia Regiment.
Major Isaac Beall, February 10, 1777-June 19, 1778. Resigned.
Major George Gibson, March 22, 1777-June 5, 1777. Resigned. Later became colonel, 1st Regiment, Virginia State Line.
Major John Brent, October 4, 1777-May 4, 1778. Resigned.
Major Charles Fleming, June 5, 1778 (?)-June 28, 1778. Promoted to lieutenant colonel, 3d Virginia Regiment.
Major William Croghan, September 14, 1778-January 1, 1783. Taken prisoner at Charleston, South Carolina, May 1780. On parole to end of war.
Major Samuel Finley, (?) 1781-January 1, 1783. Transferred to new 1st Virginia Regiment.

The 4th Virginia Regiment was authorized by the fourth Virginia convention on December 1, 1775, and accepted by Congress on February 13, 1776. Approximately half the companies were raised in southside Virginia. Many riflemen enlisted in the regiment, a fact which made drilling according to European manuals difficult. On October 17, 1776, Adam Stephen, who had recently been promoted to brigadier, begged Congress for muskets and bayonets instead of "riffles." "Only necessity," he wrote, "made me admit so many of them into the regiment." The 4th Virginia Regiment joined Washington's army late in 1776 and participated in the battles of Trenton and Germantown.[10]

Companies, February 1776-March 1777

1st Company: Captain Isaac Beall, February 10, 1776. Raised in Berkeley.
2d Company: Captain John Morton, February 19, 1776. Raised in Prince Edward.
3d Company: Captain John Brent, February 23, 1776. Raised in Charlotte.
4th Company: Captain Thomas Ridley, March 11, 1776. Raised in Southampton.
5th Company: Captain Nathaniel Mason, March 14, 1776. Raised in Sussex.
6th Company: Captain James Lucas, March 19, 1776. Raised in Brunswick.
7th Company: Captain John Watkins, Jr., March 21, 1776. Raised in Isle of Wight and Surry.
8th Company: Captain Thomas Mathews, March 25, 1776. Raised in Isle of Wight and Surry.
9th Company: Captain Arthur Smith, April 1, 1776. Raised in Isle of Wight and Surry.
10th Company: Captain John Washington, April 2, 1776. Raised in Nansemond.

Because of vacancies caused by transfers, resignations, combat losses, and absences on detached service, the following captains were commissioned in the 4th Virginia Regiment:[11]

Captain Nathaniel Lucas, May 2, 1776
Captain George Walls, September 27, 1776
Captain John Holcombe, November 23, 1776
Captain John Stith, March 12, 1777
Captain Jason Riddick, June 10, 1777
Captain William Cherry, November 29, 1777
Captain William Rogers, April 1, 1778
Captain (upon retirement) Samuel Gill, September 14, 1778

On September 14, 1778, the 4th Virginia Regiment absorbed the 8th Virginia Regiment at White Plains, New York. Within eight months, both the 3d and 4th Virginia regiments were so depleted that they were temporarily combined in the Middlebrook arrangement of May 1779, the enlisted men of the 4th Regiment entering the 3d.

Late in 1779, a new 2d Virginia Regiment was created from the remnants of the 2d, 3d, and 4th Virginia regiments for service in the Southern Department. Nearly all its personnel were captured at the fall of Charleston in May 1780.

Companies, September 1778-May 1779

Colonel's Company: Captain-Lieutenant Leonard Cooper[12]
Lieutenant Colonel's Company: Lieutenant James Curry
Major's Company: Lieutenant Christopher Myer
4th Company: Captain George Walls. Promoted to major, Crockett's Illinois Battalion, 1781.
5th Company: Captain John Stith
6th Company: Captain Jason Riddick
7th Company: Captain Abraham Kirkpatrick. From 8th Virginia Regiment.
8th Company: Captain Isaac Israel. Resigned, did not join. Captain John Steed from 8th Virginia Regiment.
9th Company: Captain James Curry, September 23, 1778

Officers, May 1779-November 1779

Colonel John Neville, 4th Virginia Regiment
Lieutenant Colonel Thomas Gaskins, 3d Virginia Regiment
Major William Croghan, 4th Virginia Regiment
Captain John Anderson, 3d Virginia Regiment
Captain John E. Blackwell, 3d Virginia Regiment
Captain Valentine Peyton, 3d Virginia Regiment
Captain William Bentley, 3d Virginia Regiment
Captain John Stith, 4th Virginia Regiment
Captain Abraham Kirkpatrick, 4th Virginia Regiment
Captain John Steed, 4th Virginia Regiment

On February 12, 1781, the board of field officers at Chesterfield Court House created a new 4th Virginia Regiment, consisting mostly of officers from the disbanded 11th Virginia Regiment, still imprisoned at Charleston, and some other officers who were then at liberty.

Officers, February 1781-January 1783

Captain Samuel Finley. Promoted to major, 1st Virginia Regiment.
Captain Samuel Booker
Captain Lawrence Butler
Captain James Curry
Captain William Lewis Lovely
Captain Reuben Fields

The 4th Virginia Regiment was officially disbanded on January 1, 1783, but in reality it had not existed as a fighting unit since its capture in May 1780.

5th Virginia Regiment of Foot, 1778-1782

(Also designated at various times: 5th Virginia Battalion of Foot in the Service of the United States, 5th Virginia Regiment on Continental Establishment.)

Field Officers, 1776-1778

Colonel William Peachey, February 13, 1776-May 7, 1776. Resigned.

Colonel Charles Scott, May 7, 1776-April 1, 1777. Promoted to brigadier general.

Colonel Josiah Parker, April 1, 1777-July 12, 1778. Resigned.

Colonel Abraham Buford, May 16, 1778-September 14, 1778. Transferred to 11th Virginia Regiment.

Lieutenant Colonel William Crawford, February 13, 1776-August 14, 1776. Promoted to colonel, 7th Virginia Regiment.

Lieutenant Colonel Josiah Parker, August 13, 1776-April 1, 1777. Promoted.

Lieutenant Colonel Abraham Buford, April 1, 1777-May 16, 1778. Promoted.

Lieutenant Colonel George Johnston, August 13, 1776-January 20, 1777. Promoted to lieutenant colonel, Washington's staff.

Lieutenant Colonel Burgess Ball, February 10, 1777-December 17, 1777. Promoted to lieutenant colonel, 9th Virginia Regiment.

Lieutenant Colonel Thomas Gaskins, November 5, 1777-May 16, 1778. Promoted to lieutenant colonel, 4th Virginia Regiment.

Lieutenant Colonel David Stephenson, May 4, 1778-September 14, 1778. Transferred to 11th Virginia Regiment.

The initial organizational history of the 5th Virginia Regiment is identical to that of the 3d and 4th regiments. Under Colonel Charles Scott the partly formed regiment was first assembled at Richmond County Courthouse and trained in Williamsburg. The command suffered severely from illness in September 1776. When it joined General Adam Stephen's brigade in December, only 14 commissioned officers and 115 enlisted men were fit for duty. In 1777 it was transferred to General Muhlenburg's brigade and served in the New Jersey campaigns of 1777-1778.[13]

Companies, February 1776-September 1776

1st Company: Captain Burgess Ball, February 10, 1776. Raised in Lancaster. (Ball was promoted to major.)

2d Company: Captain George Stubblefield, February 12, 1776. Raised in Orange.

3d Company: Captain John Pleasants, February 24, 1776. Raised in Henrico.

4th Company: Captain Thomas Gaskins, February 26, 1776. Raised in Northumberland. (Gaskins was promoted to major.)

5th Company: Captain Gross Scruggs, February 26, 1776. Raised in Bedford.

6th Company: Captain Ralph Faulkner, March 1, 1776. Raised in Chesterfield. (Faulkner was promoted to major, 2d Virginia Regiment.)

7th Company: Captain Richard Clough Anderson, March 7, 1776. Raised in Hanover.

8th Company: Captain Henry Terrill, March 12, 1776. Raised in Bedford.

9th Company: Captain Andrew Russell, March 25, 1776. Raised in Loudoun.

10th Company: Captain Henry Fauntleroy, September 15, 1776. Raised in Richmond County(?). (Fauntleroy was killed at Monmouth.)

To replace the captains who were promoted, killed, or who had resigned, the following men received commissions:

Captain William Mosby, December 18, 1776
Captain Richard Bernard, (?) 1776
Captain Samuel Colston, February 21, 1777
Captain John McAdams, March 16, 1777
Captain William Fowler, April 1, 1777
Captain John Anderson, August 12, 1777
Captain Peter Minor, February 10, 1778

At White Plains, New York, on September 14, 1778, the officers and men of the depleted 5th Virginia Regiment were absorbed into the 3d Regiment.

The designation 5th Virginia Regiment was then applied to the 7th Virginia Regiment, which was still virtually intact. Thus, from 1778 through 1782, the unit referred to as the 5th Virginia Regiment was actually composed of companies from the former 7th Regiment.

Field Officers, 1778-1782

Colonel William Russell, September 14, 1778-January 1, 1783. Taken prisoner at Charleston, South Carolina, May 1780.

Lieutenant Colonel Holt Richeson, September 14, 1778-May 10, 1779. Resigned.

Lieutenant Colonel Samuel Jordan Cabell, May 12, 1779-July 4, 1779. Transferred to 4th Virginia Regiment.

Lieutenant Colonel John Webb, July 4, 1779-February 12, 1781. Retired.

Major John Webb, September 14, 1778-July 4, 1779. Promoted.
Major John Willis, May 12, 1779-January 1, 1783. Taken prisoner at Brandywine, September 1779; exchanged, November 1780. Retired.
Major Thomas Hill, July 4, 1779-February 12, 1781. Retired.
Major Joseph Crockett, February 12, 1781-January 1, 1783. Retired. Served as lieutenant colonel of the 2d Illinois Battalion under George Rogers Clark, 1782-1783.

(For the history of the regiment prior to 1778, see "7th Virginia Regiment of Foot, 1776-1778.")

The new 5th Virginia Regiment served in General William Woodford's brigade in early 1779. Later that year the enlisted personnel of the 5th and 11th Virginia regiments were combined temporarily, but the resulting consolidation still mustered only about four hundred men.

The remnants of the 5th Virginia Regiment were consolidated with the 1st Virginia Regiment and sent south in 1779-1780. Many of its officers were captured at Charleston, South Carolina, in May 1780.

Companies, September 14, 1778-Winter 1779

Colonel's Company: Captain-Lieutenant Thomas Buckner. Promoted to captain, October 30, 1778.
Lieutenant Colonel's Company: Lieutenant William White
Major's Company: Lieutenant Henry Waring
4th Company: Captain Thomas Hill
5th Company: Captain Reuben Lipscomb. Died, October 30, 1778.
6th Company: Captain William Moseley
7th Company: Captain Henry Young
8th Company: Captain James Baytop
9th Company: Captain Adam Wallace. Killed, May 1780.
10th Company: Captain Robert Woodson
Replacement: Captain Robert Sayres

In 1779-1780 the following captains also received commissions in the regiment:

Captain Mayo Carrington, May 12, 1779
Captain William White, July 4, 1779
Captain John Nelson, May 28, 1780
Captain Tarpley White, (?) 1780

At the surrender of Charleston in May 1780, Colonel Russell and captains White, Carrington, Buckner, and Moseley were made prisoners. Captain Adam Wallace had been attached earlier to the 3d Virginia

Detachment (under Colonel Abraham Buford), which escaped the Charleston siege but was wiped out at The Waxhaws, South Carolina, on May 29, 1780.

On February 12, 1781, the 5th Virginia became a paper regiment as a result of the Chesterfield Court House arrangement and remained so until it was dissolved in January 1783.

Officers, February 1781
Captain Henry Young
Captain Joseph Scott, Sr.
Captain William Rogers
Captain Thomas Parker
Captain Custis Kendall
Captain Robert Woodson
Captain James Culbertson
Captain Charles Snead
Captain Severn Teackle
Captain Thomas Martin
Captain Isaac Webb

6th Virginia Regiment of Foot, 1776-1778, 1778-1782

(Also designated at various times: 6th Virginia Battalion of Foot in the Service of the United States, 6th Virginia Regiment on Continental Establishment.)

Field Officers, 1776-1778

Colonel Mordecai Buckner, February 13, 1776-February 9, 1777. Cashiered for cowardice.

Colonel John Gibson, October 27, 1777-September 14, 1778. Transferred to 9th Virginia Regiment.

Lieutenant Colonel Thomas Elliott, February 13, 1776-September 3, 1776. Promoted to colonel, 4th Virginia Regiment.

Lieutenant Colonel James Hendricks, August 13, 1776-September 27, 1777. Promoted to colonel, 1st Regiment.

Lieutenant Colonel Charles Simms, September 27, 1777-September 14, 1778. Transferred to 2d Virginia Regiment.

Major James Hendricks, February 13, 1776-August 13, 1776. Promoted.

Major Richard Parker, August 13, 1776-February 10, 1777. Promoted to lieutenant colonel, 2d Virginia Regiment.

Major James Johnston, April 1, 1777-August 15, 1777. Resigned.

Major Oliver Towles, August 15, 1777. Prisoner at Germantown, December 1777-fall 1780. Promoted to lieutenant colonel, 5th

Virginia Regiment, February 12, 1781, to date from February 10, 1778.

Major Samuel Hopkins, November 29, 1777-June 19, 1778. Promoted to lieutenant colonel, 14th Virginia Regiment.

Major Richard Clough Anderson, February 10, 1778-September 14, 1778. Transferred to 1st Virginia Regiment.

Like the 3d, 4th, and 5th Virginia regiments, the 6th was authorized by the fourth Virginia convention on December 1, 1775, and taken into Continental service on February 13, 1776. It went into training at Williamsburg. By September most of the men were reported ill, and in December only 25 commissioned officers and 166 soldiers were present for duty. The 6th Regiment was part of General Stephen's brigade at Trenton and part of Weedon's brigade thereafter.[14]

Companies, February 1776-April 1776[15]

1st Company: Captain James Johnson, February 16, 1776. Raised in Lunenburg.

2d Company: Captain Oliver Towles, February 16, 1776. Raised in Spotsylvania.

3d Company: Captain Thomas Patterson, February 24, 1776. Raised in Buckingham.

4th Company: Captain Samuel Hopkins, February 26, 1776. Raised in Mecklenburg.

5th Company: Captain William Gregory, February 26, 1776. Raised in Charles City. (Gregory died, May 1776.)

6th Company: Captain Thomas Ruffin, March 1, 1776. Raised in Prince George. (Ruffin was killed at Brandywine, September 1777.)

7th Company: Captain Samuel Jordan Cabell, March 4, 1776. Raised in Amherst. Riflemen.

8th Company: Captain Thomas Massie, March 11, 1776. Raised in New Kent.

9th Company: Captain Thomas Hutchings, March 21, 1776. Raised in Pittsylvania. Temporarily attached to 3d Virginia Regiment in March 1776.

10th Company: Captain John Jones, April 9, 1776. Raised in Dinwiddie.

Between April 1776 and September 1778 the following men were promoted to captain:

Captain Nicholas Hobson, April 10, 1776
Captain Nathaniel Fox, June 19, 1776
Captain Peter Dunn, June 22, 1776

Captain Alexander Rose, September 17, 1776
Captain William Haley Avery, January 4, 1777
Captain John Stokes, February 20, 1778

After the regiment had been depleted by losses at Brandywine and other battles, its officers and men were absorbed into the 2d Virginia Regiment at White Plains, New York, on September 14, 1778. The designation 6th Virginia Regiment was then applied to what had been the 10th Virginia Regiment.

Field Officers, 1778-1782

Colonel John Green, September 14, 1778-January 1, 1783. Retired.
Lieutenant Colonel Samuel Hawes, September 14, 1778-January 1, 1783. Transferred to new 1st Virginia Regiment.
Major Thomas Ridley, September 14, 1778-February 12, 1781. Retired, but became major of the 1st (Posey's) Regiment; retired, January 1, 1783.
Major David Stephenson, February 12, 1781-January 1, 1783. Was a prisoner at Charleston, May 1780-1783.

Following the White Plains arrangement the 6th Virginia Regiment underwent further internal reorganization:

Companies, September 14, 1778-1779

Colonel's Company:	Captain-Lieutenant James Williams
Lieutenant Colonel's Company:	Lieutenant Thomas Barbee
Major's Company:	Lieutenant Thomas Fox
4th Company:	Captain John Gillison
5th Company:	Captain Richard Stevens
6th Company:	Captain Thomas West
7th Company:	Captain Hughes Woodson
8th Company:	Captain Clough Shelton
9th Company:	Captain Nathan Lammé

John Spotswood, a prisoner since the battle of Germantown in October 1777, was commissioned captain later in 1778. After the retirement of Captain Thomas West, Joseph Blackwell was commissioned captain on March 22, 1779. James Williams became a full captain on September 19, 1778.

As part of the temporary 3d Virginia Regiment, the remnants of the 6th Virginia Regiment surrendered to the British at Charleston on May 12, 1780. A 6th Virginia Regiment was created on paper on February 12, 1781, made up of officers in captivity and inactive officers awaiting the end of the war.

Officers, February 1781-January 1783

Captain John Gillison

Captain John Spotswood
Captain Clough Shelton
Captain Nathan Lammé (transferred to 3d Virginia Regiment)
Captain James Williams
Captain Mayo Carrington
Captain John Henry Fitzgerald
Captain John Nelson
Captain Thomas Hoard
Captain Thomas Barbee
Captain Thomas Bowne

7th Virginia Regiment of Foot, 1776-1778, 1778-1782

(Also designated at various times: 7th Virginia Battalion of Foot in the Service of the United States, 7th Virginia Regiment on Continental Establishment.)

Field Officers, 1776-1778

Colonel William Daingerfield, February 29, 1776-August 13, 1776. Resigned.

Colonel William Crawford, August 14, 1776-March 4, 1777. Resigned. Later served with Virginia and Pennsylvania troops on the frontier near Fort Pitt.

Colonel Alexander McClanachan, October 7, 1776-May 13, 1778. Resigned.

Lieutenant Colonel Alexander McClanachan, February 29, 1776-October 7, 1776. Promoted.

Lieutenant Colonel William Nelson, October 7, 1776-October 15, 1777. Promoted to colonel, 8th Virginia Regiment.

Lieutenant Colonel Holt Richeson, October 9, 1777-September 14, 1778. Transferred to 5th Virginia Regiment.

Major William Nelson, February 29, 1776-October 7, 1776. Promoted.

Major William Davies, February 1777. Taken prisoner following the surrender at Fort Washington; apparently never served as major of the 7th; promoted to lieutenant colonel, 14th Virginia Regiment.

Major John Cropper, January 4, 1777-October 27, 1777. Promoted to lieutenant colonel, 11th Virginia Regiment.

Major John Webb, January 26, 1778-September 14, 1778. Transferred to 5th Virginia Regiment.

The 7th Virginia Regiment was the fifth of the six new regiments raised by the fourth Virginia convention in December 1775. It was taken into Continental service on February 29, 1776. The place of rendezvous was Gloucester Court House.

Most of the personnel were reported sick in September, but 150 men were well enough to be sent north two months later. The remainder of the regiment joined Washington in January 1777 and suffered great hardship for lack of tents. Attached to Woodford's brigade, the 7th Virginia Regiment was decimated at Brandywine in September 1777 but managed to recruit a full quota of replacements by September 1778.[16]

Companies, February 1776-September 1778

1st Company: Captain Gregory Smith, February 7, 1776. Raised in King and Queen.
2d Company: Captain Holt Richeson, February 26, 1776. Raised in King William.
3d Company: Captain Charles Fleming, February 29, 1776. Raised in Chesterfield.
4th Company: Captain John Webb, March 5, 1776. Raised in Essex or Middlesex.
5th Company: Captain Nathaniel Cocke, March 7, 1776. Raised in Halifax.
6th Company: Captain Charles Tomkies, March 7, 1776. Raised in Gloucester.
7th Company: Captain Matthew Jouett, March 18, 1776. Raised in Albemarle.
8th Company: Captain Thomas Posey, March 20, 1776. Raised in Botetourt.
9th Company: Captain Joseph Crockett, April 4, 1776. Raised in Culpeper and Orange.

To replace captains who resigned, transferred, or were promoted, the following men were commissioned between October 1776 and June 1778:

Captain John Nelson, October 28, 1776
Captain Thomas Hill, November 13, 1776
Captain Reuben Lipscomb, November 28, 1776
Captain William Moseley, December 13, 1776
Captain Henry Young, December 28, 1776
Captain Robert Sayres, April 4, 1777
Captain Adam Wallace, June 29, 1778

In the general arrangement of the Virginia Continental Line at White Plains, New York, on September 14, 1778, the 7th Virginia Regiment was renumbered the 5th. The former 11th Virginia Regiment became the 7th Virginia Regiment.

Virginia Continental Infantry

Field Officers, 1778-1782

Colonel Daniel Morgan, September 14, 1778-June 1779. Resigned. Appointed brigadier general, October 13, 1780.

Colonel John Gibson, February 14, 1781-January 1, 1783. Resigned.

Lieutenant Colonel John Cropper, September 14, 1778-August 16, 1779. Resigned.

Lieutenant Colonel Samuel Jordan Cabell, February 12, 1781-January 1, 1783. Prisoner at Charleston from May 1780-January 1783.

Lieutenant Colonel Thomas Posey, September 8, 1781-January 1, 1783. In service with Posey's Virginia Battalion at Yorktown and in Georgia under Wayne.

Major Thomas Posey, September 14, 1778-February 12, 1781. Transferred to 1st Virginia Regiment.

Major Charles Pelham, February 12, 1781-January 1, 1783. Prisoner at Charleston, May 1780.

After the arrangement, the old 7th (renumbered the 5th) served in Woodford's brigade. Most of its personnel were incorporated into the 1st Virginia Regiment and were captured at the surrender of Charleston, South Carolina, in May 1780.

Companies, September 1778-February 1781

Colonel's Company:	Captain-Lieutenant Philip Slaughter
Lieutenant Colonel's Company:	Lieutenant (name unknown)
Major's Company:	Lieutenant (name unknown)
4th Company:	Captain Gabriel Long
5th Company:	Captain Peter Bryan Bruin
6th Company:	Captain Charles Porterfield. Riflemen.
7th Company:	Captain William Johnston
8th Company:	Captain John Marshall
9th Company:	Captain Jesse Davis
10th Company:	Captain Thomas Ransdell

Abraham Shepherd also received a captain's commission at White Plains, but declined it because of illness contracted during two years' captivity in New York. The following men were commissioned as captains in 1779 to replace officers who were promoted:[17]

Captain Isaiah Marks, May 10, 1779
Captain James Wright, July 2, 1779
Captain Robert Porterfield, August 16, 1779

At the Chesterfield Court House arrangement of February 12, 1781, the

9th Virginia Regiment, which had been stationed at Fort Pitt at the time of the surrender of Charleston, was redesignated the 7th Virginia Regiment.

Companies, February 1781-January 1783

1st Company:	Captain Robert Beall
2d Company:	Captain Callohill Minnis
3d Company:	Captain Tarleton Payne
4th Company:	Captain Simon Morgan
5th Company:	Captain Robert Vance. Retired, December 1780.
	Captain Uriah Springer
6th Company:	Captain Benjamin Biggs
7th Company:	Captain George Berry
8th Company:	Captain Holman Minnis
9th Company:	Captain-Lieutenant Lewis Thomas

On January 1, 1783, the 7th Virginia Regiment was renumbered for the last time by the Winchester arrangement. Most Virginia Continentals still in service were transferred to the regiment, which was redesignated the 1st Virginia Regiment. It remained in service until June 1783, when most of the companies were disbanded. Three companies remained in service, guarding military stores, until July or August.

8th Virginia Regiment of Foot, 1776-1778, 1778-1782

(Also designated at various times: German Regiment, 8th Virginia Regiment of Foot in the Service of the United Colonies, 8th Battalion of Foot on Continental Establishment.)

Field Officers

Colonel John Peter Gabriel Muhlenburg, March 1, 1776-February 21, 1777. Promoted to brigadier general.

Colonel Abraham Bowman, January 30, 1777-October 1777. Resigned, December 1777.

Colonel William Nelson, October 15, 1777-December 1777.

Colonel John Neville, December 11, 1777-September 14, 1778.

Lieutenant Colonel Abraham Bowman, March 1, 1776-January 30, 1777. Promoted.

Lieutenant Colonel John Markham, December 23, 1776-October 26, 1777. Cashiered.

Major Peter Helphenstine (Helphinstone), March 1, 1776-October 1776. Died.

Major William Darke, January 4, 1777-February 12, 1781(?).

Prisoner following Germantown until November 1780. Retired, never having served with the 8th Virginia Regiment.
Major Richard Campbell, January 1777-September 29, 1777. Transferred to 13th Virginia Regiment.
Major Morgan Alexander, March 22, 1777-December 1, 1777. Resigned.
Major William Croghan, May 16, 1778-September 14, 1778.

The 8th Virginia Regiment was the last of the six regular units authorized by the fourth Virginia convention on December 1, 1775. The flag of this regiment, which was in the possession of Colonel Muhlenburg's descendants as late as 1849, was described as "made of plain, salmon-couloured silk, with a broad fringe of the same, having a simple white scroll in the centre, upon which are inscribed the words VIII Virga. Regt. The spear head is brass, considerably ornamented." A majority of the original officers and privates came from the German areas of the Virginia-Pennsylvania frontier, a fact which inspired the local designation "the German Regiment." By the time Muhlenburg received his Continental commission, five companies of the 8th Virginia Regiment already had begun recruiting, and the others were nearly completed within the next two months.[18]

Companies, December 1775-April 1776

1st Company: Captain John Stevenson, December 10, 1775. Raised in Augusta.
2d Company: Captain Jonathan Clark, January 23, 1776. Raised in Dunmore (now Shenandoah).
3d Company: Captain George Slaughter, January 26, 1776. Raised in Culpeper.
4th Company: Captain William Darke, February 9, 1776. Raised in Berkeley (now in West Virginia).
5th Company: Captain Richard Campbell, February 19, 1776. Raised in Fincastle and Dunmore. Riflemen.
6th Company: Captain Abel Westfall, March 12, 1776. Raised in Hampshire (now in West Virginia).
7th Company: Captain David Stephenson, March 25, 1776. Raised in Augusta.
8th Company: Captain Thomas Berry, March 27, 1776. Raised in Frederick.
9th Company: Captain James Knox, April 4, 1776. Raised in Fincastle.
10th Company: Captain William Croghan, April 9, 1776. Raised in West Augusta, around Fort Pitt.

In May 1776 a British fleet under Sir Henry Clinton, joined by another under Sir Peter Parker, appeared off Charleston and prepared to attack. A hastily formed army under General Charles Lee marched to Charleston to defend the city and harbor. Among the units in Lee's army was the 8th Virginia Regiment, which became the first regular unit to be sent out of the state. The enlisted men marched somewhat unwillingly, and about forty deserted along the way. On June 18, 1776, Muhlenburg's regiment arrived in the Carolinas. Aided by good gunnery and bad weather the Americans succeeded in driving the British away from Charleston on June 28, 1776.[19]

While at Charleston, Muhlenburg learned that Congress would not consider his regiment part of the Continental Line until it had filled up its ranks. On August 2, 1776, General Charles Lee protested this decision to the Continental Board of War and argued that Muhlenburg had "long thought himself on Continental Establishment, and on this presumption marched five hundred miles away from his own province, under the command of a Continental general." Even though his command was "not complete to a man, (for no regiment is ever complete to a man,) Muhlenburg's regiment was not only the most complete of the province, but I believe of the whole continent . . . the best armed, clothed, and equipped for immediate service."[20]

On August 13 Congress relented and accepted the 8th Virginia Regiment, dating from "the 27th day of May last." Most of Muhlenburg's men remained in the South, awaiting further orders from Lee, and did not return to Virginia until the following February. By that time many had contracted malarial fevers in Georgia.

After mustering at Fredericksburg the men of the 8th Virginia Regiment marched north in detachments between February and April 1777. A return of the regiment for April 11, 1777, listed seven captains sick, four of them with smallpox, and reported that Major Richard Campbell was organizing the second detachment for the march north while seven other officers were busily engaged in recruiting.

Between 1777 and 1778, the following captains were commissioned in the 8th Virginia Regiment:

> Captain Robert Higgins, March 1, 1777
> Captain Matthias Hite, August 10, 1777
> Captain Abraham Kirkpatrick, August 10, 1777
> Captain Isaac Israel, August 10, 1777
> Captain James Higgins, February 1778
> Captain Simon Morgan, March 15, 1778
> Captain John Steed, March 30, 1778

The regiment took part in the battles of Germantown and Brandywine. Major William Darke and captains Robert Higgins and Isaac Israel were captured in these engagements.[21]

At the White Plains arrangement of September 14, 1778, the depleted

8th Virginia Regiment was absorbed by the 4th Virginia Regiment. The former 12th Virginia Regiment then became the 8th.

Field Officers, 1778-1782

Colonel James Wood, September 14, 1778-January 1, 1783. Transferred to new 1st Virginia Regiment.

Lieutenant Colonel Charles Fleming, September 14, 1778-December 15, 1778. Resigned.

Lieutenant Colonel Samuel Jordan Cabell, December 15, 1778-May 12, 1779. Transferred to 5th Virginia Regiment.

Lieutenant Colonel Jonathan Clark, May 10, 1779-January 1, 1783. Prisoner at Charleston, May 1780.

Major Jonathan Clark, September 14, 1778-May 10, 1779. Promoted.

Major Andrew Waggoner, May 10, 1779-February 12, 1781. Retired. Prisoner at Charleston.

Major John Poulson, February 12, 1781-January 1, 1783. Retired, October 1777-November 1780.

Prior to the arrangement, the 8th Virginia Regiment had formed part of Muhlenburg's and Weedon's brigades. After 1778 the regiment belonged to Woodford's brigade.

Companies, September 1778-February 1781

Colonel's Company:	Captain-Lieutenant Abraham Hite
Major's Company:	Lieutenant Joseph Swearingen
3d Company:	Captain Andrew Waggoner
4th Company:	Captain William Vause
5th Company:	Captain Andrew Wallace
6th Company:	Captain Thomas Bowyer
7th Company:	Captain Benjamin Casey
8th Company:	Captain Robert Gamble
9th Company:	Captain Samuel Lapsley
10th Company:	Captain Michael Bowyer. Retired (did not transfer).

To replace those officers who had retired or received promotions, three more captains were commissioned before the Charleston surrender:

Captain Abraham Hite, April 4, 1779
Captain Presley Neville, May 10, 1779
Captain Charles Snead, May 12, 1779

A remnant of the 8th Virginia Regiment was sent to the Carolinas as part of the temporary 3d Virginia Regiment. Captain Andrew Wallace survived the massacre of Buford's detachment at The Waxhaws only to be killed at

Guilford Court House in March 1781. Robert Gamble was captured at Camden in August 1780.

Officers, February 1781
Captain Andrew Wallace
Captain Conway Oldham
Captain Thomas Bowyer
Captain Robert Gamble
Captain Thomas Buckner
Captain Abraham Hite
Captain William White
Captain John Clarke
Captain Hezekiah Morton
Captain Joseph Swearingen
Captain William Spencer
Captain Sigismund Stribling

Seven months after being arranged into the 8th Virginia Regiment, Captain Conway Oldham was killed in battle at Eutaw Springs. The handful of uncaptured veterans served in various capacities until mustered out in 1783.

9th Virginia Regiment of Foot, 1776-1778, 1779-1781

(Also designated at various times: Eastern Shore Regiment, 9th Virginia Battalion of Foot in the Service of the United States, 9th Virginia Regiment on Continental Establishment.)

Field Officers, 1776-1778
Colonel Thomas Fleming, March 2, 1776-August 1776. Died, January 30, 1777.
Colonel George Mathews, February 10, 1777-February 12, 1781. Prisoner, October 1777-December 1781.
Lieutenant Colonel George Mathews, March 4, 1776-February 10, 1777. Promoted.
Lieutenant Colonel John Sayres, January 30, 1777-October 4, 1777. Killed at Germantown.
Lieutenant Colonel George Lyne, October 4, 1777-October 14, 1777. Resigned. Later a member of Continental Board of War.
Lieutenant Colonel Burgess Ball, December 17, 1777-September 14, 1778. Transferred to 1st Virginia Regiment.
Major Matthew Donovan, January 1776-February 1776. Died.
Major James Innes, February 1776-November 1776. Promoted to lieutenant colonel, 15th Virginia Regiment.

Major Levin Joynes, February 21, 1777-December 11, 1777. Prisoner at Germantown, October 1777. Promoted to lieutenant colonel, 11th Virginia Regiment.
Major James Knox, July 6, 1778-September 30, 1778. Retired.

The Eastern Shore, with miles of exposed coastline along both the Atlantic Ocean and the Chesapeake Bay, presented special problems of defense. Throughout the war, privateers and pirates, some of them British supporters but most merely predators, raided the Eastern Shore. The battalion of minutemen which was to have been recruited in Accomack and Northampton counties in autumn 1775 was never raised, and on January 8, 1776, Congress, at the request of the Accomack County committee, ordered three companies of Maryland minutemen to the Virginia Eastern Shore "for the protection of the Association in those parts."[22] Meanwhile, the Virginia convention meeting from December 1775 to January 1776 abolished the aborted Eastern Shore minute battalion and created a seven-company regiment of regulars—the 9th Virginia. Four companies were raised on the Eastern Shore and three on the mainland. In June 1776 Congress took the 9th Regiment into Continental service (as of May 31) and brought it to the full strength of ten companies by ordering the recruitment of three more companies from Accomack and Northampton counties.[23]

Companies, February 1776-October 1777

1st Company: Captain John Cropper, February 5, 1776. Raised in Accomack.
2d Company: Captain Levin Joynes, February 10, 1776. Raised in Accomack.
3d Company: Captain Thomas Davis, February 12, 1776. Raised in Accomack or Northampton. (Davis was cashiered later in 1776.)
4th Company: Captain Thomas Snead, February 14, 1776. Raised in Accomack.
5th Company: Captain Thomas Walker, March 11, 1776. Raised in Albemarle.
6th Company: Captain Samuel Woodson, March 13, 1776. Raised in Goochland.
7th Company: Captain John Hays, March 16, 1776. Raised in Gloucester.
8th Company: Captain George Gilchrist, July 4, 1776. Raised in Accomack.
9th Company: Captain Thomas Parramore, July 4, 1776. Raised in Accomack.
10th Company: Captain John Poulson, July 17, 1776. Raised in Accomack.

Due to an oversight the officers did not received their commissions from Congress until September 1776.

To replace Captain Davis (who was cashiered), Walker (who retired), and Cropper (who was promoted to major, 7th Virginia Regiment), the following men were commissioned:

>Captain Smith Snead, August 31, 1776
>Captain John Blair, December 17, 1776
>Captain William Henderson, January 4, 1777
>Captain Thomas Parker, April 23, 1778
>Captain Nathaniel G. Morris, February 10, 1777

In the fall of 1776 the 9th Virginia Regiment joined Muhlenburg's brigade in New Jersey and fought in the battles of 1776-1777. In October 1777 Washington attacked part of Howe's army at Germantown, Pennsylvania, in a poorly timed action. The entire left wing, composed of Weedon's, Muhlenburg's, Scott's, and Woodford's brigades, was forced to retreat, and the 9th Virginia Regiment was surrounded and captured almost to a man. It then ceased to exist as a fighting unit.[24]

Until a new Continental regiment could be recruited to replace the 9th the 1st and 2d regiments of Virginia State Line were temporarily taken into Continental service.[25]

At the White Plains arrangement of September 14, 1778, the 9th Virginia Regiment, which then existed only on paper, was absorbed by the 1st Virginia Regiment. Custis Kendall, a lieutenant who had escaped capture at Germantown and had been promoted in May 1778, was the only remaining officer of the original 9th Virginia Regiment after White Plains. He became a prisoner at the Charleston surrender in May 1780.

The original 13th Virginia Regiment, then serving Fort Pitt, was renumbered the 9th Virginia Regiment in September 1778.

Field Officers, 1778-1781

>Colonel John Gibson, September 14, 1778-February 12, 1781. Regiment renumbered as 7th Virginia Regiment.
>Lieutenant Colonel Richard Campbell, September 14, 1778. Transferred to 4th Virginia Regiment.
>Major Richard Taylor, September 14, 1778-December 7, 1779. Promoted to lieutenant colonel, 2d Regiment.
>Major William Taylor, December 7, 1779-February 12, 1781. Retired.

The new 9th Virginia Regiment remained west of the Alleghenies for the remainder of its existence. It was the only Virginia Continental unit not captured at Charleston in May 1780. Colonel John Gibson commanded the so-called Western Department around Fort Pitt until December 1781, when he turned over his duties to Brigadier General William Irvine, of Pennsylvania. The 8th Pennsylvania Regiment under Colonel Daniel Brodhead, also stationed at Fort Pitt, then became the permanent garrison and continued as such until 1783.[26]

Gibson's regiment was temporarily under the jurisdiction of George Rogers Clark from 1780 to 1781 and thus took orders from both Continental and state authorities at the same time. Gibson's detachment under Clark consisted of five companies under captains Springer, Biggs, Beall, Vance, and Berry.[27]

Companies, September 1778-February 1781
Colonel's Company: Captain-Lieutenant Benjamin Biggs
Lieutenant Colonel's Company: Lieutenant George Berry
Major's Company: Lieutenant (name unknown)
4th Company: Captain Robert Beall (not Robert Beale of the 3d Virginia Regiment)
5th Company: Captain Benjamin Harrison (of Pennsylvania)
6th Company: Captain Uriah Springer. Light infantry.
7th Company: Captain Thomas Moore
8th Company: Captain James Neal
9th Company: Captain Simon Morgan
10th Company: Captain Robert Vance

Benjamin Biggs was promoted to captain on December 1, 1778, and George Berry attained a captaincy on January 13, 1779.

After the Chesterfield Court House arrangement of February 12, 1781, the 9th Virginia Regiment ceased to exist as such. It was redesignated the 7th Virginia Regiment. Either through oversight or through desire to maintain a paper establishment, Thomas Payne was commissioned a captain in the 9th Virginia Regiment on May 14, 1782. Payne had been a prisoner twice: from 1777 to 1778 after Germantown and from 1780 to 1783 after Charleston.

10th Virginia Regiment of Foot, 1776-1778, 1778-1781

(Also designated at various times: 10th Virginia Battalion of Foot in the Service of the United States, 10th Continental Virginia Regiment, 10th Virginia Regiment on Continental Establishment.)

Field Officers, 1776-1778
Colonel Edward Stevens, November 12, 1776-January 31, 1778. Resigned.

Colonel John Green, January 26, 1778-September 14, 1778. Transferred to 6th Virginia Regiment.
Lieutenant Colonel Lewis Willis, November 13, 1776-March 1, 1778. Resigned.
Lieutenant Colonel Samuel Hawes, March 1, 1778-September 14, 1778. Transferred to 6th Virginia Regiment.
Major George Nicholas, November 13, 1776-October 15, 1777. Promoted to lieutenant colonel, 11th Virginia Regiment.
Major Samuel Hawes, October 4, 1777-March 1, 1778. Promoted.
Major Thomas Ridley, March 1, 1778-September 14, 1778. Transferred to 6th Virginia regiment.

The 10th Virginia Regiment was one of the six new regiments ordered raised by the General Assembly in October 1776 to meet Virginia's quota of fifteen regiments set by Congress on September 16, 1776. Edward Stevens, formerly lieutenant colonel of the Culpeper Minute Battalion, was commissioned on November 12, 1776, to raise this regiment. Unlike the nine regiments already in Continental service, which had been raised by districts, the 10th Regiment was raised at large in the counties of Augusta, Amherst, Fairfax, Culpeper, Orange, Spotsylvania, Fauquier, Cumberland, Caroline, Stafford, and King George.[28]

The regiment marched north in the spring of 1777. By April two companies were reported on the road: four at Baltimore and four at Newcastle, Delaware. After reaching the main army in June the regiment was placed in General George Weedon's brigade.[29]

Companies, November 1776-March 1777

1st Company: Captain Thomas West, November 10, 1776. Raised in Fairfax.
2d Company: Captain John Gillison, November 18, 1776. Raised in Culpeper. (Gillison was wounded at Brandywine.)
3d Company: Captain James Franklin, November 19, 1776. Raised in Amherst.
4th Company: Captain Richard Stevens, November 25, 1776. Raised in Orange(?).
5th Company: Captain John Spotswood, November 29, 1776. Raised in Spotsylvania. (Spotswood was wounded at Brandywine.)
6th Company: Captain Tarleton Woodson, December 3, 1776. Raised in Albemarle.
7th Company: Captain David Laird, December 3, 1776. Raised in Caroline or King George(?).
8th Company: Captain John (or Jonathan) Symmes, December 3, 1776. Raised in Augusta.

Virginia Continental Infantry 63

9th Company: Captain John Mountjoy, January 14, 1777.
   Raised in Stafford.
10th Company: Captain Clough Shelton, March 1, 1777.
   Raised in Fauquier or Cumberland(?).

To replace Captain Tarleton Woodson (who was promoted to major of the 2d Canadian Regiment), John Symmes (who resigned), and David Laird (who was dismissed), the following men were commissioned:

Captain Thomas Blackwell, March 2, 1777
Captain James McIlhaney, November 5, 1777
Captain Nathan Lammé, December 31, 1777

The regiment served at Brandywine and through the remainder of the campaigns in New Jersey and Pennsylvania.

On September 14, 1778, the 10th Virginia Regiment was arranged with the rest of the Virginia Continental units at White Plains, New York. It was renumbered the 6th Virginia Regiment, and the 14th Virginia Regiment was renumbered the 10th.

Field Officers, 1778-1781

Colonel William Davies, September 14, 1778-February 12, 1781. Transferred to 1st Virginia Regiment.
Lieutenant Colonel Samuel Hopkins, September 14, 1778-February 12, 1781. Prisoner at Charleston, May 1780; exchanged; transferred to 1st Virginia Regiment.
Major Samuel Jordan Cabell, September 14, 1778. Promoted to lieutenant colonel, 8th Virginia Regiment.
Major Andrew Waggoner, December 15, 1778-May 10, 1779. Transferred to 8th Virginia Regiment.
Major William Lewis, May 12, 1779-February 12, 1781. Prisoner at Charleston, May 1780; transferred to 3d Virginia Regiment.

The new 10th Virginia Regiment was part of Muhlenburg's brigade in 1778-1779 and part of Scott's brigade in 1779. In May 1779 the regiment was combined with the 1st Virginia Regiment. Nine officers of the 10th Virginia Regiment were at Charleston when it fell in May 1780.

Companies, September 1778-1779

Colonel's Company: Captain-Lieutenant Thomas Holt
Lieutenant Colonel's Company: Lieutenant Henry Conway. Promoted to captain, December 15, 1779.
Major's Company: Lieutenant Nathaniel Terry. Promoted to captain.
4th Company: Captain Nathan Reid

5th Company:	Captain John Marks
6th Company:	Captain John Winston
7th Company:	Captain Peter Jones
8th Company:	Captain John Overton

On February 12, 1781, the regiment was disbanded when a board of field officers at Chesterfield Court House reduced the Virginia Continental regiments to eight. Colonel William Davies was appointed the governor's special assistant in charge of military affairs in March 1781, with the title of commissioner of the war office, and served until that post was abolished in December 1782. Although he was nominally the commander of the 1st Virginia Regiment, Davies's duties kept him in Richmond until the end of the war.

In 1781 Alexander Ewing, General Nathanael Greene's aide-de-camp, was promoted to a captaincy in the defunct 10th Virginia Regiment. He continued on detached service with Greene until the end of the war and was wounded at Guilford Court House in March 1781.

11th Virginia Regiment of Foot, 1776-1778, 1778-1781

(Also designated at various times: 11th Virginia Battalion of Foot in the Service of the United States, 11th Virginia Regiment on Continental Establishment.)

Field Officers, 1776-1778

Colonel Daniel Morgan, November 12, 1776-September 14, 1778. Regiment renumbered 7th Virginia Regiment in 1778.

Lieutenant Colonel Christian Febiger, November 13, 1776-September 26, 1777. Promoted to colonel, 2d Virginia Regiment.

Lieutenant Colonel George Nicholas, October 15, 1777-November 27, 1777. Resigned.

Lieutenant Colonel John Cropper, October 26, 1777-September 14, 1778. Regiment renumbered 7th Virginia Regiment in 1778.

Major William Heth, November 13, 1776-April 1, 1777. Promoted to lieutenant colonel, 3d Virginia Regiment.

Major Thomas Snead, April 1, 1777-March 8, 1778. Resigned.

Major Thomas Massie, February 20, 1778-September 14, 1778. Transferred to 2d Virginia Regiment.

The initial organization of the 11th Virginia Regiment was identical to that of the 10th. Raised in Prince William, Amelia, Loudoun, and Frederick counties, it was closely associated with Daniel Morgan's rifle company of 1775 and with Morgan's elite rifle corps of 1777-1778. Morgan, Febiger, and

Heth were all veterans of Arnold's expedition against Quebec and had recently been released from their paroles. Most of the captains had served as enlisted men on the same expedition.[30]

Companies, November 1776-February 1777

1st Company: Captain Thomas West, commission dated from July 21, 1776. County of origin unknown.

2d Company: Captain Gabriel Long, commission dated from July 23, 1776. Raised in Culpeper(?).

3d Company: Captain William Blackwell, commission dated from July 31, 1776. County of origin unknown.

4th Company: Captain William Johnson, November 22, 1776. County of origin unknown.

5th Company: Captain William Smith, November 22, 1776. County of origin unknown.

6th Company: Captain Peter Benjamin, December 13, 1776. County of origin unknown.

7th Company: Captain Peter Bryan Bruin, December 19, 1776. County of origin unknown.

8th Company: Captain George Rice, January 18, 1777. County of origin unknown.

9th Company: Captain Charles Gallahue, January 1777. Raised in Prince William.

10th Company: Captain Charles Porterfield, February 3, 1777. Raised in Amelia(?).

Thomas West died late in 1776 or early in 1777, and his company was placed under Captain James Calderwood for a short time.

Six captains from Colonel Moses Rawlings's rifle regiment were officially transferred to the 11th Virginia Regiment early in 1777 but never actually served with the regiment:

Captain Abraham Shepherd (remained with rifle regiment)
Captain Alexander Lawson Smith (remained with rifle regiment)
Captain Samuel Finley (prisoner in New York, 1776-1780)
Captain William Brady (remained with rifle regiment)
Captain William George (prisoner in New York, 1776-1780)
Captain Nathaniel Pendleton (prisoner in New York, 1776-1780)

Enlisted men from West and Calderwood's company and those destined for the companies under Shepherd and Brady were assigned to Long's company. From May 1777 through May 1778, Long's company of seventy-one men served with a special detachment of Morgan's Rifle Corps commanded by Lieutenant Philip Slaughter. After the victory at Saratoga the special rifle companies were gradually phased out, and their members rejoined their respective regiments in 1778.[31]

In September 1778 at White Plains, New York, the 11th Virginia Regiment was renumbered the 7th Virginia Regiment. At this time Slaughter's detachment of riflemen was combined with Captain Charles Porterfield's company, and the 15th Virginia Regiment was renumbered the 11th Virginia Regiment.

Field Officers, 1778-1781

Colonel Abraham Buford, September 14, 1778-February 12, 1781. Transferred to 3d Virginia Regiment.

Lieutenant Colonel Gustavus Brown Wallace, September 14, 1778-February 12, 1781. Prisoner at Charleston, South Carolina. May 1780-January 1783; transferred to 2d Virginia Regiment.

Major David Stephenson, September 14, 1778-February 12, 1781. Prisoner at Charleston, South Carolina, May 1780; transferred to 6th Virginia Regiment.

Major Joseph Crockett(?), May 20, 1779-December 1779. Commanded Illinois Battalion, Virginia State Line, 1779-1781.

Companies, September 1778-November 1779

Colonel's Company:	Captain-Lieutenant Lawrence Butler
Lieutenant Colonel's Company:	Lieutenant Philip Mallory(?)
Major's Company:	Lieutenant Samuel Booker
4th Company:	Captain John Gregory
5th Company:	Captain James Gray
6th Company:	Captain Thomas Edmunds
7th Company:	Captain Thomas Wells
8th Company:	Captain David Mason
9th Company:	Captain Samuel Smith

Captain Edwin Hull, of the 15th Virginia Regiment, became supernumerary on September 30, 1778. Philip Mallory, Lawrence Butler, and Samuel Booker received commissions as captains in 1779 and 1780.

With the rest of the Virginia Continentals, the remaining officers and enlisted men of the new 11th Virginia Regiment were placed in the temporary 1st Virginia Regiment and sent to Charleston in 1780. Colonel Buford, commanding the 3d Virginia Detachment, returned to Virginia to assemble recruits in Richmond and Petersburg. Having thus avoided the capitulation of Charleston in May, Buford's detachment was defeated by the British Legion of Banastre Tarleton on May 29, 1780, near The Waxhaws, South Carolina.

On February, 12, 1781, the Chesterfield Court House arrangement reduced the Virginia Continental Line to eight regiments, and the 11th Virginia Regiment ceased to exist.

12th Virginia Regiment of Foot, 1776-1778

(Also designated at various times: 12th Virginia Battalion of Foot in the Service of the United States, 12th Virginia Regiment on Continental Establishment.)

Field Officers

Colonel James Wood, November 12, 1776-September 14, 1778. Regiment renumbered 8th Virginia Regiment.

Lieutenant Colonel James Neville, November 12, 1776-December 11, 1777. Promoted to colonel, 8th Virginia Regiment.

Lieutenant Colonel Levin Joynes, December 11, 1777-September 14, 1778. Wounded and taken prisoner at Germantown; retired, February 1781.

Major Charles Simms, November 12, 1776-September 26, 1777. Promoted to lieutenant colonel, 6th Virginia Regiment.

Major George Slaughter, October 9, 1777-November 4, 1777. Resigned. Commanded Illinois detachment of Indian fighters, May 1780.

Major Jonathan Clark, January 10, 1778-September 14, 1778. Regiment renumbered 8th Virginia Regiment.

The third of the six additional regiments authorized by the General Assembly in October 1776 was the 12th Virginia Regiment. It was raised mostly in the western frontier counties of Dunmore (Shenandoah), Augusta, Berkeley, Hampshire, and Botetourt, with one company from Prince Edward. These companies were augmented in April 1777 by the independent companies stationed at Fort Pitt and Fort Randolph (Point Pleasant). Most of these garrison troops had been in service on the frontier since late in 1774, guarding Tygart's Valley and other strategic points on or near the Ohio River.

Companies, November 1776-December 1776

1st Company: Captain Andrew Waggener, commission to date from June 30, 1776. Raised in Augusta.

2d Company: Captain Benjamin Casey, commission to date from September 1, 1776. Raised in Hampshire.

3d Company: Captain Stephen Ashby, commission to date from September 9, 1776. Raised in Hampshire.

4th Company: Captain Michael Bowyer, commission to date from September 30, 1776. Raised near Tygart's Valley, West Augusta District.

5th Company: Captain Matthew Arbuckle, November 1776. Raised in Botetourt for Fort Randolph.

6th Company: Captain William McKee, November 1776. Raised in Rockbridge for Fort Randolph.

68   *Virginia Military Organizations*

> 7th Company: Captain Jonathan Langdon, November 27, 1776. Raised in Dunmore (Shenandoah).
> 8th Company: Captain Joseph Mitchell, December 9, 1776. Raised in Berkeley or Augusta.
> 9th Company: Captain Rowland Madison, December 16, 1776. Raised in Prince Edward(?).
> 10th Company: Captain Thomas Bowyer, December 16, 1776. Raised in Botetourt.

From 1777 to 1778 the regiment served in General Scott's brigade. After losses through death, disease, and desertion, the regiment became sadly depleted. Consequently, four additional captains were commissioned in the unit:

> Captain William Vause, January 3, 1777
> Captain Andrew Wallace, March 13, 1777
> Captain Samuel Lapsley (of Gist's Additional Regiment; served briefly in 1777).
> Captain Robert Gamble, March 7, 1778

At the White Plains arrangement of September 14, 1778, the regiment was renumbered the 8th Virginia Regiment. There was no 12th Virginia Regiment after 1778.

13th Virginia Regiment of Foot, 1776-1778

(Also designated at various times: 13th Virginia Battalion in the Service of the United States, 13th Virginia Regiment on Continental Establishment, West Augusta Regiment.)

Field Officers

Colonel Samuel Meredith, November 12, 1776. Declined.
Colonel William Russell, November 19, 1776-September 14, 1778. Transferred to 5th Virginia Regiment.
Lieutenant Colonel John Gibson, November 12, 1776-October 27, 1777. Promoted to colonel, 6th Virginia Regiment.
Lieutenant Colonel Richard Campbell, February 20, 1778-September 14, 1778. Regiment renumbered 9th Virginia Regiment.
Major George Lyne, November 12, 1776-October 4, 1777. Promoted to lieutenant colonel, 9th Virginia Regiment.
Major Richard Campbell, September 29, 1777-February 20, 1778. Promoted.
Major Richard Taylor, February 4, 1778-September 14, 1778. Regiment renumbered 9th Virginia Regiment.

The West Augusta Regiment was the fourth of the six regiments authorized by the General Assembly in October 1776. Recruiting in Yohogania, Monongalia, and Ohio counties began in December 1776.

Five of the companies served with Muhlenburg's brigade in the northern campaigns, while the remaining five were stationed at Fort Pitt and Fort Randolph (Point Pleasant).

Companies, December 1776-January 1778

1st Company: Captain Robert Beall, December 16, 1776. Raised in Yohogania. (Not to be confused with Robert Beale of the 3d Virginia Regiment.)
2d Company: Captain Benjamin Harrison, December 16, 1776. Raised in Yohogania.
3d Company: Captain George McCormick, December 16, 1776. Raised in West Augusta.
4th Company: Captain David Steele, December 16, 1776. Raised in Yohogania.
5th Company: Captain James Sullivan, December 16, 1776. Raised in West Augusta.
6th Company: Captain John Lemon, December 18, 1776. Raised in West Augusta.
7th Company: Captain James Hook(e), December 19, 1776. Raised in Yohogania.
8th Company: Captain James Neal, December 19, 1776. Raised in Monongalia.
9th Company: Captain Silas Zane, February 9, 1777. Raised in West Augusta.
10th Company: Captain David Scott, 1777. Raised in Monongalia.

In 1778, the following officers received captains' commissions in the 13th Virginia Regiment:

Captain Thomas Moore, January 23, 1778
Captain Simon Morgan, March 15, 1778
Captain Robert Vance, August 19, 1778
Captain Uriah Springer, August 25, 1778

Uriah Springer's company was organized as a light infantry unit trained for rapid movement through rough country.

On September 14, 1778, at White Plains, New York, the 13th Virginia Regiment was renumbered the 9th. There was no 13th Virginia Regiment after this.

When the regiment was renumbered it was stationed at Fort Pitt, together with Colonel Daniel Brodhead's 8th Pennsylvania Regiment, and thus escaped the Charleston surrender in May 1780.[32]

14th Virginia Regiment of Foot, 1776-1778

(Also designated at various times: 14th Virginia Battalion of Foot in the Service of the United States, 14th Virginia Regiment on Continental Establishment, 5th Battalion of the New Raised Virginia Continental Regulars.)

Field Officers

Colonel Charles Lewis, November 12, 1776-March 28, 1778. Resigned.

Colonel William Davies, March 20, 1778-September 14, 1778. Regiment renumbered 10th Virginia Regiment.

Lieutenant Colonel Richard Kidder Meade, November 12, 1776-March 12, 1777. Appointed to Washington's staff.

Lieutenant Colonel William Davies, February 21, 1777-March 20, 1778. Promoted.

Lieutenant Samuel Hopkins, June 19, 1778-September 14, 1778. Promoted.

Major Abraham Buford, November 13, 1776-April 1, 1777. Promoted to lieutenant colonel, 5th Virginia Regiment.

Major George Stubblefield, April 1, 1777-February 22, 1778.

Major Samuel Jordan Cabell, December 20, 1777-September 14, 1778. Regiment renumbered 10th Virginia Regiment.

The 14th Virginia Regiment was the fifth of the six regiments ordered raised by the General Assembly in October 1776. In March 1777 Colonel Charles Lewis was ordered to send all the men raised at that time to join the main army. To speed the march the soldiers were required to supply their own arms, blankets, and clothes, all of which were to be replaced from Continental sources in Philadelphia. The companies from Albemarle, Bedford, Fincastle, Pittsylvania, Halifax, Charlotte, and Lunenburg counties were to rendezvous at Charlottesville, while those from Prince George, Dinwiddie, Hanover, Goochland, and Louisa were to meet at Fredericksburg. In July 1777 the first companies reached Washington's headquarters at Morristown, New Jersey, after having passed through Baltimore, "Trentown," and Middlebrook, leaving sick soldiers in each of those towns. As part of General Weedon's brigade, the regiment fought in the battles of Brandywine and Germantown.[33]

Companies, October 1776-February 1777

1st Company: Captain John Overton, October 4, 1776. Raised in Hanover.

2d Company: Captain Peter Johnes, November 18, 1776. County of origin unknown.
3d Company: Captain Edward Garland, November 20, 1776. Raised in Lunenburg.
4th Company: Captain Henry Conway, November 28, 1776. County of origin unknown.
5th Company: Captain Thomas Thweatt, December 2, 1776. County of origin unknown.
6th Company: Captain John Winston, December 5, 1776. Raised in Hanover(?).
7th Company: Captain Nathan Reid, January 28, 1777. County of origin unknown.
8th Company: Captain Moses Hawkins, February 6, 1777. County of origin unknown.
9th Company: Captain John Marks, February 12, 1777. County of origin unknown.
10th Company: Captain Joseph Michaux, February 19, 1777. Raised in Charlotte.

In February 1777 Lieutenant Drury Oliver was reported to be in command of a company in the regiment. George Lambert and Cyrus L. Roberts were commissioned captains on February 24, 1777, and on January 15, 1778, respectively.

At the White Plains, New York, arrangement the 14th Virginia Regiment was renumbered the 10th Virginia Regiment. There was no 14th Virginia Regiment after 1778.

15th Virginia Regiment of Foot, 1776-1778

(Also designated at various times: 15th Virginia Battalion in the Service of the United States, 15th Virginia Regiment on Continental Establishment.)

Field Officers

Colonel David Mason, November 12, 1776-July 1, 1777. Resigned.
Lieutenant Colonel James Innes, November 13, 1776-(?) 1777. Resigned.
Lieutenant Colonel Gustavus Brown Wallace, March 20, 1778-September 14, 1778. Regiment renumbered 11th Virginia Regiment.
Major Holt Richeson, November 13, 1776-October 9, 1777. Promoted to lieutenant colonel, 7th Virginia Regiment.
Major Gustavus Brown Wallace, October 4, 1777-March 20, 1778. Promoted.

Major Francis Taylor, March 20, 1778-September 14, 1778. Retired. Later commanded Convention Army Guards, Virginia State Line.

This regiment, the sixth of those authorized by the General Assembly in October 1776, was the last numbered Virginia Continental regiment of foot. Throughout its two-year existence the regiment was part of General Woodford's brigade.[34]

The 15th Virginia Regiment was raised in Princess Anne, Nansemond, King William, Richmond, Westmoreland, Isle of Wight, Sussex, Southampton, Surry, Brunswick, and Amelia counties. An ensign raised his quota of men in Norfolk and Chesterfield counties.

Companies, November 1776-December 1776

1st Company: Captain John Gregory, November 19, 1776. Raised in Nansemond.
2d Company: Captain William Grymes, November 21, 1776. Raised in Princess Anne.
3d Company: Captain James Gray, November 22, 1776. County of origin unknown.
4th Company: Captain Samuel Smith, November 22, 1776. County of origin unknown.
5th Company: Captain William Johnston, December 24, 1776. County of origin unknown.
6th Company: Captain James Mason, November 25, 1776. Raised in Brunswick.
7th Company: Captain Edwin Hull, November 25, 1776. Raised in Northumberland.
8th Company: Captain Thomas Edmunds, November 25, 1776. Raised in Sussex.
9th Company: Captain James Foster, November 28, 1776. County of origin unknown.
10th Company: Captain George Lee Turberville, December 2, 1776. Raised in Westmoreland.

To replace officers who were promoted, killed, or transferred to other units, the following officers were commissioned between 1777 and 1778:

Captain James Harris, July 4, 1777
Captain Thomas Willis (or Wells), July 21, 1777
Captain Samuel Booker, August 1, 1777
Captain John Marshall, July 1, 1778

On September 14, 1778, at White Plains, New York, the 15th Virginia Regiment was renumbered the 11th Virginia Regiment. There was no 15th Virginia Regiment after 1778.

The Additional Continental Regiments, 1777-1781

4

ON December 27, 1776, three months after the Continental army had been fixed at eighty-eight battalions, Congress authorized General Washington to raise sixteen regiments at large as a supplementary force. Although some of the additional regiments were recruited on a Continental basis, most of them were raised within fairly limited geographical areas.

Four of these units were composed largely of Virginians, with smaller numbers coming from Pennsylvania and Maryland. Although these units were not considered a part of Virginia's Continental quota during the war, many of the officers and soldiers received land bounties from the state afterwards.

Colonel Nathaniel Gist's Additional Continental Regiment was the only one of the four still in existence at the surrender of Charleston, South Carolina. Grayson's Regiment was weakened by an epidemic of smallpox, while Thruston's Regiment failed to recruit enough men to be militarily effective. Both were absorbed into Gist's Regiment in 1779. The fourth additional regiment with a significant Virginia contingent was a rifle regiment under Colonel Moses Rawlings. This regiment never completed its organization, and those men recruited were assigned to other units.

Colonel William Grayson's Additional Continental Regiment of Infantry, 1777-1779

(Also designated at various times: Grayson's Regiment, 16th Virginia Regiment.)

Field Officers

Colonel William Grayson, January 11, 1777-April 22, 1779. Promoted to commissioner of the Continental Board of War.

Lieutenant Colonel Levin Powell, January 11, 1777-November 15, 1778. Resigned.
Lieutenant Colonel John Thornton, November 15, 1778-April 20, 1779. Retired.
Major David Ross, January 11, 1777-December 20, 1777. Resigned.
Major John Thornton, March 20, 1777-November 15, 1778. Promoted.
Major Nathaniel Mitchell, December 23, 1777-April 22, 1779. Transferred to Gist's Regiment.

William Grayson, assistant secretary and aide-de-camp to General Washington, was promoted to the colonelcy of one of the sixteen additional infantry regiments authorized by Congress on December 27, 1776. Raised at large in Virginia and Maryland, the regiment was attached to General Charles Scott's brigade in 1777. In April 1779 the regiment, whose ranks had been ravaged by smallpox, merged with Nathaniel Gist's additional regiment, and Grayson was put in command of the Continental War Office.[1]

Companies, January 1777-April 1779

1st Company:	Captain Thomas Triplett, January 13, 1777
2d Company:	Captain Francis Willis, January 14, 1777
3d Company:	Captain John Willis, January 14, 1777
4th Company:	Captain Cleon Moore, January 29, 1777
5th Company:	Captain Granville Smith, February 4, 1777
6th Company:	Captain Hebard Smallwood, February 4, 1777
7th Company:	Captain James McGuire, February 5, 1777
8th Company:	Captain John McGuire, February 5, 1777
9th Company:	Captain Strother Jones, May 14, 1777
10th Company:	Captain Peter Grant, August 20, 1777

The regiment fought in the Pennsylvania campaigns of 1777. Captain Moore was wounded at Brandywine and Captain John McGuire at Germantown. Before the merger with Gist's Regiment, Lieutenant Thomas Bell was promoted to the captaincy of the 10th Company.

Colonel Nathaniel Gist's Additional Continental Regiment of Infantry, 1777-1781

(Also designated at various times: Gist's Regiment, Gist's Rangers.)

Field Officers
Colonel Nathaniel Gist, January 11, 1777-January 1, 1783. Taken prisoner at Charleston, South Carolina, May 1780. Retired.

Major Nathaniel Mitchell, April 22, 1779-January 1, 1781. Retired.

On January 11, 1777, Nathaniel Gist (pronounced "guest"), of Virginia, was authorized by Washington to raise a corps of rangers in his home state and in Maryland. Three companies were recruited and were attached to Muhlenburg's brigade in 1777-1778. On January 1, 1779, the enlisted men from Colonel Charles Mynn Thruston's additional regiment were absorbed by Gist's Rangers, and on April 22, 1779, three companies of Grayson's Regiment, by then disbanded, were attached to the ranger corps.[2]

Companies, March 1777-April 1779
1st Company: Captain John Gist, March 9, 1777. Raised near Frederick, Maryland.
2d Company: Captain Samuel Lapsley, March 9, 1777. Raised in Virginia.
3d Company: Captain Joseph Smith, May 31, 1777. Raised in Maryland.

Companies added after April 22, 1779
4th Company: Captain Strother Jones, April 22, 1779. From Grayson's Regiment.
5th Company: Captain Thomas Bell, April 22, 1779. From Grayson's Regiment.
6th Company: Captain Alexander Breckinridge, April 23, 1779
7th Company: Captain Francis Muir, April 1779
8th, or "Major's," Company: Major Nathaniel Mitchell, April 1779. From Grayson's Regiment.

Gist's enlarged regiment was sent south in late 1779, and most of its officers and men were captured when Charleston fell on May 12, 1780. On November 1, 1780, a general order disbanded Gist's Regiment, effective January 1, 1781.[3]

Colonel Charles Mynn Thruston's Additional Continental Regiment, 1777-1779

(Also designated at various times: Thruston's Regiment.)

Field Officers
Colonel Charles Mynn Thruston, January 15, 1777-January 1, 1779
Lieutenant Colonel Angus McDonald, April 1777. Declined to serve.
Lieutenant Colonel John Thornton, April or May 1777-January 1779
Major John Thornton, March 20, 1777. Promoted.

Charles Mynn Thruston, of Frederick County, was the second of Virginia's "fighting parsons" in the Revolution. Like Peter Muhlenburg, Thruston had had prior military experience, serving as a lieutenant in Colonel William Byrd's 2d Virginia Regiment of 1756-1758. In 1758 both Thruston and Colonel George Washington had been members of Forbes's expedition against Fort Duquesne.

Thruston was one of the most active members of the Frederick committee of safety in 1775, and in 1776 he raised a company of gentlemen volunteers and joined Washington in the north. In January 1777 the company became the nucleus of one of the sixteen additional regiments. Thruston's luck, which had carried him unscathed through the French and Indian War and the battles of Harlem Heights, White Plains, and Trenton, ran out in March 1777. While storming a small redoubt at Quibbletown (Piscataway), near Amboy, New Jersey, Parson Thruston had his arm shattered by a musket ball. John Thruston, the colonel's twelve-year-old son, and Lieutenant Colonel Thornton managed to drag him to safety.

Since Thruston was the motivating spirit behind the partially raised regiment, recruiting trickled to a halt while he recovered from his wound. The unit, which never reached regimental strength, took part in the battle of Monmouth, but its small size made it almost useless. On January 1, 1779, the remaining personnel were transferred to Gist's Regiment. After the war Colonel Thruston abandoned both the army and the church and turned to politics. He served in the House of Delegates from 1782 through 1788, representing Frederick County. His son John, whose military career began at the age of twelve, became a cornet in John Rogers's troop of Illinois Dragoons under George Rogers Clark.[4]

Companies, January 1777-January 1779

Frederick Volunteer Company: Captain (Colonel) Charles Mynn Thruston, late 1776-March 8, 1777. Wounded.

2d Company: Captain S. William Snickers, March 1777-January 31, 1778. Resigned.

3d Company: Captain William Scott, April 3, 1777-April 4, 1778. Dismissed and transferred to Colonel Thomas Hartley's additional regiment.

4th Company: Captain George Scott, ?-October 1778

5th Company: Captain Van Swearingen, March 1777. This company of the 8th Pennsylvania Regiment was temporarily attached during the Amboy battle.

[6th Company]: Lieutenant James Chapline, 1777

7th Company: Captain John Byrn, June 4, 1777-August 1, 1778. Resigned.

8th Company: Captain James Monroe, July 1777. Only fifteen

men were raised, and Monroe became a major on Lord Stirling's staff on November 20, 1777.

Colonel Moses Rawlings's Additional Continental Regiment, 1777-1780

Field Officers
Colonel Moses Rawlings, January 12, 1777-May 1779
Major Alexander Lawson Smith, September 11, 1777-September 6, 1780

While Moses Rawlings, who had been captured at Fort Washington, was still a British prisoner, Congress authorized General Washington to appoint the colonels of the sixteen additional Continental regiments. Washington ordered the creation of a new rifle regiment, leaving the colonelcy vacant until Rawlings's release or escape. Lieutenants Samuel Finley and William George, also of the original rifle regiment, were promoted to captaincies, but both remained prisoners until 1780.

Seven companies of riflemen were raised for Rawlings's regiment in 1777 and 1778, but six of them were subsequently transferred to the 11th Virginia Continental Regiment. After Rawlings's captivity ended in 1778, he and seven captains attempted to recruit a full regiment, but their efforts were doomed to failure. Most of the available riflemen had been drafted into Daniel Morgan's battalion the previous year. Furthermore, units already established took precedence over the rifle regiment in filling their quotas of recruits. On January 23, 1779, Rawlings was ordered to raise three companies for the defense of Fort Pitt, but he could only muster seventy men. In April even these men were requisitioned for Baron de Arendt's German battalion. Rawlings resigned in disgust a month later.[5]

Companies, January 1777-May 1779
1st Company: Captain Abraham Shepherd, January 1777
2d Company: Captain Alexander Lawson Smith, January 1777
3d Company: Captain William Brady, January 1777
4th Company: Captain Adamson Tannehill, April 1, 1778
5th Company: Captain Elijah Evans, April 10, 1778
6th Company: Captain Thomas Warman, November 1, 1778. Prisoner from 1776 until 1781.
7th Company: Captain James McCubbin Lingan, December 10, 1778
8th Company: Captain William Blackwell, 1777

Moses Rawlings was not forgotten by Congress. In 1780 he received a staff appointment as assistant quartermaster general at Fort Frederick, Maryland. He supervised the moving of the Saratoga Convention prisoners from Albemarle and Winchester barracks to Fort Frederick in 1781 and 1782. He retired from Continental service in November 1783.[6]

 *Miscellaneous and Special Units and the Partizan Legions* 5

ONE of the major causes of weakness in the central organization of the Continental army was the wide variety of independent and semiofficial military units that continued to appear and disappear from the payrolls. The earliest independent companies raised in Virginia, which are discussed in chapter 1, were not the last such units to be raised during the war. The later organizations were generally part of the Virginia State Line and as such will be covered in chapter 8.

This chapter deals with units that either were created with official Continental status or soon achieved it, whether they served on a temporary or a permanent basis. The frontier independent companies were first organized to garrison the important outposts at Fort Pitt and Fort Randolph. These were gradually absorbed into the Virginia and Pennsylvania Continental lines. The companies of bodyguards who protected General Washington from 1776 to 1783 and General Charles Lee in 1776 were handpicked for their important duties and were paid by Congress. The remaining units covered in this section, while not strictly Virginia organizations, are included because one or more full companies of Virginians served with them, and their members received Virginia bounty lands after the war.

The partizan, or *freikorps*, organizations were radical departures from the traditional Anglo-American concept of static formations fighting in line of battle. The partizan legions were small, highly mobile units and were composed of cavalrymen, infantry, and artillerymen. On forced marches the foot soldiers either rode double with the cavalry or ran beside the horsemen, holding on to a stirrup. The artillery pieces carried by the legions were small field guns (one- or three-pounders) mounted on light galloper or grasshopper carriages. Each legion was, in effect, a miniature army. Virginians served in the two main partizan legions raised by Congress: those commanded by Charles Armand Tuffin, marquis de la Rouerie, and by Henry "Light Horse Harry" Lee.

Washington's Life Guard, 1776-1783

(Also designated: Commander in Chief's Guard, Washington's Bodyguard.)

Field Officers

Major-Commandant Caleb Gibbs, March 13, 1776-January 1, 1783
Major-Commandant William Colfax, January 1, 1783-September 5, 1783
Major-Commandant Bezaleel Howe, September 5, 1783-December 1783

On March 12, 1776, Congress authorized a company of infantry to protect General George Washington and his not inconsiderable personal baggage in the field. The original company was disbanded in February 1777, but a new detachment of guards was created on May 1, 1777, from Colonel George Baylor's 3d Regiment of Continental Light Dragoons, it being felt that cavalry were more suited to the task.[1]

After September 26, 1778, the personnel of the life guard were put on a rotating basis so that other cavalry units could share in the honor. In 1782 Captain Bartholomew von Heer's Merechausée, or provost guard company, composed largely of Germans and Pennsylvania Dutch, became the permanent guard. Besides guarding the commander in chief, the men of the unit also had the duty of serving as drill instructors to the rest of the army. Continental Inspector General von Steuben personally trained the life guardsmen at Valley Forge and then sent them out to train other drillmasters. Von Heer's provost guard became the forerunners of the modern military police.[2]

Companies, 1776-1783

Infantry

Captain Bezaleel Howe, 1776-1778. Raised in New Hampshire.
Captain Henry Philip Livingston, 1778-1779. Raised in New York.

Cavalry

Captain George Lewis, 1777-1778. Raised in Virginia.
Captain Bartholomew Von Heer (Company of Provost Guards), 1782-1783

General Charles Lee's Life Guard, 1776

Field Officers

Captain-Commandant John Holland, April 1776

On March 12, 1776, Congress authorized an infantry company to protect Commander in Chief George Washington. Not to be outdone, General

Charles Lee, commanding the Southern Department, raised his own life guard. Since no official mention of such a unit is made in congressional accounts nor in Lee's correspondence with John Hancock, it may be that the life guard was paid for out of Lee's own pocket.[3]

On April 12, 1776, the regimental store in Williamsburg sold one pair of shoes and a pair of stockings to "the capt. of General Lee's Life Guard." The receipt book was signed "John Holland." This is the only known reference to Lee's bodyguard discovered to date.[4]

Independent Virginia Frontier Companies, 1775-1778

Unlike the gentlemen independents who flocked to the liberty poles after the gunpowder incident of April 1775, the independent companies formed by the third Virginia convention in July 1775 were regular troops in every sense. Throughout the period from 1750 to 1794 the western frontier, which stretched from Georgia to Upper Canada, was a hotbed of unrest. After the first armed clashes between colonists and royal troops Lord Dunmore attempted to create a counterrevolutionary militia at Fort Pitt, renamed Fort Dunmore after the Indian war of 1774.

On August 18, 1775, Purdie's *Virginia Gazette* reported that Captain Neville's independent company from Winchester had been ordered to Fort Pitt. It arrived on September 11, shortly after garrisons at Wheeling and Point Pleasant (Fort Randolph) had been established to check tory activities and guard the frontier.

On January 8, 1777, Congress assumed control of the frontier forts and requested the Virginia Council of State to raise garrison companies for that purpose. Several months later, five companies of the 13th Virginia Continental Regiment were sent to Fort Pitt as a permanent reinforcement. The independent companies were then consolidated under captains Henry Heth and James O'Hara.

The garrisons were increased in 1778, when the 8th Pennsylvania Continental Regiment was sent to the frontier. The independent companies seem to have passed out of existence by 1779 and the enlisted men transferred to other units.[5]

Companies, 1775-1776

Captain John Neville, July 1775. Raised in Winchester and sent to Fort Pitt.

Captain Matthew Arbuckle, July 1775. Raised in Botetourt and sent to Fort Randolph.

Captain William McKee, July 1775. Raised in West Augusta and sent to Fort Randolph and Wheeling.

Companies, 1777-1779

Captain Robert Campbell, January 1777. Raised in Botetourt and sent to Fort Pitt.

Captain John Robinson, January 1777. Raised in Botetourt and sent to Fort Randolph.

Captain Henry Heth, 1777-1779. In garrison at Fort Pitt.

Captain James O'Hara, 1777-1779. In garrison first at Fort Randolph and then at Fort Pitt.

Captain Samuel Brady's (Ranger) Company, 1777(?)

2d Canadian ("Congress' Own") Regiment, 1776-1783

Field Officers

Colonel Moses Hazen, January 22, 1776-June 1, 1783

Lieutenant Colonel Edward Antil, January 22, 1776-May 1, 1782

Lieutenant Colonel Joseph Torrey, May 1, 1782-June 1, 1783

Major John Taylor (of Caroline), November 13, 1776-February 10, 1779

Major Joseph Torrey, January 9, 1777-May 1, 1782

Major Tarleton Woodson, May 1, 1777-March 1782. Declined commission in Thruston's Regiment and accepted majority in Hazen's.

Major James R. Reid, September 1, 1777-June 1, 1783

Major Lawrence Olivia, May 1, 1782-June 1, 1783

Major Anthony Selin, ?-January 1, 1783

Two regiments of Canadians were recruited by Congress in 1776, one commanded by Colonel Joseph Livingston and one by Colonel Moses Hazen, a former British officer. Congress favored Hazen's regiment and kept it well supplied at public charge. In 1777 two Maryland companies and one company from Connecticut were added to the regiment. On January 1, 1781, all foreigners in the service of the United States (except Armand's Legion) were incorporated into Hazen's command. Although Washington proposed that German prisoners of war who took the oath of allegiance be enlisted under Hazen, nothing came of the plan, and the regiment was disbanded on June 9, 1783, along with most of the other Continental units.[6]

A number of Virginians served as officers and enlisted men under Hazen, notably John Taylor, of Caroline, later judge advocate for the Virginia Continental Line, and Tarleton Woodson, of Albemarle County, both of whom held the rank of major. Apparently all the Virginians in the regiment served in Captain Reuben Taylor's company.

2d Georgia Battalion of Foot, 1776-1780

Field Officers
Colonel Samuel Elbert, July 5, 1776-close of war
Lieutenant Colonel Stephen Drayton, January 7, 1776-July 5, 1776
Lieutenant Colonel John Stirk, July 5, 1776-March 20, 1778
Lieutenant Colonel Daniel Roberts, March 21, 1778-November 18, 1779
Lieutenant Colonel Benjamin Porter, November 18, 1779-May 12, 1780
Major Seth John Cuthbert, January (?) 1776-July 1776
Major Joseph Pannill, July 5, 1776-April 16, 1778
Major Benjamin Porter, April 16, 1778-November 18, 1779
Major Francis Moore, November 18, 1779-(?) 1782

The Georgia Continental Line was created in January 1776, but only one regiment could be raised from the state's small population. On July 5, 1776, Congress resolved that "for the defence of the colony of Georgia, there be an addition of two battalions" (one of them to consist of riflemen) which were to be raised within the states of Virginia, North Carolina, and South Carolina. In August the Virginia Council of State grudgingly allowed Georgia recruiters into the commonwealth, but by December, after the Georgia legislature had authorized a fourth battalion, the permission was withdrawn. Virginia's quota of Continental troops had been raised from nine to fifteen regiments in September 1776, and the Virginia recruiters had enough difficulties raising troops without competition from the Georgians. By October 1776 at least two South Carolina recruiters were also attempting to raise troops in Virginia.[7]

The Georgia government protested the restriction so loudly that the council was obliged to countermand its own order on February 7, 1777, stipulating that henceforth only one battalion of Georgia forces could be raised in Virginia. Recruits were offered high bounties by the Georgia officers, and many men enlisted, claimed the money, and then deserted. Only a few of the Virginia recruits ever reached Georgia. Each recruit was promised twenty dollars' worth of clothing, including two hunting shirts, two pairs of overalls, a sleeved waistcoat of leather or wool, and two pairs of shoes. After signing up, the recruit received seventy dollars in hand and the promise of 100 acres of land upon discharge. The Georgia officers were also empowered to purchase muskets, enough rifles for two "flying companies," and musical instruments. By May 1777 the Georgia forces, traveling aboard the transport *Polly*, reached the Saint Marys River, on the Georgia-Florida border. Colonel Elbert deployed "flying Parties of my Virginians" to search for parties of Florida loyalists and Indians and "keep those Rascals out of Georgia." The promised clothing never arrived, and the Virginians were issued "as much Osnabrigs as will make Coats and Kilts." Ammunition was in short supply, and spanish moss was used for wadding in each cartridge. Each soldier had only six cartridges and had to carry a powder horn and pouch with loose bullets.[8]

On February 13, 1778, Congress ordered that the four Georgia battalions be consolidated into two. Although the Georgia legislature refused to obey, it soon became apparent that there were not enough men to fill four battalions. By November 1779 only about two hundred soldiers were in service, and the four battalions were officially merged into one, presumably designated the 2d Georgia Battalion. At the surrender of Charleston, South Carolina, in May 1780, the six Georgia officers still in service became prisoners of war.[9]

Companies, August 1776-May 1777[10]

1st Company: Captain Benjamin Porter, July 1776 (promoted to major). Lieutenant William D. Strother (promoted to captain). Lieutenant John Cunningham (promoted to captain).

2d Company: Captain Francis Moore, July 5, 1776. Grenadiers. (Moore was promoted to major.) Lieutenant Daniel Duval (Virginia)

3d Company: Captain Jesse Hughes Walton

4th Company: Captain Robert Walton

5th Company: Captain Thomas Scott, Jr.

6th Company: Captain William Smith (Virginia). Lieutenant Alexander Baugh

7th Company: Captain William Lane, Jr. (Virginia). Lieutenant Elisha Miller

8th Company: Captain Isham (or Shem) Cook

9th Company: Captain Samuel Scott

10th Company: Captain John Bard (or Baird)

In addition, lieutenants Robert Ward, George Hancock, John Clarke, J. Winfrey, and John Hawkins, of Virginia, and ensigns Abraham Jones and John Morrison were on the Georgia recruiting service in Virginia in 1776.

In October 1777, John Mosby, of Virginia, was promoted to a captaincy in the 2d Georgia Regiment, as was his brother, Littleberry Mosby. Many of the men in their companies served their enlistments under the impression that they were in the Virginia Continental Line but attached to the Georgia battalions. Because of bounty jumping and other reasons, few Virginians served their full three-year enlistments and consequently were not eligible for bounty land. Notices published in the *Virginia Gazette* indicate that deserters from the 2d Georgia Battalion outnumbered the faithful soldiers.[11]

3d Georgia Battalion of Foot, 1776-1780

Field Officers
Colonel James Screven, July 5, 1776-March 20, 1778
Colonel John Stirk, March 20, 1778-close of war
Lieutenant Colonel Robert Rae, July 5, 1776-March 21, 1778
Lieutenant Colonel John McIntosh, April 1, 1778-close of war
Major Daniel Roberts, July 5, 1776-March 21, 1778
Major Joseph Lane, April 2, 1778-October 1780

The organizational history of the 3d Georgia Battalion is virtually identical with that of the 2d Georgia Battalion. Its officers were recruiting in Virginia in 1776 and 1777. It is unlikely that the unit raised a full ten companies. Only four recruiters were mentioned in the *Virginia Gazette:*[12]

Captain Isaac Hicks, July 1776
Captain Thomas Scott, 1777
Captain Andrew Jeter
Lieutenant James McKenny

Like the 2d and 4th Georgia battalions, the 3d Battalion was merged into one unit of two hundred men in November 1779.

4th Georgia Battalion of Foot, 1776-1780

Field Officers
Colonel John White, February 1, 1777-October 1781
Lieutenant Colonel Thomas Hovenden, February 1, 1777-April 16, 1778
Lieutenant Colonel Joseph Pannill, April 16, 1778-October 22, 1782
Major John Skey Eustace, 1776. Although assigned to the 4th Georgia Battalion, Eustace served as an aide-de-camp to generals Lee, Sullivan, and Greene from 1776 to 1780.
Major Thomas Chisholm, February 1, 1777-March 21, 1778
Major Philip Lowe, June 18, 1778-October 1, 1780

The Georgia legislature authorized a fourth battalion of infantry in December 1776. Except for the late date of its creation, its purpose and overall history are virtually identical with that of the 2d and 3d Georgia battalions. Four recruiting officers advertised for deserters in the *Virginia Gazette:*[13]

Captain William Scott
Lieutenant Walter Dixon
Lieutenant Patrick Fitzpatrick
Lieutenant Bernard Paty

The Continental Corps of Invalids, 1777-1783

Field Officers

Colonel Lewis Nicola, June 20, 1777-June 1783

Following a long-established European custom, Congress raised a corps of invalids (i.e., wounded soldiers who could perform limited duties) to free able-bodied men for active service. Originally the corps was planned as a cadre of military instructors for officer candidates, but the proposed military academy was never established. Instead, the commander in chief's guard, trained directly by Baron von Steuben, acted as instructors to the rest of the Continental Line officers.[14]

Colonel Lewis Nicola, of Pennsylvania, a valuable and energetic leader, was chosen to command the regiment of invalids. In September 1783 Nicola was brevetted to the rank of brigadier general as a belated reward for his faithful services.

Companies, 1777-November 1783

Captain Thomas Arnold, Rhode Island
Captain Moses McFarland, Massachusetts
Captain John McGowan, Pennsylvania
Captain John Riely, Pennsylvania
Captain Ebenezer Hills, Connecticut
Captain Philip Liebert, Canada
Captain John D. Woelper, Pennsylvania
Captain William Williams, North Carolina
Captain Leonard Cooper, Virginia
Captain-Lieutenant William McHatton

Nearly fifty Virginians were transferred to the corps during the war.[15]

Colonel Hugh Stephenson's Virginia and Maryland Rifle Battalion, 1775-1776

Field Officers

Colonel Hugh Stephenson, June 27, 1776-September 1776
Lieutenant Colonel Moses Rawlings, September 1776-December 1776
Major Otho Holland Williams, June 27, 1776-November 16, 1776

In June 1775 Virginia ordered that two volunteer rifle companies be raised to assist Washington's army, encamped near Boston. Daniel Morgan, of Frederick County, and Hugh Stephenson, of Berkeley County, received commissions to raise the rifle companies. Although the two companies were expected to rendezvous at Frederick, Maryland, and travel together, Morgan and Stephenson raced each other to the camp at Roxbury, with Morgan's company arriving first after a record march of six hundred miles in three weeks. On August 4, 1775, Purdie's *Virginia Gazette* reported that rifle companies under Morgan and "Stinson's," of Virginia, and Michael Cresap and Thomas Price, of Maryland, were close to Boston.[16]

Companies, June-October 1775

Captain Hugh Stephenson, June 27, 1775. Virginia.
Captain Daniel Morgan, June 2, 1775. Virginia.
Captain Michael Cresap, June 21, 1775. Maryland.
Captain Thomas Price, June 1775. Maryland.

After Cresap's death in October 1775, Lieutenant Moses Rawlings was promoted to the captaincy of his company. Although the unit was credited to Maryland, a large number of its enlisted men were Virginia residents.

While Morgan's company moved north with Benedict Arnold's expedition against Quebec in the fall of 1775, Stephenson's remained at Roxbury for a short time and then participated at Dorchester Heights and Staten Island before it returned to Virginia early in 1776. Morgan and his men were captured at Quebec, not to be released until January 1777, and so command of the Virginia riflemen naturally fell to Hugh Stephenson. Washington personally recommended him to Congress. On July 29, 1776, Congress resolved that a rifle battalion of nine companies should be raised in Virginia and Maryland.[17]

Companies, July-September 1776

1st Company: Captain Abraham Shepherd, July 9, 1776. Raised in Virginia.
2d Company: Captain Philemon Griffith, July 11, 1776. Raised in Virginia.
3d Company: Captain Alexander Lawson Smith, July 13, 1776. Raised in Maryland.
4th Company: Captain Thomas West, July 21, 1776. Raised in Virginia. (West died in late 1776 or early 1777.)
5th Company: Captain William Brady, July 23, 1776. Raised in Virginia.
6th Company: Captain Samuel Finley, July 9, 1776. Raised in Virginia.

Stephenson died in the fall of 1776, and his second-in-command, Moses Rawlings, of Maryland, was commissioned in his place. Late in the same year, Rawlings's rifle regiment became part of the 2,900-man garrison at Fort Washington on Manhattan Island. This stronghold, together with Fort Lee on the Jersey side of the Hudson River, commanded the passage of the river. Colonel Robert Magaw, in command of Fort Washington, posted Rawlings's men in a small redoubt called Fort George just north of the main fort. The British realized the importance of opening the Hudson and concentrated in force against Fort Washington. Eighteen regiments of British regulars, including the Royal Welsh Fusileers, the Black Watch, and the Coldstream Guards, supported by at least fourteen Hessian regiments with the Royal Artillery and the 17th Light Dragoons, attacked the fort on November 15, 1776. The riflemen, who were reported by Dixon and Hunter's *Virginia Gazette* as lightheartedly "Hessian-hunting" a few days earlier, were forced to retreat from Fort George, Fort Tryon, and Cock-Hill Fort and take refuge in Fort Washington. The two Hessian divisions under von Knyphausen and von Rall surrounded the fort, and after a fierce battle Magaw surrendered the entire garrison. Rawlings remained a prisoner in New York until he was exchanged late in 1778, and many of his men remained captives until 1780 or 1781.[18]

Colonel Daniel Morgan's Battalion of Riflemen, 1777-1778

(Also designated at various times: Morgan's Riflemen, Morgan's Rifle Corps, Virginia Riflemen.)

Field Officers

Colonel Daniel Morgan, summer 1777-fall 1778. Virginia.
Lieutenant Colonel Richard Butler, summer 1777-fall 1778. Pennsylvania.
Major Joseph Morris, summer 1777-fall 1778. New Jersey.

In 1777 Colonel Daniel Morgan, 11th Virginia Continental Regiment, was chosen by Washington to raise a picked corps of sharpshooters as flankers to the main army. Leaving his regiment in the hands of his subordinate, Christian Febiger, Morgan canvassed the army in May and June of 1777 for the ablest sharpshooters. By the fall of the year he had raised five hundred men from the Virginia and Pennsylvania Continental lines and organized them into ten companies.

Washington had originally planned to place the rifle battalion under Colonel Moses Rawlings, of Maryland. Rawlings had been captured at the surrender of Fort Washington in November 1776 and was still a prisoner in New York. Thus Morgan's riflemen were considered only a temporary unit, and they were supposed to become the nucleus of a planned regiment to be commanded by Rawlings after his release.

While attached to the northern army under General Horatio Gates, Morgan's riflemen played a crucial part in the victory at Saratoga in September 1777. During the 1778 campaign a portion of the corps was attached to Captain Charles Porterfield's company of the 11th Virginia Continental Regiment. On September 14, 1778, the White Plains arrangement renumbered this regiment as the 7th Virginia Regiment and transferred the riflemen into existing Virginia and Pennsylvania units. Although Moses Rawlings was released late in 1778, his efforts to recruit a full regiment of riflemen failed.[19]

Companies, July 1777-September 1778

1st Company: Captain Hawkins Boone. Raised in Pennsylvania.
2d Company: Captain Samuel Jordan Cabell. Raised in Virginia.
3d Company: Captain William Henderson. Raised in Virginia.
4th Company: Captain James Knox. Raised in Virginia.
5th Company: Captain Gabriel Long. Raised in Virginia.
6th Company: Captain James Parr. Raised in Pennsylvania.
7th Company: Captain Michael Simpson. Raised in Pennsylvania.
8th Company: Captain Thomas Posey. Raised in Virginia.
9th Company: Captain Benjamin Taliaferro. Raised in Virginia.
10th Company: Captain Van Swearingen. Raised in Pennsylvania.
Detachment: Lieutenant Philip Slaughter. Raised in Virginia.

Volunteer Battalions for the Grand Army, June-August 1778

In response to Continental requests for additional Virginia troops to serve in the main army under General Washington, the Virginia General Assembly authorized four volunteer battalions in June 1778. The battalions, to be made up of men enlisted for six months, were of the usual size and strength—ten companies of fifty men each, rank and file, per battalion. A bounty of thirty dollars and a suit of clothes was voted for each volunteer. To obtain a captain's commission, a candidate had to enlist a quota of twenty-four men, two sergeants, a drummer, and a fifer. A lieutenant's quota was sixteen men and a sergeant. Ensigns had to enlist ten men and one sergeant. The officers were to be chosen according to an elaborate county quota system. On August 6, 1778, Congress advised Virginia that the men would not be needed after all, and the partially formed units were accordingly disbanded.[20]

1st Battalion

Lieutenant Colonel Edward Stevens (resigned from 10th Virginia Continental Regiment)

Major David Jameson (Culpeper Militia)

2d Battalion

Lieutenant Colonel George Slaughter (resigned from 12th Virginia Continental Regiment)

Major Edward Garland (resigned from 14th Virginia Continental Regiment)

3d Battalion

Lieutenant Colonel Lewis Burwell (Mecklenburg Militia)

Major Richard Waugh (militia unknown)

4th Battalion

Lieutenant Colonel Nicholas Cabell (Buckingham Militia)

Major William Haley Avery (resigned from 6th Virginia Continental Regiment)

Colonel Christian Febiger's Light Infantry, 1779

Field Officers

Commander: General Anthony Wayne

Colonel Christian Febiger

Lieutenant Colonel François Louis de Fleury

Major Thomas Posey

After the battle of Monmouth, General Anthony Wayne was given command of the various companies of light infantry in the Continental army. He created a brigade of four provisional regiments, the first two of which were commanded by Colonel Christian Febiger, formerly commander of the 2d Virginia Continental Regiment. Both of these units were officered largely by Virginians. Febiger was a Dane, born in 1746, who settled in Massachusetts before the Revolution. He served as a volunteer in Gerrish's Massachusetts regiment at Bunker Hill and was a member of Benedict Arnold's march on Quebec in the winter of 1775. Captured by the British, he remained a prisoner until August 1776. On November 13, 1776, he was commissioned lieutenant colonel of the 11th Virginia Continental Regiment, which was commanded by his former fellow prisoner, Daniel Morgan. On September 26, 1777, Febiger was promoted to the colonelcy of the 2d Virginia Continental Regiment following the resignation of Alexander Spotswood.[21]

By the summer of 1779 Wayne and Febiger had assembled and trained about sixteen hundred light infantrymen. At midnight on July 16, 1779, Wayne's corps assaulted and captured the well-guarded fort at Stony Point, New York, using only their bayonets. Although the British regained Stony Point shortly afterward, the victory proved that Americans could accept discipline equal to that of the British regulars. The morale of Washington's army rose accordingly. Febiger's two battalions were in the forefront of the American attack, and Febiger himself received a slight wound. ("A musket ball scraped my nose—no other damage to Old Denmark," he wrote his wife afterward.) Lieutenant Colonel Fleury was voted a medal by Congress for being the first into the fort.

1st Battalion
Lieutenant Colonel François Louis de Fleury (France)
Captain Benjamin Lawson (Virginia), 4th Virginia Regiment
Captain Robert Gamble (Virginia), 8th Virginia Regiment
Captain John Jordan (Pennsylvania)
Captain Jacob Ashmead (Pennsylvania)

2d Battalion
Major Thomas Posey (Virginia)
Captain Clough Shelton (Virginia), 6th Virginia Regiment
Captain Joseph Smith (Virginia), Morgan's Riflemen
Captain Abraham Kirkpatrick (Virginia), 4th Virginia Regiment
Captain John Overton (Virginia), 1st Virginia Regiment
Captain John Steed (Virginia), 4th Virginia Regiment

In December 1779 Wayne's elite corps was disbanded, and Febiger returned to Virginia to supervise recruiting for the southern campaign.[22]

Colonel Thomas Gaskins's Virginia Regiment, 1781

Field Officers
Colonel Thomas Gaskins, from 3d Virginia Continental Regiment
Major John Poulson, from 8th Virginia Continental Regiment

Although contemporary accounts refer to this unit as a regiment, it was actually a four-hundred-man detachment made up of eighteen-month recruits and a handful of veterans who had escaped capture at Charleston. The unit served at Yorktown on the right flank of the first line as part of Anthony Wayne's brigade. After Yorktown most of its personnel were incorporated into Posey's Virginia Battalion for service in Georgia.[23]

Companies, October 1781
Captain Alexander Parker
Captain Thomas Warman
Captain William Lewis Lovely
Captain Andrew Lewis
Captain John Harris

In addition to the companies listed above, the detachment included four company-sized units commanded by lieutenants and sergeants.

Colonel Thomas Posey's Virginia Battalion, 1782-1783

(Also designated at various times: 1st Virginia Battalion, Febiger's Battalion.)

Field Officers
Colonel Thomas Posey, February(?) 1782-June 1783

Following the capture of the Virginia Continental Line at Charleston in May 1780, desperate efforts were made to raise a new army through militia conscription. Although Virginia failed to enroll the required 5,000 men, two small battalions were created for service with Nathanael Greene's forces in the South. Meanwhile, recruiting stations were established at Richmond, Chesterfield Court House, Winchester Barracks, and Cumberland Old Court House.[24]

Colonel Christian Febiger, 2d Virginia Continental Regiment, was nominally in charge of recruiting reinforcements for Greene, but he became so embroiled with supply problems in Philadelphia that he could not take the field. Major Thomas Posey, who had served with Febiger at Stony Point, became his proxy in Virginia. Working under Baron von Steuben, the senior Continental officer in the state, Posey began collecting recruits at Cumberland Old Court House late in 1780.

Recruiting came to a virtual halt during the two British invasions under Benedict Arnold in January and April 1781. By the late summer of 1781, however, Posey had raised a unit for service in the Yorktown campaign.

Companies, 1781-1782[25]

1st Company:	Captain Nathan Reid
2d Company:	Captain Thomas Thweatt
3d Company:	Captain John Overton
4th Company:	Captain Thomas Holt
5th Company:	Captain Archibald Denholm
6th Company:	Captain Nathaniel Terry
7th Company:	Captain Francis Minnis
8th Company:	Captain Joseph Scott, Jr.
9th Company:	Captain John Boswell Johnston

With Cornwallis's army out of action, the American forces under Nathanael Greene stood a good chance of recapturing Charleston and Savannah, but they would succeed only if reinforcements were sent. Congress organized an expedition under General Arthur St. Clair to go to Greene's assistance: all the light infantry troops, including Posey's battalion; the remnants of Gaskins's regiment; and a detachment of the 2d Virginia Continental Regiment from Philadelphia. They were joined by the 1st Legionary Corps, which was made up of drafts from the 1st and 3d regiments of Continental Light Dragoons.[26]

The expedition crossed the Edisto River in South Carolina on January 4, 1782. Wayne's light infantry spent the next few months fighting Indian and loyalist partizans, led by Chief Alexander McGillivray, of the Creeks, and Lieutenant Colonel Thomas Brown, of the Georgia loyalists. On June 23, 1782, McGillivray and Brown ambushed Wayne's troops at Sharon, near Savannah. A prompt recovery by Posey's battalion and the dragoon company under Captain James Gunn turned the affair into an American victory, but it was a costly one.

After the battle at Sharon, the Anglo-Indian raids on Georgia became less severe, but sporadic skirmishing along the frontier continued. By late October, so Greene informed Virginia's Governor Benjamin Harrison, Posey's battalion was on the march home. The battalion seems to have been disbanded early in 1783.

Armand's Legion, 1777-1783

(Also designated at various times: Armand's Partizan Corps, 1st Partizan Corps, Free and Independent Chasseurs.)

Field Officers

Colonel Charles Armand Tuffin, marquis de la Rouerie, May 10, 1777-November 25, 1783. Promoted to brigadier general.

Lieutenant Colonel Jean Baptiste Ternant, 1778-1783. Succeeded Armand as colonel, March 26, 1783.

Major John Baptisti, viscount de Lomagne, 1781-1783

Charles Armand Tuffin, marquis de la Rouerie, was one of the more colorful characters of the Revolution. Born in Brittany in 1756, Armand came to America as a volunteer in 1777. Commissioned a colonel at the age of twenty-one, he was permitted by Washington to raise a partizan, or guerrilla, force of two hundred men. On June 11 he was given command of three companies from Ottendorff's Independent Corps. Major Nicholas Dietrich, Baron von Ottendorff, had inherited the command of an independent Pennsylvania company raised by John Paul Schott in September 1776. Ottendorff's *freikorps* was a failure, and Ottendorff himself resigned, ultimately to desert to the British and join Benedict Arnold in 1780.[27]

By June 1777 Armand's corps numbered about eighty. On the 26th of that month, his men were defending a gun emplacement at Short Hills, New Jersey, against great odds. Thirty-two enlisted men were killed or wounded, and by November, Armand's force consisted of only forty-two privates. The small size of the unit prompted Congress to consider scrapping the partizan corps and "to throw the Men into some Regiment." In an effort to save his unit Armand recruited prisoners, deserters, and other undesirables to swell his ranks. With Washington's personal support Armand got Congress to countermand its resolve, and on June 25, 1778, he was authorized to raise three companies of infantry (Free and Independent Chasseurs) with 14 officers and 438 men. Later in the year a company of mounted troops was joined to the corps. Slightly over half the quota of enlisted men was actually raised, enough to satisfy Congress.[28]

In 1780 the partizan corps was attached to Gates's army in the Southern Department. Both Armand's and Lee's legions were engaged at Camden on August 15, 1780, when Gates's army was roundly defeated by Cornwallis. Lighthorse Harry Lee blamed Armand for much of the confusion and panic but admitted that the poor quality of his recruits was more responsible than any want of bravery on the part of the officers.

By 1781 Armand's corps was again down to forty light dragoons. In May the remnant was attached to Lafayette's light infantry on the James River station. Under Lafayette the partizan legion served at Jamestown and Yorktown from July to October. After the surrender of Cornwallis's army at Yorktown Armand remained in Virginia, where he conducted a vigorous recruiting effort. The Continental War Office on December 11 authorized him to enlist "free men between the ages of sixteen and forty [but] . . . no deserters . . . or Seamen." George Washington allowed him to recover any and all horses "that become public property by the Capitulation of the 19th. . . ."[29]

Armand took his instructions so seriously that complaints of civilian oppression flooded Governor Benjamin Harrison's office from late 1782 to 1783. Horses and forage were impressed on suspicion of having once been British property. After being transferred from Yorktown to the James River station to Staunton, Armand's force, now grown to 300, was ordered disbanded in October 1783. Toward the end, it was feared that Armand and his private army of foreigners might attempt a coup d'état against Congress. To placate him, Congress appointed Armand a brigadier general on March 26, 1783.[30]

Companies, 1777-1783

Captain Frederick William Rice, 1777-1781
Captain Le Brun de Bellecoeur, 1778-1783
Captain Charles Markle, 1778-1783
Captain Claudius de Bert, 1778-1783
Captain Louis de Sigonnier, 1778-1783
Captain George Schaffner, 1778-1783
Captain Augustine Briffault (Brissault?), 1779-1783
Captain John Sharp, 1780-1783
Brevet-Captain de Trenson, 1779
Brevet-Captain le Chevalier de Vaudore, 1780
Brevet-Captain Jean-Baptiste Georges, chevalier de Fontevieux, 1783-1784

One hundred and twenty-nine noncommissioned officers, musicians, and privates received bounty land from Virginia for service in Armand's Legion.[31]

Lee's Legion, 1778-1781

(Also designated at various times: Light Horse Harry Lee's Legion, 2d Partizan Corps, Lee's Partizan Corps.)

Field Officers

Major-Commandant Henry Lee, April 7, 1778-November 6, 1780. Promoted to lieutenant colonel.

Major Henry Peyton, February 17, 1780-May 12, 1780. Killed at Charleston, South Carolina.

Major Joseph Eggleston, 1780-1781. Retired.

As a reward for his services during the campaigns of 1777-1778, Captain Henry Lee, of the 5th Troop, 1st Regiment, Continental Light Dragoons, was promoted by Congress to major-commandant of his own unit. On April 7, 1778, Lee was authorized to raise two troops of horse for special missions. A third troop was authorized on May 28.[32]

Companies, April 1778-July 1779

1st Troop:	Captain William Lindsay, April 7, 1778
2d Troop:	Captain Robert Forsyth, July 1, 1778
3d Troop:	Captain Henry Peyton, July 2, 1778

By November 1778 the corps had almost attained its authorized strength of ten commissioned officers, nineteen noncommissioned officers, and ninety-two men. The mounted corps was turned into a legion in 1779 by the addition of a company of foot soldiers from Delaware.[33]

4th Troop (dismounted):	Captain Allen McLane, July 13, 1779

Major Lee and his men distinguished themselves at the battle of Paulus (Powles') Hook, on August 19, 1779. Congress voted Lee a handsome medal in September.[34]

On February 14, 1780, the corps was consolidated into three troops, although McLane's dismounted dragoons seem to have remained as an unofficial fourth troop.[35]

Companies, February 1780-November 1780

1st Troop:	Captain James Armstrong, January 1, 1779
2d Troop:	Captain John Hord, 1779
	Captain Michael Rudolph, November 1, 1779

3d Troop: Captain Joseph Eggleston, September 5, 1779

As part of the general reorganization of the Continental Line following the Charleston surrender, Lee's Legion was expanded by a general order of November 1, 1780, into a six-company unit. Three companies were cavalry and three were infantry, although all personnel were paid according to the higher cavalry scale.[36]

Companies, January 1781-June 1782

1st Troop:	Captain Allen McLane
2d Troop:	Captain James Armstrong
3d Troop:	Captain Michael Rudolph
4th Troop:	Captain Patrick Carnes
5th Troop:	Captain Ferdinand O'Neal
6th Troop:	Captain George Handy

The legion's services in the Southern Department from 1781 to 1782 are ably chronicled in Lee's two-volume *Memoirs of the War*.[37] In June 1782 General Nathanael Greene split up the legion by combining the horsemen with the consolidated legionary corps, which included the 3d and 4th Continental Light Dragoons. The dismounted dragoons were put under Lieutenant Colonel John Laurens in Gist's light corps. All of Lee's former officers resigned in protest, but most of them were persuaded to remain with their men until the end of the war.

 # The Continental Artillery, 1776-1783

6

VIRGINIA raised two regiments of artillery during the Revolution, one for Continental service and one for local defense. Unlike infantry units, a regiment of artillery rarely fought as a single organization. In most cases one or more field guns and the necessary personnel for each piece accompanied a regiment of infantry. Only in case of a prolonged siege did entire regiments of artillery form themselves into massed batteries.

Although cannon of any sort were scarce in the American Revolution, between twenty-eight and thirty different styles of ordnance were in common use. Naval cannon were often adapted to land use by mounting them on different carriages. This diversity caused untold headaches for the relatively few foundrymen who had to cast the shells and solid shot required for the different calibers. (A major source of artillery ammunition was salvaged British projectiles picked up on the field after an engagement.)

Because of the specialized nature of artillery, the enlisted men were ranked as bombardiers, gunners, or matrosses according to their experience and mathematical skill. The first two ranks included the men capable of estimating range and of loading, sighting, and firing a cannon. The matrosses were the unskilled privates who manhandled the guns.

1st Regiment of Continental Artillery, 1776-1783

(Also designated at various times: Harrison's Regiment, Harrison's Train of Artillery.)

Field Officers

Colonel Charles Harrison, November 30, 1776-June 17, 1783
Lieutenant Colonel Edward Carrington, November 30, 1776-June 17, 1783

Major Christian Holmer, November 30, 1786-January 1, 1783
Major William Brown, January 31, 1781-June 17, 1783

In February 1776 Monsieur O'hickey d'Arundel, a French volunteer from Alsace, was recommended to the Continental Congress by delegate Francis Lewis, of New York. He was sent to General Philip Schuyler on February 8 for the purpose of being examined as a capable artillerist for the Canadian troops. On March 19 Congress commissioned "Dohickey Arundel" a captain in the American artillery and ordered him to report to General Charles Lee, commanding the Southern Department. Lee was empowered on the same day "to set on foot the raising of a company of artillery" in Virginia.[1]

Lee arrived in Williamsburg on March 29, a week after two new field pieces had been delivered there from Philadelphia. The Virginia Committee of Safety had already appointed officers for an artillery company. The captain, James Innes, of Williamsburg, was a faithful officer who had commanded the Williamsburg Independent Company during the gunpowder incident of 1775. On April 19 Lee wrote to John Hancock, advising him that Innes was "totally ignorant of this particular branch [the artillery]" but was a good officer and capable of replacing the late Matthew Donovan, of the 9th Virginia Regiment. Arundel, who had arrived earlier in the month, was given the command of the Williamsburg artillery company. On May 18 Congress authorized two subalterns and forty matrosses for this unit.[2]

Virginia Artillery of 1776[3]

Captain James Innes, February 16, 1776-April 1776
Captain O'hickey d'Arundel, April 1776-July 8, 1776
1st Lieutenant Charles Harrison, February 16, 1776-November 26, 1776. Acting captain from July 8, 1776.
2d Lieutenant Edward Carrington, February 16, 1776-November 26, 1776. Acting captain from July 8, 1776.
3d Lieutenant Samuel Denny, February 16, 1776-November 26, 1776. Acting 1st lieutenant from July 8, 1776.

The Virginia artillery first saw combat duty during the expulsion of Lord Dunmore from Virginia in June and July 1776. Andrew Lewis divided the company into two batteries during the battle for Gwynn's Island. Captain Arundel, inventor of a wooden mortar, determined to test his invention against Dunmore's fleet. On July 8, 1776, Arundel became the mortar's first and only casualty when it exploded. Acting Captain Charles Harrison commanded a battery of two eighteen-pounders, and Lieutenant Denny directed the fire of several six-pounders and nine-pounders after the death of the eccentric Frenchman. Although Arundel was the only American casualty of the entire engagement, the artillery inflicted great damage on Dunmore's men, who boarded their "floating town" and limped out of the Chesapeake.[4]

Congress had had its difficulties in creating a workable corps or train of artillery, although some form of the branch had existed since April 1775. After the loss of Fort Washington in November 1776 it became apparent that more cannoneers were needed to save New York and perhaps the whole patriot cause. In consultation with Henry Knox, Washington drew up a plan to enlarge the American artillery, beginning with the creation of a regimental-sized unit in Virginia. On November 26, 1776, Congress resolved "that a regiment of artillery, to be armed with musquets and bayonetts, instead of fusees, be raised in Virginia" and then issued commissions to Charles Harrison, Edward Carrington, and Christian Holmer four days later. Since the new unit was a Continental organization from the outset, ten captains were also chosen on November 30, 1776.[5]

Companies, as organized November 1776

1st Company: Captain Samuel Denny, November 30, 1776
2d Company: Captain William L. Pierce, Jr., November 30, 1776. From Georgia.
3d Company: Captain Nathaniel Burwell, November 30, 1776
4th Company: Captain Buller Claiborne, November 30, 1776. Declined; already captain, 2d Virginia Regiment.
5th Company: Captain Joseph Scott, November 30, 1776
6th Company: Captain William Murray, November 30, 1776
7th Company: Captain Spotswood Dandridge, November 30, 1776. Declined; already captain, Virginia Dragoons. (Also known as Alexander Spotswood Dandridge.)
8th Company: Captain Matthew Smith, November 30, 1776
9th Company: Captain (Sir) John Pettus, November 30, 1776
10th Company: Captain William Waters, November 30, 1776

Although Congress reserved the right to appoint field officers and captains, the Virginia government was allowed to appoint all subalterns. On January 13, 1777, the council of state named a first, second, and third lieutenant for each company. The latter was to consist of a captain, three lieutenants, a sergeant, four bombardiers, eight gunners, four corporals, and forty-eight matrosses. As 1777 began, Washington's need for artillerymen became desperate since the bulk of his Massachusetts gunners had ended their period of enlistment on New Year's Day. Only Major Proctor's Pennsylvania detachment and a temporary company taken from the 2d Pennsylvania Regiment of Foot were left to handle the cannons of the main army. Harrison was requested to recruit his regiment as soon as possible, and in the summer of 1777 it was designated the 1st Regiment of Continental Artillery. Colonel John Lamb's regiment became the 2d, Colonel John Crane's the 3d, and Proctor's the 4th. Only Harrison's regiment was raised in Virginia.[6]

By May 1778 the 1st Regiment of Continental Artillery had joined the main army under Washington, which was considerably understrength. Because gun crews and officers were parceled among the infantry regiments and officers served for years on detached duty, it is impossible to reconstruct the actual composition of Harrison's regiment for most of the time between 1778 and 1783.

>Captain John Dandridge, February 7, 1777
>Captain Anthony Singleton, February 7, 1777
>Captain Drury Ragsdale, February 7, 1777
>Captain James Pendleton, February 7, 1777
>Captain Jacob Walker, February 7, 1777
>Captain John Henry, February 20, 1777. (From Pennsylvania ?)
>Captain John Champe Carter, October 30, 1777
>Captain Samuel Eddins, January 1, 1778

On January 8, 1778, two companies of Maryland artillery, under captains William Brown and Richard Dorsey, were incorporated into Harrison's regiment.[7] The remaining officers commissioned after were:

>Captain Thomas Baytop, February 5, 1778
>Captain Whitehead Coleman, August 15, 1778
>Captain-Lieutenant William Meredith, 1778
>Captain-Lieutenant Thomas Finn, 1780
>Captain-Lieutenant Ambrose Bohannon, 1782

On October 3, 1780, Congress reduced the four artillery regiments to nine companies of sixty-four matrosses each. Since a large part of Harrison's regiment had become prisoners at the fall of Charleston, the reorganization made little difference. The Winchester arrangement of December 1782 reduced the artillery to two companies, one under Captain William Pierce and one under Captain-Lieutenant Ambrose Bohannon. They remained at Winchester Barracks until mustered out in the fall of 1783.[8]

The Continental Light Dragoons, 1776-1783

7

CONGRESS raised four regiments of cavalry during the Revolution, three of them from Virginia. The term *cavalry*, however, was rarely used in the eighteenth century, possibly because of its close etymological relation to *cavalier*. Cromwell's army reforms of the 1640s had established both heavy and light dragoons to distinguish his horsemen from the gay blades who served Charles I. The early dragoons carried infantry equipment and were considered mobile infantry. Light dragoons, on the other hand, were trained to fight on horseback, using the saber as their principal weapon. Pistols and light carbines were only secondary arms. Light dragoons were among the most versatile of troops and were used as scouts, flank troops, videttes (mounted sentinels), messengers, and military police.

1st Regiment of Continental Light Dragoons, 1776-1783

(Also known unofficially as: Bland's Horse, 1st Legionary Corps.)

Field Officers

Colonel Theodorick Bland, March 31, 1777-December 10, 1779

Colonel Anthony Walton White, February 16, 1780-November 9, 1782

Lieutenant Colonel Benjamin Temple, March 31, 1777-December 10, 1779

Lieutenant Colonel Anthony Walton White, December 10, 1779-February 16, 1780

Major John Jameson, March 31, 1777-August 1, 1779

Major Epaphras Bull, August 1, 1779-September (?) 1781

Major John Swan, October 21, 1780-November 9, 1782

101

In April 1776 General Charles Lee, commanding the Southern Department, sent out a call for "gentlemen volunteers" to "form themselves into companies of LIGHT DRAGOONS" armed with short, rifled carbines, eight-foot pikes, and tomahawks. The fifth Virginia convention, which met that May, passed an ordinance creating six troops of horsemen for one year's service. This measure was supplemented by a subsequent ordinance in June 1776 that fixed pay scales and allowances for horses, forage, and equipment and created the rank of major-commandant.[1]

The Committee of Safety issued commissions to the captains, lieutenants, and cornets of the six troops, and recruiting began almost immediately, continuing through June and July. On July 5, 1776, Captain Theodorick Bland, of the 1st Troop, advertised for thirty geldings from four to six years old, offering ready money for them.[2]

Companies, June 1776-November 1776

1st Troop: Captain and Major-Commandant Theodorick Bland, June 14, 1776
2d Troop: Captain Benjamin Temple, June 15, 1776
3d Troop: Captain John Jameson, June 16, 1776
4th Troop: Captain Llewellin Jones, June 17, 1776
5th Troop: Captain Henry Lee, June 18, 1776
6th Troop: Captain John Nelson, June 19, 1776

The original Virginia dragoons under Major-Commandant Bland represented the cream of the state's society, talent, and military leadership. All the officers would rise in rank before the war ended, and Henry Lee would be voted a medal by Congress for gallantry at Paulus Hook.[3]

Although Washington originally had little faith in cavalry, the success of American horsemen during the New York campaign of 1776 altered his views. Learning of the existence of Bland's squadron, Washington requested that Governor Patrick Henry order the Virginia horsemen to the north. In December 1776 they marched to New York, although not fully raised or equipped. The troops were accepted into Continental pay on January 14, 1777, the pay commencing from November 25, 1776, and the officers' commissions taking effect from that date.[4]

Companies, December 1776-January 1778

1st Troop: Captain William Penn, November 25, 1776. Promoted from 1st lieutenant upon Bland's promotion to major-commandant.
2d Troop: Captain Richard Call, December 4, 1776
3d Troop: Captain John Nelson, June 19, 1776. Resigned, February 1777.
Captain Alexander Spotswood Dandridge, March 15, 1777
4th Troop: Captain Cuthbert Harrison, February 12, 1777

5th Troop: Captain John Belfield, March 15, 1777
6th Troop: Captain Addison Lewis, March 15, 1777

Like the artillery, the light dragoons were rarely kept together as a regiment. Normally, troops and detachments of light dragoons served with the various infantry regiments and brigades as flankers, scouts, videttes, and couriers. Nevertheless, Bland's horsemen made significant contributions during the battles of Wilmington on July 23, 1777, and Brandywine on September 11, 1777. At Germantown on October 4, Lee's troop acted as Washington's personal bodyguard.[5]

After much detached duty in the Jerseys the regiment lost Henry Lee's troop on April 7, 1778. Lee was promoted to major-commandant of an elite corps combining infantry and cavalry, which was to be known as Lee's Legion. In March 1779 Colonel Bland left the regiment, having been ordered by Washington to take charge of the British prisoners interned at Albemarle Barracks near Charlottesville. Lieutenant Colonel Benjamin Temple commanded the regiment until December 10, 1779, when he was succeeded by Anthony Walton White, of New Jersey.[6]

Most of the dragoons' enlistments were over by the end of 1778, and only eight men were fit for duty in March 1779. In the fall of that year the regiment was recruited up to strength and sent to Savannah, Georgia, to assist General Benjamin Lincoln. Early in 1780 the detached horsemen, commanded by Major John Jameson, were sent to Charleston, South Carolina, to remove military stores from the threat of British capture. Lieutenant Colonel White assumed command in April 1780 and managed to get most of the horsemen out of Charleston before the town surrendered to Clinton on May 12.[7]

Companies and Squads ("Troops"), January 1778-November 1782

Captain Berryman Green, January 1, 1778
Captain John Watts, April 7, 1778
Captain Thomas Pemberton, June 12, 1779
Captain William Watts, 1779
Captain Baylor Hill, 1780
Captain Andrew Nixon, 1780
Captain John Hughes, March 31, 1781
Captain William Gray, 1781
Captain James Gunn, 1782
Captain William Armistead, 1782

After the Charleston debacle White and the other officers returned to Virginia to rebuild the regiment. The troopers who remained in the Carolinas were temporarily merged with the 3d Regiment of Continental Light Dragoons under Lieutenant Colonel William Washington. This amalgam was known as the 1st Legionary Corps.[8]

Back in Virginia, White managed to raise about two hundred recruits but was only able to equip sixty for active service because of the British invasion of Virginia in 1781. Horses, even when available, were selling for $150,000 in depreciated Continental currency—worth about $150 in hard cash. White was forced to equip some of the men out of his own resources.

The reconstituted regiment fought at Spencer's Ordinary, Green Spring, and Yorktown, where it served under the duc de Lauzun at Gloucester Point. After Yorktown, the regiment was ordered to reinforce General Greene at Charleston, arriving on January 4, 1782. Major John Swan took command of the regiment after White was transferred to Moylan's 4th Regiment of Continental Light Dragoons. The 1st Continental Light Dragoons were assigned to the Cherokee expeditions under generals Pickens and Wayne.[9]

On November 9, 1782, the 1st and 3d regiments of Continental Light Dragoons were merged into a unit of five troops, nominally commanded by the ailing George Baylor, but actually commanded by Major Swan. The consolidated regiments remained in South Carolina until peace was declared. On hearing of the peace, about half the men elected Sergeant-Major William Dangerfield as their leader, seized the remaining horses, and rode homeward. By their mutiny they forfeited their pensions and bounty lands. The other cavalrymen, unhorsed by the mutineers, were eventually picked up by a troop transport and taken home by sea to collect their discharges.[10]

3d Regiment of Continental Light Dragoons, 1777-1783

(Also designated at various times: Baylor's Regiment, Baylor's Dragoons, Lady Washington Dragoons, 3d Legionary Corps, Washington's Dragoons.)

Field Officers

Colonel George Baylor, January 9, 1777-close of war

Lieutenant Colonel Benjamin Bird, March 14, 1777-November 20, 1778

Lieutenant Colonel William Washington, November 20, 1778-November 9, 1782

Major Alexander Clough, January 8, 1777-September 28, 1778. Killed at Tappan, New York.

Major Richard Call, October 2, 1778-November 9, 1782

Major John Swan, November 9, 1782-close of war

In December 1776 Congress authorized General Washington to appoint officers to three additional regiments of light dragoons. Elisha Sheldon, of Connecticut, became colonel of the 2d Regiment, and George Baylor, one of Washington's aides, became colonel of the 3d Regiment. By September

1777 six troops were raised, mostly made up of Virginians, although one troop included some Pennsylvanians. The first served as Washington's personal life guard in 1777-1778.[11]

Companies, December 1776-September 1777

1st Troop: Captain George Lewis, December 12, 1776. Served as commander in chief's life guard.
2d Troop: Captain Cadwallader Jones, February 6, 1777
3d Troop: Captain John Swan, April 26, 1777
4th Troop: Captain Chiswell Barrett, April 1777
5th Troop: Captain Churchill Jones, June 1, 1777
6th Troop: Captain Peter Presley Thornton, September 6, 1777

On September 27, 1778, Baylor's Regiment, numbering about 104, was billeted at Tappan, New York. After the men were asleep a British detachment burst in and massacred the officers and troopers. Major Alexander Clough was mortally wounded, and Colonel Baylor was shot through the lungs. He eventually recovered but had to take an extended leave of absence and limit his activities for the rest of his life. Field command passed to Lieutenant Colonel William Washington, a relative of the commander in chief. The dragoons were part of the Continental troops sent to the Carolinas in 1779. Captain William Barrett, a native of North Carolina, was captured at the fall of Charleston, South Carolina, in May 1780.[12]

Companies, 1778-1780

Captain Carter Page, April 10, 1778
Captain Peregrine Fitzhugh, May 5, 1778
Captain William Barrett, May 1779
Captain William Parsons, November 1779
Captain John Kilty, 1780. Maryland.
Captain John Baylor, 1780
Captain Walker Baylor, 1780

The horsemen suffered heavy casualties in the mobile warfare of the southern campaign, especially at Camden, South Carolina, in August 1780. The other Virginia troops of light dragoons were also depleted, and early in 1781 the 1st, 3d, and 4th regiments were temporarily consolidated into the 1st Legionary Corps under William Washington. When Colonel Anthony White returned to Virginia to reconstitute the 1st Regiment of Continental Light Dragoons, the men of the 3d and 4th regiments remained under Lieutenant Colonel Washington's command.

On June 13, 1782, Washington's dragoons were transferred to General Mordecai Gist's light corps, along with Lee's Legion and light infantry under Major William Beall and Lieutenant Colonel John Laurens. The following

Virginia companies served with the 3d Regiment of Continental Light Dragoons in 1782:

>Captain John Hughes
>Captain John Watts
>Major Richard Call

By November 9, 1782, the remnants of the 1st and 3d regiments were merged into five troops. The companies remained in South Carolina under the command of Major John Swan until peace was declared. Fearing that they had been forgotten about half the men commandeered the remaining horses and mutinied. Those who stayed behind were eventually picked up and taken home, receiving their furloughs by September 1783.[13]

4th Regiment of Continental Light Dragoons, 1777-1782

(Also designated unofficially: Moylan's Regiment, Moylan's Dragoons, 4th Legionary Corps.)

Field Officers

Colonel Stephen Moylan, January 5, 1777-December 1782. Promoted to brigadier, 1783.

Lieutenant Colonel Anthony Walton White, February 15, 1777-December 10, 1779. Transferred to 1st Continental Light Dragoons.

Lieutenant Colonel Benjamin Temple, December 10, 1779-close of war

Major William Washington, January 27, 1777-November 20, 1778. Promoted to lieutenant colonel, 3d Regiment, Continental Light Dragoons.

Major Moore Fauntleroy, August 1, 1779-(?) 1780

Major David Hopkins, (?) 1780-(?) 1782

In December 1776 Congress authorized Washington to appoint officers of the 2d, 3d, and 4th regiments of light dragoons. On January 5, 1777, Stephen Moylan was commissioned colonel to the 4th Regiment. In the fall of 1777 Count Casimir Pulaski was placed in charge of the Corps of Continental Light Dragoons, which was made up of the four numbered regiments. Since the cavalrymen were split into small detachments, serving in every combat area from New York to Georgia, Pulaski's command was only nominal. When the Polish nobleman resigned to form a partizan legion in March 1778, command of the corps went to Stephen Moylan until it was dissolved in May 1779.[14]

Companies, January 1777-December 1777

1st Troop: Captain Thomas Dorsey, January 10, 1777. Raised in Pennsylvania.

2d Troop: Captain David Plunkett, January 10, 1777. Raised in Maryland.

3d Troop: Captain Moore Fauntleroy, January 21, 1777. Raised in Virginia.

4th Troop: Captain David Hopkins, January 21, 1777. Raised in Virginia.

5th Troop: Captain Vashel D. Howard, January 24, 1777. Raised in Virginia.

6th Troop: Captain George Gray, December 7, 1777. Raised in Virginia.

To replace Captain Howard, who died in March 1778, and Captain Dorsey, who resigned, and to increase the strength of the regiment, the following officers were commissioned:

Captain John Heard, February 8, 1778. Raised in New Jersey.
Captain Nicholas Ruxton Moore, March 15, 1778. Raised in Maryland.
Captain John Craig, December 25, 1778. Raised in Pennsylvania.
Captain Zebulon Pike, December 25, 1778. Raised in New Jersey.
Captain Erasmus Gill, December 25, 1778. Raised in Virginia.
Captain Lawrence Trent, 1779. Raised in Virginia.

In 1779 Moylan's Dragoons were sent south and suffered heavy casualties. The following companies were assigned to the regiment after the fall of Charleston, South Carolina:

Captain Larkin Smith, April 1, 1780. Raised in Virginia.
Captain John Cook, 1780. Raised in Virginia.
Captain Thomas Overton, April 24, 1780. Raised in Virginia.
Captain Henry Willis, 1780. Raised in Pennsylvania.

Two companies of Delaware dragoons were also temporarily attached to Moylan's Regiment. These were commanded by captains Peter Jaquett and Robert H. Kirkwood.

After its consolidation with the 3d Regiment of Continental Light Dragoons in December 1782, the 4th Regiment passed out of existence.[15]

The Virginia State Line, 1776-1783

8

IN December 1776 the Virginia General Assembly created a body of regular troops (distinct from the units in the Continental Line) for local defense. Three numbered infantry regiments were authorized to serve within the boundaries of Virginia. Within the year, however, they were temporarily placed in the Continental Line to offset the loss by capture of the 9th Virginia Continental Regiment at Germantown. After the White Plains reorganization of 1778 the state regiments were allowed to return home.

During their absence a special regiment of garrison troops was created to man the fortifications at Williamsburg, Portsmouth, and Yorktown. These troops were augmented by Colonel Thomas Marshall's State Artillery Regiment and Loyeauté's artillery cadets. A company of French volunteers under Decrome de la Porte served briefly in Williamsburg at the same time. Following the capture of Burgoyne's army at Saratoga in 1777, a special regiment was raised in Albemarle County to guard the prisoners at a camp near Charlottesville.

Because the Continental army had priority in enlistments, recruiting for the state line was a constant problem. The 3d Regiment of state line infantry failed to complete its quota, and its personnel eventually merged with the 1st Virginia State Regiment. In 1779 Lieutenant Colonel James Monroe attempted to raise a state infantry regiment and thereby earn a colonel's commission, but his efforts were doomed to failure for lack of recruits.

Because the three-fourths of the Continental Light Dragoons who were raised initially in Virginia for local defense were taken by Congress, the General Assembly was forced to authorize a separate cavalry regiment on the state establishment. In December 1779 Major John Nelson received a commission to raise and equip four troops of horsemen. Like the other state line organizations, this one was levied by Congress for service in the Carolinas several months later.

The largest unit raised by either Congress or Virginia was George Rogers Clark's Illinois Regiment, which originally was made up of four companies of frontiersmen. Between 1778 and 1783 Clark and his successors enlarged the regiment into a force almost as large as Washington's main army just prior to Yorktown. Clark's regiment was reinforced by Joseph Crockett's Western Battalion, which also supplied companies for the Convention Army Guard Regiment.

Like the Continental Line, the state line underwent at least four arrangements to compensate for attrition. In January 1778 the 1st and 3d regiments of infantry were merged. Following the defeat of Porterfield's State Detachment at Camden in August 1780, the state line was drastically reduced on February 6, 1781.

All state units, except for Clark's and Crockett's Illinois troops, were merged into Charles Dabney's Virginia State Legion in February 1782. Two other legions under General Alexander Spotswood were still in process of recruiting, but these units were never fully completed.

In February 1783 Charles Dabney was ordered to trim his state legion to a minimum and declare most of its officers supernumerary. On April 24, 1783, the legion was disbanded. Spotswood's legions were not dismissed until November.

1st Regiment, Virginia State Line, 1776-1782

Field Officers[1]

Colonel William Grayson, December 19, 1776-January 1777. Declined.
Colonel Haynes Morgan, June 5, 1777-June 24, 1777. Declined.
Colonel George Gibson, June or July 1777-February 1, 1782
Lieutenant Colonel Haynes Morgan, December 20, 1776-June 5, 1777
Lieutenant Colonel Nathaniel Cocke, June 5, 1777-February 1778
Lieutenant Colonel John Allison, February 1778-February 1782
Major Nathaniel Cocke, December 20, 1776-June 5, 1777
Major John Allison, June 5, 1777-February 2, 1778
Major Thomas Meriwether, February 2, 1778-February 1782

In December 1776 the Virginia General Assembly authorized three battalions of eight companies each, one of which was designated the 1st State Regiment. These units were not supposed to serve outside the state's boundaries, but on October 4, 1777, Virginia troops experienced their worst military disaster since the capture of Rawlings's rifle regiment in December 1776; at the battle for Germantown, Pennsylvania, the entire 9th Virginia Continental Regiment was either captured or killed, and Congress ordered a full Virginia regiment to replace it until new levies could be trained. The 1st and 2d state regiments were sent to join Muhlenburg's brigade late in 1777, and they served in the Continental Line until late 1779. By 1780 the 1st State Regiment was back in Virginia for the campaigns that led to Yorktown. In February 1782 it was incorporated into Dabney's Legion, having shrunk to 195 men enlisted "for the war."[2]

Companies, January 1, 1777-March 1, 1777

1st Company: Captain John Lee, January 1, 1777. Raised in James City County.
2d Company: Captain Thomas Meriwether, January 3, 1777. Raised in Caroline County.
3d Company: Captain William Hoffler, January 9, 1777. Raised in Norfolk County.
4th Company: Captain Thomas Winder Ewell, January 31, 1777. County of origin unknown.
5th Company: Captain John Nicholas, February 1, 1777. Raised in Albemarle County(?).
6th Company: Captain William Payne, February 3, 1777. Raised in Fauquier County.
7th Company: Captain Robert Windsor Brown, February 28, 1777. Raised in Fairfax County.
8th Company: Captain Gabriel Jones. (Died 1777.) Captain John Camp, March 1, 1777. Raised in Gloucester County (?).

Companies, March 1777-January 1778 (additions)[3]

Captain Thomas Hamilton, March 3, 1777. Raised in Fairfax County.
Captain John Shields, March 5, 1777. Raised in Henrico County (?).
Captain John Hunter Holt, April 29, 1777. Raised in Chesterfield County (?).
Captain Abner Crump, May 10, 1777. Raised in New Kent County.

Companies, February 1, 1778-January 1782 (additions)

Captain Jacob Valentine, February 1, 1778. Raised in Norfolk County.
Captain Thomas Armistead, April 6, 1778. Raised in New Kent County. Grenadiers.
Captain Charles Ewell, June 1, 1778. Raised in Prince William County.
Captain William Campbell, January 17, 1779. Raised in King and Queen County.
Captain Angus Rucker, July 3, 1779. Raised in Culpeper County.
Captain Frederick Woodson, 1780. Raised in Henrico County.

2d Regiment, Virginia State Line, 1776-1782

Field Officers
Colonel James Duncanson, December 20, 1776-June 1777
Colonel Gregory Smith, June 1777
Colonel George Gibson, June 1777. Transferred to 1st Regiment.
Colonel William Brent, January 1779-April 1782
Lieutenant Colonel Thomas Blackburn, December 20, 1776-June 12, 1777
Lieutenant William Brent, June 14, 1777-January 1, 1779
Lieutenant Charles Dabney, January 1779-January 1782
Major William Brent, December 20, 1776-June 14, 1777
Major Alexander Dick, June 14, 1777-January 1778
Major John Lee, February 1, 1778-February or April 1782

Like the 1st Regiment, Virginia State Line, the 2d Regiment of infantry was created by act of assembly in December 1776. After Germantown it and the 1st State Regiment joined Muhlenburg's brigade. In 1779 it returned to Virginia. The 3d Virginia State Regiment was merged with it in January 1778, and several officers from the 3d joined the 2d Regiment. The 2d Regiment was reduced to thirty-one men by the time it merged with Dabney's Legion in February 1782.[4]

Companies, January 1777-April 1778
1st Company: Captain James Quarles, January 4, 1777. Raised in Albemarle County (?).
2d Company: Captain John Quarles, January 4, 1777. Raised in Norfolk (?).
3d Company: Captain John Lee, March 1777. From 1st Regiment.
4th Company: Captain John Dudley, March 1777
5th Company: Captain Peter Bernard, April 10, 1777. Raised in Gloucester.
6th Company: Captain Benjamin C. Spiller, May 9, 1777
7th Company: Captain Harry Dudley, October 15, 1777
8th Company: Captain Thomas Minor, April 23, 1778

The regiment seems to have been reorganized in mid-1778, since its officer personnel changed radically at that time. Of the original captains only Captain Harry Dudley remained. After the change he automatically became the senior company commander.[5]

Companies, September 1778-January 1782
1st Company: Captain Harry Dudley
2d Company: Captain Augustine Tabb, September 10, 1778
3d Company: Captain Machen Boswell, September 15, 1778

4th Company: Captain John Hudson, October 1, 1778.
  Grenadiers, or light infantry.
5th Company: Captain William Long, January 1, 1779
6th Company: Captain James Moody, April 30, 1779
7th Company: Captain Nathaniel Welch, September 1, 1779
8th Company: Captain John McElhaney, August 25, 1779
9th Company: Captain John Lewis, January 1, 1779
10th Company: Captain Thomas Quarles, 1781

3d Regiment, Virginia State Line, 1776-1778

Field Officers
Colonel Philip Love, December 20, 1776. Declined.
Colonel George Gibson, June-July 1777. Transferred to 2d Regiment.
Colonel Gregory Smith, July 1777. Transferred to 2d Regiment.
Lieutenant Colonel Gregory Smith, December 20, 1776-July 1777
Lieutenant Colonel Charles Dabney, July 1777-February 16, 1778
Major Charles Dabney, December 20, 1776-July 1777

Like the 1st and 2d numbered regiments of the Virginia State Line, the 3d State Regiment was raised under the authority of an act of assembly passed in December 1776. The large calls for manpower from Continental and state authorities made recruiting difficult. Colonels Gibson and Smith both transferred to the 2d Virginia State Regiment, and Lieutenant Colonel-Commandant Charles Dabney was appointed to a similar rank in the 2d Virginia Continental Regiment for a year. By 1779 he was lieutenant colonel of the 2d Virginia State Regiment, a rank he held until January 1782, when all state line units were consolidated under his command as the Virginia State Legion.

In January 1778 the 3d Regiment ceased to exist, and its remnants were incorporated into the 1st Virginia State Regiment.[6]

Companies, December 1776-January 1778
Captain Thomas Bressie, December 1776
Captain Jacob Valentine (?)
Captain Thomas Armistead (?)
Captain Tully Robertson. (Later served in the Georgia Line.)

Virginia State Engineer Department, 1775-1781

Officers
Deputy Adjutant General and Engineer Thomas Bullitt, August 17, 1775-early 1776

> State Engineer Major John Stadler, December 30, 1776-October 1777
> State Engineer Major Frederick Warnecke, October 18, 1777-January 1781
> State Engineer Major John Christian Senf, February 21, 1781. Appointed by Jefferson but declined the office.
> Assistant Engineer Major J. F. Fournier, 1777-1778
> Sergeant Jacob Diener, April 26, 1777-?
> Inspector of Artillery and Fortifications St. François A. M. D. de Loyeauté, January-May 1778; January 1781-October (?) 1781
> Assistant Adjutant General Thomas Jones, Jr., January 27, 1778-?

At the outbreak of the Revolution, Virginia lacked a talented engineer to plan and superintend the state's defenses. On August 17, 1775, the third convention appointed Thomas Bullitt, of Fauquier County, deputy adjutant general. Bullitt's chief contribution as engineer pro tem was to fortify the powder magazine at Williamsburg with a ditch and some light chevaux-de-frise, which were still standing two years later.[7]

When General Charles Lee assumed command of the Southern Department in the spring of 1776, he instituted some sweeping reforms in Virginia's Continental Establishment, including the creation of a paid engineer's post. In March 1776 John Stadler, a German volunteer, offered his services to Congress as an engineer. This pleased Lee, who believed that only a foreign-trained engineer would have the skill in mathematics and the science of fortification that was needed. On May 7, 1776, Lee persuaded Congress that a mere twenty dollars per month would enable an engineer "to eat, drink, and wear linen, or indeed any kind of Cloaths." He concluded his report by complaining that "I have as yet heard nothing of Mr. [John] Stabler [sic] the Engineer. I ought in fact to have at least half a dozen, for we have a variety of posts to throw up, and there is not a Man or Officer in the Army, that knows the difference betwixt a chevaux de Frize and a Cabbage Garden."[8]

Stadler finally arrived in the fall of 1776 and worked for a year, strengthening earthwork forts, moving cannon, and performing the other routine duties of his office. On December 30, 1776, the Virginia Council of State appointed him "Engineer in the Service of this Common wealth," pursuant to an act of assembly. After he resigned in 1777, another German, Frederick Warnecke, was hired by the state as his replacement. Warnecke seems to have had a fondness for the bottle. When British raiders under Benedict Arnold attacked Richmond and Westham Foundry in January 1781, Warnecke was too drunk to flee and was captured at Westham. Although he pleaded with Jefferson to exchange him for Colonel Jacob Ellegood, the Tory, Jefferson had him relieved of command and exchanged Ellegood for Colonel George Mathews, of the 9th Virginia Regiment. Since he was of no further value Warnecke was paroled soon afterwards.[9]

Although Virginia maintained an engineer throughout the greater part of the war, most of the earthworks were constructed by the state's artillery officers. From Harrison's Regiment of Continental Artillery and from Marshall's Regiment of State Artillery officers were regularly detached to infantry units to provide artillery cover and build fortifications. A certain number of matrosses, or common privates of artillery, were designated artillery artificers or pioneers. They were issued spades, axes, and fascine knives, or primitive machetes, to construct earthworks. In the fall of 1781, when Washington's Grand Army came to the defense of Virginia, the engineer work was carried out mostly by French specialists under Duportail.

Captain Decrome de la Porte's French Company, 1777-1778

Officers[10]

Captain Decrome de la Porte, April 16, 1777-August 1778
1st Lieutenant Joseph André Carlivan, April 30, 1777-1778
2d Lieutenant Joseph Louis de Beaulieu, March 31, 1778-?
Ensign André la Baud, March 1778-?
Ensign Edmund Clark, September 29, 1777-?
Recruiter Pierre du Chatelier, March 21, 1778
Recruiter Pierre Dubar, April 1777

Decrome de la Porte (also spelled Delaporte or Laporte), a French merchant and adventurer residing in Williamsburg, petitioned the council of state early in 1777 to allow him to form a volunteer company of French nationals. The journal of the council for April 16, 1777, records that:

> ... application has been made to this Board by several french gentlemen for permission to raise a corps of french troops, and to form, discipline, and dress them in the manner of french troops, and whereas it appears that such forming a Corps wou'd be the most likely method of introducing good discipline, neatness in the dress and laudable spirit of emulation amongst our troops and wou'd most probably interest the french in general as well as a great number of gentlemen of that gallant Nation in our behalf, whose assistance we the more stand in need of from the great Backwardness of our men to engage in the service of the state or in that of the Unites States. Resolved . . . therefore that recruiting instructions be given to Monsieur Delaporte . . . and that he shall receive a captain's command.

The council issued warrants to de la Porte and his subordinates to recruit men throughout the state and in North Carolina. Lieutenant Carlivan's company served as garrison troops in Williamsburg, while de la Porte travelled in the recruiting service.[11]

On April 23, 1778, the French company was ordered to Portsmouth to perform garrison duty, except for one detachment that was sent to Hampton. One of the members of the company, Charles Bellini, was appointed the governor's French interpreter on March 25. In order to bring his company up to the assigned strength of fifty, de la Porte was forced to accept some non-Frenchmen. On May 1, 1778, he advertised in Purdie's *Virginia Gazette* for an Irishman who had deserted from the company. De la Porte's efforts to clothe his men as befitted French regulars led him into heavy debt at the public store in Williamsburg, and he was arrested in August 1778. Governor Patrick Henry arranged security for him and ordered his release, but his company was disbanded and absorbed by other units of the state line. By 1779 de la Porte was a private citizen and a merchant once again. No further French units were raised in the east, but several companies of Kaskaskia volunteers were to form a part of George Rogers Clark's Illinois battalion.[12]

Lieutenant Colonel James Monroe's Regiment, Virginia State Line, July-December 1779

Field Officers

Colonel James Monroe, July 1779-December 1779

Lieutenant Colonel John Francis Mercer, October 26, 1779-December 4, 1779

Major Charles de Klaumann, July 1779-December 1779

Major James Monroe resigned from the 3d Virginia Continental Regiment in December 1778, hoping for a promotion within the state line. He was granted permission to raise a regiment for local defense with the understanding that a promotion to a colonelcy would be forthcoming. Captain Charles de Klaumann, a Danish veteran of the Norwegian army who was serving in Marshall's artillery regiment, became Monroe's subaltern.[13]

The regiment never became active, since Continental, state, and militia organizations had prior claims on Virginia's manpower. De Klaumann attempted to get a major's commission in the State Garrison Regiment, but failed. On March 10, 1780, Monroe was paid "for commanding a regiment from August 15 to December 15, 1779," although his unit never reached company size, much less regimental proportions.

Monroe spent the remainder of the war as a special assistant representing Governor Jefferson in the Carolinas. He narrowly avoided capture while delivering dispatches to Porterfield's detachment. After the war Monroe served as governor of Virginia and as president of the United States.[14]

Companies, 1779
1st Company: Captain Edward Digges, 1779

The Convention Army Guard Regiment, 1779-1781

(Also designated at various times: Colonel Francis Taylor's Guard Regiment, Taylor's State Regiment, State Guard Regiment, Albemarle County Battalion, Convention Guard Regiment.)

Field Officers

Post Commandant (Albemarle Barracks) Colonel Theodorick Bland, March 29, 1779-August 1779

Post Commandant (Albemarle and Winchester) Colonel James Wood, August 1779-1782

Post Commandant (Fort Frederick, Maryland) Colonel Moses Rawlings, 1782-1783

Colonel Charles Lewis, December 23, 1778-March 5, 1779

Colonel Francis Taylor, March 5, 1779-June 15, 1781

Lieutenant Colonel Francis Taylor, December 24, 1778-March 5, 1779

Lieutenant Colonel William Fontaine, March 5, 1779-June 15, 1781

Major William Fontaine, December 24, 1778-March 5, 1779

Major John Roberts, March 5, 1779-May 1, 1781

On October 17, 1777, the British general, John Burgoyne, surrendered his six-thousand-man army to an American force commanded by General Horatio Gates, thus ending his grandiose but ill-conceived effort to seize control of the Hudson and thus split the northern colonies in two. Refusing Gates's demand for an unconditional surrender, the wily Burgoyne persuaded the Americans to accept a convention, whereby the British would lay down their arms, permit themselves to be taken to Boston, and then sail for home on parole. This extraordinary document was signed on October 17, after all hopes of reinforcements from British-held New York had passed.[15]

Almost immediately the convention was violated by both sides. Weapons and flags were not surrendered; some of the British escaped; and Congress feared that once Burgoyne's men were back in England on garrison duty, an equal number of troops would be freed for active service in America.

Congress stalled, ostensibly waiting for George III to ratify the convention and when the ratification arrived refused to believe that the royal signature was genuine. In the meantime the convention army had been escorted to Cambridge to wait for transportation home, but even as the prisoners marched north Congress had already made plans to send them far to the south. Delegate John Harvie, of Virginia, offered his own land outside Charlottesville as a site for a prisoner-of-war camp, and his offer was accepted. Harvie's brother Richard was paid $23,000 by Congress to construct log cabins on the site. Thinking that the prisoners would not arrive before late spring, Harvie's workmen moved slowly, but Congress, spurred by food shortages in Massachusetts, decided not to wait and began marching the British south in six divisions at the end of November. Under the direction of Colonel Theodorick Bland, the prisoners covered 623 miles in two months, crossing the Potomac on New Year's Eve, 1778. After passing through Fauquier, Culpeper, and Orange counties, the last of the conventioners arrived in Charlottesville on January 13, 1779.

Notified of the transfer of the troops from Massachusetts to Virginia almost while it was happening, Governor Patrick Henry had little time to prepare. On December 23, 1778, he had transmitted to Charles Lewis, the county lieutenant, the General Assembly's authorization for a small battalion of guards (about one hundred men) from Albemarle. While these men were being raised by Lieutenant Colonel Francis Taylor and Major William Fontaine, Henry instructed Lewis to call on the county lieutenants of Amherst, Buckingham, Louisa, Orange, Culpeper, and Goochland for one hundred militiamen each to augment the force from Albemarle.[16]

A few days before Burgoyne's men arrived at the unfinished Albemarle Barracks, Congress had approved a resolution of the Continental Board of War "that a battalion of 600 men, properly officered, be forthwith raised on Continental establishment in Virginia for the space of one year . . . that these troops be stationed at, and not removed . . . from the barracks in Albemarle county, as guards over the convention troops." In March, Francis Taylor was promoted to colonel, William Fontaine to lieutenant colonel, and Captain John Roberts to major. Four companies of regular guards were raised at this time, augmented by militia detachments:[17]

Companies, March-October 1779

1st Company:	Captain Garland Burnley
2d Company:	Captain Ambrose Madison
3d Company:	Captain Benjamin Timberlake
4th Company:	Captain Robert Barrett
Albemarle Militia:	Captain James Garland (accidentally shot by a sentinel).
Amherst Militia:	Captain John Sale

    Captain David Woodrup
    Captain Richard Ballinger
    Captain (?) Jacob
    Captain Richard Pamplin
    Captain (?) Shelton

Culpeper Militia: Captain John Strother
Fluvanna Militia: Captain Samuel Richardson
    Captain Joseph Hayden
Goochland Militia: Captain Holman Rice

For the first few months of their internment on Ivy Creek, the convention troops busied themselves by finishing the miserable roofless and unchinked log huts provided for them. The officers fared somewhat better, being allowed to rent lodgings within a one-hundred-mile radius. Thus, some of them took up residence as far away from their men as Staunton and Richmond. Governor Henry became alarmed at the fact that German officers were roaming freely about the streets of Richmond, and he curtailed the radius to twenty-five miles. His successor, Thomas Jefferson, was on friendly terms with several of the officers, including his new neighbors at Colle, Baron and Baroness Riedesel, and General William Phillips, who was living at Blenheim. Jefferson and Baron Geismar played the violin together, and Louis de Unger was given free access to Jefferson's library.[18]

Late in August 1779 Theodorick Bland resigned as commander of the barracks, leaving the post vacant for a few months. Some time between August and December, Colonel James Wood was appointed his successor. Bland had been popular with the prisoners, largely because he did not censor their correspondence. During his administration, however, "considerable desertions" had taken place, mostly among the British prisoners. Although large numbers of Hessians had slipped out of ranks and disappeared into the Pennsylvania and Maryland backcountry, only a few attempted to escape after reaching Charlottesville. Those who did run away were conspicuous, dressed as they were in "short coarse linen coats or coatees, and linen overalls; and carrying their regimental coats in knapsacks."[19]

By October 8, 1779, nine companies of guards had been raised at least to half-strength.[20]

Companies, October 8-25, 1779

1st Company: Captain Garland Burnley
2d Company: Captain George Rice. Retired.
    Captain Ambrose Madison
3d Company: Captain Benjamin Timberlake
4th Company: Captain Robert Barrett
5th Company: Captain William Kirtley. Retired.
    Captain James Purvis
6th Company: Captain Thomas Porter
7th Company: Captain James Burton
8th Company: Captain Richard P. White
9th Company: Major John Roberts
    Lieutenant Edward Herndon

On October 25 the partly raised regiment was consolidated from nine into seven companies, and captains Madison and Timberlake were retired. Since the guard regiment now only numbered about 270 men fit for duty, detachments of militia were maintained also:[21]

Amherst Militia:	Captain Henry Dawson
	Captain (?) Loving
	Captain Philip Thurmond
Buckingham Militia:	Captain Peter Bernard
Culpeper Militia:	Lieutenant Robert Johnson
Goochland Militia:	Captain Humphrey Parrish
Louisa Militia:	Lieutenant Joseph Street
Orange Militia:	Captain Robert Miller

Life for the convention troops became more pleasant as they finished their cabins, built churches, planted gardens, and cleared roads. By June four recreational huts containing billiard tables had been built, as were a theatre, a coffeehouse, and a sutler's store. There were still major discomforts, the worst of which were the weather, rattlesnakes, and sporadic food shortages. In some respects the men of the guard regiment suffered more than the prisoners. They went months without pay, fresh food, or essential clothing. On April 8, 1780, 121 were without shoes of any kind, and by July 1, 38 were reported "naked."[22]

During April the first companies of Lieutenant Colonel Joseph Crockett's Western Battalion arrived at Albemarle Barracks. While the enlisted personnel of this unit were being recruited for service in the Illinois country, the battalion was assigned to augment Taylor's regiment at the barracks, thus relieving the militia drafts. Crockett's men remained at Charlottesville until February 1781, then mustered with George Rogers Clark in May, after serving briefly near Guilford Court House, North Carolina.

Companies, Crockett's Detachment, April 1780-February 1781
Captain William Cherry
Captain Benjamin Kinley
Captain John Millen
Captain John Chapman
Captain Thomas Young
Captain Abraham Tipton

Sometime between September and November 1780, Captain Kinley died, and his company was commanded subsequently by Lieutenant John Kearney. At least three militia companies were assigned to the barracks after Crockett's regiment departed:[23]

Albemarle Militia: Captain Nicholas Hammer
Fluvanna Militia: Captain Anthony Henderson
Prince Edward Militia: Captain Richard Holland

Late in 1779 the British and German commanders of the convention troops had both been exchanged. General William Phillips returned to Virginia at the head of an army of invasion a year later. Baron Riedesel was given command of German troops in New York. After their commanders left the prisoners became more docile in captivity, and many of the Germans hired themselves out to local farmers and craftsmen.[24]

Because of the blurred distinction between their status as troops in Continental pay and their role as special state forces the convention guards remained on the verge of mutiny from late 1780 through the summer of 1781. Most were sick, poorly clad, and half-starved, and the sight of their prisoners earning good wages while they suffered was intolerable. On February 7, 1781, at the height of Benedict Arnold's invasion, only three companies were left, commanded by lieutenants Thomas Porter and Thomas Pettus, and Ensign Nicholas Meriwether. The noncommissioned officers petitioned Governor Jefferson for relief, but the beleaguered government could offer little help.[25]

During the summer of 1779 additional barracks had been constructed at Winchester, the residence of Colonel James Wood. In the dark days of 1780, Jefferson had instructed Wood to stay in readiness to remove the convention troops to the Winchester Barracks. The distressed situation of Taylor's regiment, combined with Arnold's invasion, made the move imperative, and on February 20, 1781, the prisoners left the barracks and began the march to Winchester and Warm Springs (in Berkeley County). Captain Edmund Read's troop of state cavalry was assigned as a mounted guard. On April 3 Francis Taylor reported that the German prisoners had reached Winchester, "very orderly and easily governed." The British prisoners had already been moved to Fort Frederick, Maryland.[26]

James Wood returned from Maryland on April 9 and convened a board of officers to decide about discharging the guard regiment from Albemarle. Captains Burnley, White, Purvis, Porter, Meriwether, and James Kennedy had returned to their commands. Three companies were discharged in April and the rest on May 16, except for a few men in Captain Purvis's company. While the last of Taylor's regiment was being discharged, a new guard regiment was being raised in Frederick County under Colonel Joseph Holmes and Captain Robert White, a disabled officer from the 8th Virginia Continental Regiment.[27]

On June 8, 1781, while a force under Tarleton and Simcoe was pushing west toward Charlottesville, the German prisoners were moved to Shepherdstown on the Potomac by order of Lafayette. Militia from Frederick,

Berkeley, Hampshire, and Shenandoah counties were hastily mobilized as additional escorts. The situation remained stable until November. About two thousand prisoners from Cornwallis's army were moved from Yorktown to Winchester Barracks, and Colonel Holmes was appointed commander over the new contingent. On November 6 Holmes complained that there were more prisoners than available cabin space. Nearly a thousand of the Yorktown captives were "obliged to camp out" in the winter weather. In January 1782 County Lieutenant John Smith was ordered to escort the prisoners to Maryland. Since Colonel Holmes could not furnish a proper escort, Smith had to request an executive order without which militia could not be ordered out of the state. By May nearly all of the convention and Yorktown troops were at Fort Frederick, except those too ill to be moved. A one-hundred-man contract guard in Continental pay was maintained at Winchester through the summer to guard the last of these prisoners.[28]

The Virginia State Garrison Regiment, 1777-1782

Field Officers

Colonel George Muter, June 24, 1778-April 1, 1781
Lieutenant Colonel Nicholas George Moëballé, December 1778-August 1779
Lieutenant Colonel Charles Porterfield, August 14, 1779-January 10, 1781
Major Charles Porterfield, July-August 1779
Major Edmund Waller, April 5, 1779-September 26, 1780
Major Charles Magill, September 1780-April 1, 1781
Major Alexander Dick, 1781-January 1782

In June 1778 the Virginia General Assembly authorized a "Battalion of Infantry for Garrison Duty" to be enlisted for three years. The eight companies making up the battalion were divided among the forts and batteries defending Virginia's tidewater harbors. Separate organizations were raised for the frontier forts. (See "Independent Virginia Frontier Companies.") Detachments of the State Garrison Regiment were stationed in Williamsburg, Portsmouth, Hampton, and Yorktown from 1777 to 1781; there was also a sergeant's detachment serving in Richmond in 1780.[29]

Companies, 1777-1781

Captain Peter Grant (from Grayson's Regiment)
Captain Edmund Waller (State Marine Corps)
Captain Thomas Upshaw
Captain Edward Digges (Williamsburg recruiter)
Captain Joseph Kidd
Captain Nicholas George Moëballé

Captain Charles Magill
Captain Frederick de Blankenburg
Captain Alexander Dick (State Marine Corps)
Captain Henry Garnett

On February 6, 1781, the war office ordered the State Garrison Regiment reduced to 9 officers and about 130 noncommissioned officers and enlisted men. The next month 132 volunteers joined the state detachment, which marched to the Carolinas under Lieutenant Colonel Charles Porterfield.[30] This unit was destroyed at Camden, South Carolina, on August 16, 1781. In January 1782 the garrison regiment, then numbering 140 men, was incorporated into Charles Dabney's State Legion.

Companies, 1781-1782
Captain Thomas H. Drew
Lieutenant Obadiah (Opie) Davenport
Lieutenant John Vaughan
Liuetenant David Mann
Lieutenant James Kennedy
Ensign Robert Boush
Surgeon Anthony Tucker Dixon

Lieutenant Colonel Charles Porterfield's State Detachment, 1780

Field Officers
Lieutenant Colonel-Commandant Charles Porterfield (State Garrison Regiment)
Major Thomas Mathews (State Artillery Regiment)
Quartermaster Gideon Johnston (State Artillery Regiment)

In March 1780 Lieutenant Colonel Charles Porterfield was appointed commandant of a special detachment of state troops that was raised for service with the Continental troops in the Southern Department. The detachment, which numbered about three hundred men, was drawn from different units. Porterfield, a veteran of Arnold's expedition against Quebec in 1775, had served in Daniel Morgan's Rifle Corps and in the 11th Virginia Continental Regiment. After he resigned from the Continental service in July 1779 he entered the state line.[31]

Porterfield's command escaped the surrender of Charleston in May 1780 and joined Horatio Gates's army. When Gates and Cornwallis clashed at Camden, South Carolina, on August 16, 1780, Porterfield's men were assigned to the left flank. They held firm after the militia and Armand's Legion panicked, and Porterfield and most of his men were killed or captured when the British overran the American lines.[32]

Companies, March 1780-August 1780

Garrison Company: Captain Edward Digges (132 men)
Artillery Company: Captain Gideon Johnston (134 men)
1st Cavalry Troop: Major John Nelson (33 men)
2d Cavalry Troop: Captain Charles Fierer (29 men)

Virginia State Artillery Regiment, 1777-1782

(Also designated at various times: Marshall's Artillery, Edmunds's Corps.)

Field Officers

Colonel Thomas Marshall, November 15, 1777-February 1782. Captured at Charleston.
Lieutenant Colonel George Muter, November 15, 1777-June 1778
Lieutenant Colonel Elias Edmunds, June 1778-February 1782
Major Thomas Mathews, November 15, 1777-1780. Captured at Charleston.
Major John Mazarett, April 15, 1780-1781. Dropped from the service for "Unofficer like & ungentlemanly conduct."

In June 1777 the General Assembly authorized a regiment, or train, of artillery for local defense purposes. In August 1777 the council of state appointed the captains and subalterns and in November of the same year the field officers. By August 1778 the ten companies, numbering between three and four hundred men, had been fully completed. An eleventh company consisted of artillery artificers, or ordnance repairmen.[33]

In 1780 Colonel Thomas Marshall and Major Thomas Mathews led a detachment of 134 men and eight brass field pieces to the south. The main portion went to Charleston and were captured, and one company joined Charles Porterfield's detachment in the Carolinas. The remnants of Marshall's Artillery were incorporated into Dabney's Legion in February 1782. In its last year of independent existence the State Artillery Regiment was known as Edmunds's Corps, after its lieutenant colonel.[34]

Companies, 1777-1778

Captain Elias Edmunds
Captain George Ancram
Captain Griffin Port
Captain Edward Moody
Captain Harry Quarles
Captain Nicholas George Moëballé
Captain James Lewis
Captain Turner Richardson

Captain Samuel Timson
Captain John Mazarett
Captain David Mossom. Artificers.

The State Artillery Regiment originally included the new State Garrison Regiment, organized as a separate unit in June 1778 under Colonel George Muter. Captain Decrome de la Porte, a French adventurer, apparently served in Marshall's artillery until early 1778, when his newly formed French company was detached as an infantry unit guarding Hampton.[35]

Companies, 1778-1780
Captain Samuel Crawley
Captain Patrick Wright
Captain Richard Booker
Captain David Pennell
Captain Charles de Klaumann[36]
Captain John Trigg
Captain John Watlington
Captain Thomas Pollard
Captain Samuel Blackwell
Captain Gideon Johnson
Captain Lawrence House. Artificers.

Companies, 1780-1782
Captain James Bradley (no command)
Captain Thomas Clay (no command)
Captain Christopher Roane (to Dabney's Legion)
Captain William Spiller (no command)
Captain John Williams (no command)
Captain William Thompson (no command)
Captain Peter Kemp (no command)
Captain Thomas Marshall, Jr.
Captain Humphrey Marshall
Captain Edward Valentine
Captain John Allan. Artificers.

St. François de Loyeauté's Corps of State Artillery Cadets, 1777-1778

Officers
Captain and State Inspector General of Artillery and Fortifications, St. François Arnert Michel Dieudonné de Loyeauté, November 11, 1777-May 21, 1778
Major Guillaume Pierre, 1777

On November 11, 1777, the Virginia House of Delegates resolved to establish an academy "for the advancement of knowledge in military architecture and gunnery." The academy was to be headed by St. François de Loyeauté, a young French volunteer, who had been sent by Louis XVI as an instructor to Knox's artillery brigade. Loyeauté had arrived in America earlier in the year on the staff of Major General Phillippe Charles Baptiste Trenson de Coudray, who had brought cannon and muskets for Washington's army. After de Coudray's accidental death, Richard Henry Lee befriended Captain Loyeauté and persuaded him to remain in America and direct the academy for artillery cadets in Virginia. The French officer demurred at first, preferring "military honor" to "the business of an academician better suiting age and infirmity." The promise of a high salary and the title of inspector general of artillery, fortification, and military stores caused him to change his mind and travel to Virginia.[37]

The first class of cadets was to be made up of men detached from Thomas Marshall's State Artillery Regiment and from Decrome de la Porte's French company, and these men were supposed to serve on a rotating basis. As Loyeauté's students graduated they were to become instructors in their own or in other state units.

On January 27, 1778, Thomas Jones, Jr., was appointed assistant adjutant general to aid Loyeauté in overseeing the state's artillery, military stores, and fortifications. By the spring of 1778 Loyeauté had begun to take his own importance too seriously and to interfere with normal recruiting for the state artillery and state garrison regiments. Thomas Marshall believed that Loyeauté was attempting to take over the state artillery and forced his resignation. On May 21, 1778, Loyeauté returned his commission, gallantly refusing to accept any pay for his past year's services. Late in 1780 or early in 1781 he was reappointed Virginia's inspector of state artillery, with the rank of lieutenant colonel. Assigned to General George Weedon's command he superintended the transfer of heavy ordnance from New Castle to Hanover Court House. He spent time at the Fredericksburg manufactory and acted as a dispatch rider between Governor Jefferson and Baron von Steuben.[38]

Companies, November 1777-May 1778
1st Company: Captain Coyette
2d Company: Captain Bagarre (or Beyard)

Major John Nelson's Regiment of Virginia State Cavalry, 1779-1782

Field Officers

Major-Commandant John Nelson, May 1779-February 1782

In May 1779 the Virginia General Assembly authorized the governor, with the advice of the council, to raise as many companies of volunteer cavalry as they felt were necessary for local defense. The following October the assembly limited this body of cavalry to three troops. (A number of volunteer and militia units of light horse were also raised between 1778 and 1782 and eventually drew state pay for their services.)[39]

In March 1780 Major Nelson and Captain Charles Fierer, a Hessian defector, took sixty-two volunteers from their regiment into the Carolinas as part of Lieutenant Colonel Charles Porterfield's detachment. Arriving after the capture of Charleston, Porterfield's detachment joined Gates's army and was engaged at the battle of Camden in August 1780. Although Nelson's and Fierer's troops were greatly reduced as a result of this action, Captain Vogluson's company was virtually intact and thus could be the nucleus for a reconstructed regiment. Recruiting went slowly, however, and further trouble occurred when Captain Fierer, who had absented himself without leave, was dismissed in 1781.[40]

Companies, May 1779-January 1782

1st Troop: Captain Edmund Read, 1779. Temporarily commanded by Major Nelson while part of Porterfield's detachment.

2d Troop: Captain Martin Armand Vogluson, 1779. Transferred to Dabney's Legion, 1782.

3d Troop: Captain Charles Fierer, 1779. Dismissed, 1781. Captain Thomas Armistead, 1781. Promoted from a lieutenancy to replace Fierer. Transferred to Dabney's Legion, January 1782.

In January 1782 a board of state officers consolidated the remnants of the Virginia State Line into a legion commanded by Lieutenant Colonel Charles Dabney. Captains Vogluson and Armistead were transferred to the state legion, as were the cavalrymen whose terms of service had not yet expired. It is believed that Virginia's only known woman soldier of the Revolution, Anna Maria Lane, served with Nelson's cavalry in 1780.[41]

George Rogers Clark's Illinois Regiment, Virginia State Forces, 1778-1783

Field Officers

Colonel George Rogers Clark, December 1778-January 1781
Lieutenant Colonel George Rogers Clark, December 1777-December 1778
Lieutenant Colonel John Montgomery, December 1778-1783
Major Joseph Bowman, December 14, 1778-August 17, 1779
Major Thomas Quirk, August 17, 1779-1782
Major William Lynn, 1778?-1781

Major George Slaughter, 1778?-1780?. Commanded detachment.
Major Walker Daniel (?)

The largest and most complex unit raised by Virginia during the Revolution began its existence in January 1778 as a special militia regiment for the defense of the Western Department. Governor Patrick Henry's instructions to Lieutenant Colonel Clark on January 2, 1778, authorized him to raise seven companies of fifty men each and to attack the British outpost of Kaskaskia on the Mississippi. Clark was also ordered to establish a post on the Falls of the Ohio.[42]

Clark set out in May 1778 with two companies under captains Joseph Bowman and Leonard Helm and mustered with two militia companies under captains William Harrod and John Montgomery, from Kentucky. The combined force that left the Falls of the Ohio on June 24 numbered about 150, but Clark succeeded in taking Kaskaskia by surprise attack on the night of July 4, 1778. Philippe de Rastel, sieur de Rocheblave, commandant of Kaskaskia's Fort Gage, was sent back to Virginia with a guard detachment led by Captain Montgomery and lieutenants Levi Todd and John Rogers.[43]

After Clark's men established themselves at Kaskaskia a detachment of thirty mounted soldiers under Joseph Bowman captured the nearby posts of Prairie du Rocher, St. Philippe, and Cahokia (Cohoes). Companies of French-speaking volunteers under captains François Bosseron, François Charleville, and J. M. P. Legrace joined Clark and acted as garrison troops for Kaskaskia, Cahokia, and the town of Vincennes, 180 miles east of Kaskaskia, which had surrendered to the Virginians. On December 17, 1778, a British force under Henry Hamilton recaptured Vincennes, taking Captain Leonard Helm and Lieutenant John Bailey prisoners. By early February 1779 Clark had gathered a 200-man force, in five companies, under captains Joseph Bowman, John Williams, Richard McCarty (a British deserter), Edward Worthington, and François Charleville. Unaware that reinforcements under George Slaughter were on the way from Kentucky, Clark's force marched overland from Kaskaskia, laid siege to the British works at Vincennes (then called Fort Sackville), and captured it on February 25, 1779.[44]

In March an artillery company under Captain Robert George and a militia company from Kentucky under Captain Hugh McGary arrived, followed by other militia units at irregular intervals. George Slaughter's detachment of Indian fighters arrived in May and participated in all of Clark's activities from Vincennes through the Shawnee campaigns of 1780-1782.[45]

In 1781 Clark returned to Virginia to accept a commission as brigadier general and to plan an expedition against Fort Detroit. Soon after his arrival Virginia was attacked by British forces under Arnold and Phillips, and Clark commanded several sorties along the James River. After a few months he returned to Fort Pitt for supplies and reinforcements. He hoped to take a detachment of men from Colonel John Gibson's 7th Virginia Continental Regiment but was unable to get them. Then long-awaited reinforcements under Lieutenant Colonel Joseph Crockett arrived at Wheeling on May 23, after service at Albemarle Barracks and in the Carolinas. Clark took most of Crockett's men back to the west, leaving some at Fort Pitt to replace volunteers from the 7th Virginia Regiment. After the long Shawnee campaign ended the remnants of Crockett's unit were absorbed into the garrision at the Falls of the Ohio by late 1781. A force of Pennsylvanians under Colonel Archibald Lochry, destined for Clark's army, never reached him. The entire unit was massacred on August 24, 1781, by an Indian raiding party under Thayendanegea, better known as Chief Joseph Brant.

Although the Old Northwest was fairly settled and pacified by April 1783, when Clark turned his command over to Major George Walls, remnants of his army continued to defend the frontier against Indian raids until about 1786.[46]

Companies, June 1778
No. 1:   Captain Joseph Bowman
No. 2:   Captain William Harrod
No. 3:   Captain Leonard Helm
No. 4:   Captain John Montgomery

Infantry Companies, July 1778-December 1782
Captain Joseph Bowman
Captain John Williams
Captain Thomas Quirk
Captain Jesse Evans
Captain James Shelby
Captain Richard McCarty
Captain Benjamin Roberts
Captain Robert Todd
Captain Abraham Kellar
Captain Richard Brashear
Captain John Bailey
Captain Isaac Ruddell
Captain William Harrod
Captain Leonard Helm
Captain William Shannon
Captain-Lieutenant Richard Harrison
Captain Issac Taylor

French Volunteer Infantry Companies from Kaskaskia, 1778
Captain François Charleville
Captain François Bosseron

Captain J. M. P. Legrace
Captain Joseph Allery
Captain John Gerault
Captain Michael Perrault
Captain Godfrey Linitot

Cavalry Companies, 1778-1782

Captain Edward Worthington
Captain William McCracken
Captain John Rogers
Lieutenant William Gillespie

Artillery Companies, 1778-1782

Captain Robert George
Captain Alexander Craig

Companies of Marines

Captain John Pyeatt. Aboard the row galley *Willing*.

Companies of Rangers

Captain Charles Gatliffe
Captain Bland Ballard. Mounted rangers.
Lieutenant Thomas Stevenson
Ensign Thomas Montgomery
Ensign William Casey
Ensign William Harlan

Major George Slaughter's Detachment, Companies, 1779-1782

Captain Mark Thomas
Captain Jesse Evans
Captain Thomas Ravenscroft
Captain Benjamin Roberts
Captain Benjamin Fields. Mounted company.

Colonel John Gibson's Detachment in the Western Department, Fort Pitt, Companies, January 1780-December 6, 1781

Captain Uriah Springer
Captain Benjamin Biggs
Captain Robert Beall
Captain Robert Vance
Captain George Berry

Colonel Archibald Lochry's Pennsylvania Detachment Companies, July-August 1781

Captain Robert Orr. Riflemen.
Captain William Campbell. Cavalry.

Captain Samuel Shannon. Rangers.
Captain Thomas Stockley. Rangers.

Colonel Zachquill Morgan's Monongalia County Volunteers Companies, 1781

Colonel Zachquill Morgan, county lieutenant
Colonel Daniel McFarlin
Lieutenant Colonel Thomas Gaddis
Major John Evans
Major James Chew
Captain Michael Catt
Captain William Cross
Captain Thomas Crooks

Captain John Rogers's Troop of Dismounted Illinois Dragoons, 1779-1782
(Raised in Bedford County)

Captain John Rogers
Lieutenant James Meriwether
Cornet John Thruston

Volunteer Militia Units in the Western Department Companies, 1779-1783

The militia companies listed below served for brief periods on a rotating basis:

Kentucky County (formed in 1777)

Colonel John Bowman, county lieutenant
Captain William Harrod
Captain Squire Boone
Captain George Owens
Captain David Gass
Captain Charles Gatliffe
Captain Hardy Hill
Captain William Hogan
Captain Daniel Hall
Captain John Kennedy
Captain John Holder
Captain Charles Polk
Captain Michael Humble
Captain William McAfee
Captain William Oldham
Captain Robert Patterson
Captain Henry Prather
Captain John Swan

Captain Parmenas Briscoe
Captain Peter Asturgus

Fayette County (formed in 1780)

Colonel Daniel Boone, county lieutenant
Captain Charles Hazlerigg
Captain Robert Johnson
Captain Samuel Kirkham
Captain William McConnell
Captain Robert Patterson
Captain Charles Polk
Lieutenant John South
Lieutenant Francis McDonnal
Lieutenant John Constant
Ensign John Pleak

Lincoln County (formed in 1780)

Captain William Hays
Captain Nathan Huston
Captain Nathaniel Hart
Captain John Irvine
Captain Simon Kenton
Captain Joseph Kinkead. Light horse.
Captain Andrew Kinkead
Captain Samuel Kirkham
Captain Thomas Moore
Captain John Snoddy
Captain John Martin
Captain Gabriel Madison
Captain William McBride
Captain Samuel McAfee
Captain Samuel Scott
Lieutenant James Brown
Lieutenant George Adams
Lieutenant Benjamin Pettot
Lieutenant John Cowan
Ensign John Smith. Light horse.
Ensign Laurence Thompson
Ensign John Wood
Ensign John Dougherty
Ensign James Downing
Ensign James Estill
Ensign David Cook
Ensign Elisha Clary

Ensign Robert Barnett
Ensign John Boyle
Ensign William Casey. Rangers.
Ensign John McMurtry
Sergeant John South

Jefferson County (formed in 1780)
Colonel John Floyd, county lieutenant
Captain Lewis Hinchman
Captain William McClure
Captain Andrew Hynes
Captain James Patton
Captain James Rogers
Captain James Samuels
Captain John Vartreese
Captain Jacob Vanmeter
Captain Aquilla Whitaker
Lieutenant George Wilson
Lieutenant James Davis
Lieutenant Richard Chenowith
Lieutenant James Asturgus. Light horse.
Sergeant Richard Lee

Lieutenant Colonel Joseph Crockett's Western Battalion, Virginia State Forces, 1779-1782

Field Officers
Lieutenant Colonel-Commandant Joseph Crockett, 1779-1782
Major George Walls, 1780-1782

The second unit raised for service in the Old Northwest had an even more checkered history than Clark's Illinois Regiment. In December 1779 Joseph Crockett, 5th Virginia Continental Regiment, was commissioned lieutenant colonel-commandant of a new battalion to be raised in Botetourt, Berkeley, and Hampshire counties for western defense. George Slaughter's detachment of Indian fighters, while nominally attached to Crockett's command, spent most of its existence as part of the Illinois regiment.[47]

In 1780 seven of Crockett's companies were assigned to assist Taylor's Convention Army Guard Regiment at Albemarle Barracks. From February to May 1781 Crockett's men were part of the Virginia forces in the Guilford Court House, North Carolina, area. The battalion finally joined Clark at Wheeling on May 23, 1781, and marched west. After hard service against the Indians the remnants of the battalion were incorporated into Clark's garrison at the Falls of the Ohio.[48]

Companies, 1779-1782
Captain Isaac Craig
Captain William Cherry
Captain Thomas Young
Captain John Kearney
Captain Abraham Tipton
Captain Peter Moore
Captain Benjamin Kinley
Captain Abraham Chapline
Captain-Lieutenant James Lloyd
Lieutenant Richard Clark

The 1st and 2d Virginia State Legions, 1781-1783

(Also designated as Spotswood's Legions)

Field Officers
Brigadier General-Commandant Alexander Spotswood, 1781-1783
Lieutenant Colonel (1st Legion) John Taylor, 1781-1783
Major (1st Legion) William Lindsay, 1781-?
Major (1st Legion) Robert Forsyth, 1782-?
Lieutenant Colonel (2d Legion) Everard Meade, 1781-1783
Major (2d Legion) Cole Digges, 1781-?
Major (2d Legion) John Nicholas, 1782-?

On March 1, 1781, the General Assembly passed an act creating "two Legions for the Defense of the State," which were to serve under the command of General Alexander Spotswood, formerly colonel, 2d Virginia Continental Regiment. Each legion was to consist of six companies of foot and one of horse, a combined total of 400 men. When Phillips and Arnold raided Virginia between April and June 1781, the legions were still not completely organized and ready for field service. Spotswood, whose resignation from the Continental Line for personal reasons had been attended by much unpleasantness, yearned for military glory and spent more time designing showy uniforms and planning an eight-man band than he did in the field. Approximately 350 men had been recruited by November 1782, but their service was limited to drilling and guard duty. The legions were officially disbanded on November 4, 1783, but for all practical purposes they had ceased to exist as a military force much earlier.[49]

Companies, 1781-1783
1st Legion: No companies identified
2d Legion: Captain Peter Randolph. No other companies identified.

Colonel Charles Dabney's Virginia State Legion, 1782-1783

Field Officers
Lieutenant Colonel-Commandant Charles Dabney
Major Alexander Dick
Captain-Commandant Windsor Brown, 1782-1783
Captain-Commandant Abner Crump, 1783

On January 18, 1782, Governor Benjamin Harrison ordered that "the [1st] State regiment of Infantry, Major Nelson's corps of Cavalry, Captain Roger's company of dismounted Dragoons, and the company of Artillery commanded by Captain Roan, should be consolidated into a legionary Corps." Lieutenant Colonel Charles Dabney, 2d Regiment, Virginia State Line, was chosen as commandant by a special board of field officers in state service.[50]

Dabney, who had commanded a company of Hanover District minutemen and had served as lieutenant colonel of the 2d and 3d regiments, Virginia State Line, and lieutenant colonel of the 2d Virginia Continental Regiment, had been an officer since 1775. His fine record included participation in the northern campaigns and at the siege of Yorktown. The formation of Dabney's Legion out of the debris of the state line was greeted with opposition from a number of officers who "hoped to win promotion in their own corps." These men were dropped from the roll of active officers when they refused to join the legion, thereby forfeiting their claims to half-pay.[51]

The new legion, which bore no relationship to the legions under Alexander Spotswood (except in that its formation indicated the state's displeasure with Spotswood), numbered about 225 officers and men throughout 1782. It garrisoned Yorktown, Hampton, and Richmond and performed shipboard service on flag vessels. At one time Dabney tried to interest the governor in a wild scheme to capture Bermuda, but this idea was rejected. During the Shawnee campaigns of 1782 George Rogers Clark requested the legion as a reinforcement. Although the legionnaires were held in readiness for service in the west, they were needed in the tidewater area and could not be spared. Clothing and foodstuffs were in short supply, and Dabney's men often suffered from exposure and malnutrition in the midst of a heavily populated area. Roane's artillery and company mutinied on one occasion, refusing to cross the York River until they had received their back pay.[52]

From late 1782 through the spring of 1783 Dabney was absent from his command at the York, leaving Captain Windsor Brown as the garrison's commanding officer. In March and April 1783 Captain Abner Crump succeeded Brown as commandant pro tem of the state troops. On April 24,

1783, Dabney's Legion was ordered disbanded. Lieutenants David Mann and Pratt Hughes were reenlisted to recruit detachments to guard the state supply depots at Point of Fork and Richmond. These small companies of about eighteen men each continued in service until the middle of 1784. The guards at Point of Fork were then permitted to reenlist for three years. Under the command of successive commissaries of military stores the state guards remained in existence until 1802, when Point of Fork was decommissioned as the state's arsenal. Several of Charles Dabney's old veterans joined the new Public Guard at Richmond and served until 1807, when they were mustered out for medical reasons.[53]

Companies, 1782-1783

Infantry:	Captain Windsor Brown
	Captain Abner Crump
	Captain Frederick Woodson
Cavalry:	Captain Martin Armand Vogluson
	Captain Thomas Armistead
Artillery:	Captain Christopher Roane

The Virginia Militia, 1775-1783

9

THE Virginia common militia was first organized under the authority of Governor Thomas Dale's famous martial laws, imposed on the struggling colony in 1611. The militia, made up of all white males between the ages of sixteen and fifty, existed as an institution from Dale's time until 1865. During the Revolution the militia provided the principal manpower pool for both the Continental and the state forces.

It is difficult to determine how many men actually served in the militia during the war for independence because available population statistics for the period are extremely crude. Various historians, using these statistics, have estimated that between 30,000 and 50,000 Virginians were of military age in 1775. Thomas Jefferson, making an educated guess in 1781, set the number at just under 50,000 (his actual figure was 49,971). If one deducts the 8,000 men who served in the Continental and state forces between 1775 and 1781, a total of about 40,000 enrolled militiamen remains.

The militia was never considered to be an effective or even a unified fighting force. The monthly and quarterly musters were generally something of a joke, since those who reported to the rendezvous were usually untrained, unarmed, and uninterested. Officers were most often elected by the men, and the ones who retained their popularity between elections did so by permitting lax discipline and even major infractions of regulations.

On the positive side, however, the militia system provided authorities with the only workable method of registering eligible males of military age. It also gave many young men their first experience in handling of and drilling with muskets. On the frontier, membership in the militia provided a social bond as well as a means of defending widely separated communities. For these reasons, the militia remained strong for over two centuries.

The Virginia legislation that regulated the militia was based largely on the English yeomanry tradition, which in turn had its distant origins in the wars against Danish Vikings during the reign of Alfred the Great. Throughout the Middle Ages all able-bodied freeholders were liable for service to their landlords in time of war. By the seventeenth century each English shire had a lord lieutenant in charge of summoning and equipping the militia foot soldiers. The wealthier young men often formed themselves into trained bands and independent companies of volunteers, and they dressed in gaudily expensive regalia for state occasions.

In colonial Virginia the lord lieutenant had his counterpart in the county lieutenant, usually a man of education and wealth, like Colonel William Byrd. Most county lieutenants at the time of the Revolution were justices, lawyers, surveyors, planters, or members of the General Assembly. The county lieutenant outranked all other militia officers, although he nominally held only the rank of colonel.

Virginia's population and boundaries both expanded during the Revolution. In 1775 there were sixty established counties; by 1781 there were seventy-four.

Usually no more than one-tenth of the total militia force was on active duty at a given time. Much of this duty consisted of guarding supplies and chasing suspected tories and felons. From 1779 to 1782, however, the militia was a key factor in the southern campaign. Because the regular line troops were suddenly eliminated after Charleston and Camden, the two Virginia militia brigades under generals Robert Lawson and Edward Stevens constituted a large part of General Greene's forces in the Carolinas. The militiamen's poor record at Camden was offset by surprising bravery at Cowpens and at Guilford Court House, but their lack of training and short tours of duty made them unreliable troops.

Hundreds of militia companies existed during the war, but only the temporary regiments that served at Point Pleasant, Camden, Kings Mountain, Cowpens, and Guilford Court House are discussed in this section. Extant militia records for the period are fragmentary at best, and the limitations of space prohibit a more detailed listing.

Militia Regiments on the Frontier, 1774-1775

As Virginians pushed their land companies and settlements into the Ohio River Valley following the French and Indian War, the Shawnee Indians commenced retaliating for the intrusion into their lands. Scattered incidents between white frontiersmen and peaceful Indians sparked a wave of violence in early 1774. The most serious affair occurred at Yellow Creek, a tributary of the Ohio River, when a party of traders under Daniel Greathouse massacred the family of Logan, a war chief of the Mingo Confederation. Logan blamed Michael Cresap, one of Greathouse's associates, although Cresap probably was not present at the time of the killings.

Captain John Gibson, of West Augusta, husband to Logan's murdered sister, became an intermediary between Logan and Lord Dunmore, but he was unable to prevent an uprising of the Shawnees in retaliation for Yellow Creek. Both Gibson and Cresap commanded militia companies in the ensuing Indian war.

Colonel Andrew Lewis, a prime mover in the Greenbrier Land Company, collected about three thousand men in two divisions, or regiments, at Camp Union on the Great Levels of the Greenbrier during late September and early October 1774, and he then marched them to Point Pleasant, arriving on October 6. On Monday, October 10, 1774, Cornstalk attacked the Virginians. After a daylong battle, in which about a hundred of Lewis's men (the figures range from 87 to 160) were killed or wounded, the Indians were defeated. Lord Dunmore, commanding a second expeditionary force, did not reach the battlefield, stopping instead at Fort Gower.[1]

Militia Companies in Service, 1774-1775[2]

Augusta
Captain John Bell
Captain Anthony Bledsoe
Captain John Gilmore
Captain William Leftwich
Captain Alexander Long
Captain William Lowther
Captain George Moffatt
Captain William Nalle
Captain John Vanbeaver

Bedford
Captain John Bell
Captain James Ewing
Captain Jonas Friend
Captain John Hopkins
Captain Henry Paulling
Captain James Smith
Captain Ralph Stewart
Captain William Trigg
Captain John Wilson
Ensign James Alexander
Sergeant Robert Davis
Sergeant Joseph Dictorn(?)

Botetourt
Captain Edward Cowan
Captain James Cooke

Captain James Henderson
Captain Robert McAfee

Fincastle
Captain William Cock
Captain William Campbell
Captain Walter Crockett
Captain Joseph Cloyd
Captain David Campbell
Captain Hugh Crockett
Captain Robert Doak
Captain William Edmondson
Captain John Floyd
Captain James Harrod
Captain David Looney
Captain Henry Patton
Captain William Robinson
Captain David Smith
Captain Henry Skeggs
Captain James Thompson

Between October 1774 and October 1775 about seventy-five of the organized companies of frontier militia raised for Dunmore's War remained on scouting and patrol duty. The majority of these men became a nucleus for the regular western companies in the Continental and state lines. Many did not receive their pay for frontier duty until the Revolution was well underway.

Northern Division Officers

Commander in Chief John Murray, earl of Dunmore, governor of Virginia
Major Angus McDonald
Colonel William Crawford, Frederick County Regiment
Colonel Adam Stephen, Berkeley County Regiment
Major John Connolly, West Augusta Battalion

Companies
Captain Michael Cresap, Sr.
Captain Michael Cresap, Jr.
Captain Hancock Lee
Captain Daniel Morgan, Frederick County
Captain Daniel Cresap
Captain (?) Teabaugh
Captain (?) Hoagland

Captain John Gibson, West Augusta
Captain George Rogers Clark, West Augusta
Captain James Parsons, West Augusta

Southern Division Officers

Commander in Chief Colonel Andrew Lewis
Commissary Charles Simms
Commissary Thomas(?) Posey
Adjutant James Newell
Spy: Thomas Baker
Spy: Simon Kenton
Spy: Simon Girty

Augusta Regiment Companies

Colonel Charles Lewis
Major John Field
Captain John Dickenson
Captain Benjamin Harrison
Captain Samuel Wilson
Captain John Lewis (son of Thomas Lewis)
Captain Andrew Lockridge

Botetourt Regiment Companies

Colonel William Fleming
Major William Inglis (Ingles)
Captain Thomas Burford (Buford)
Captain Philip Love
Captain John Murray
Captain Robert McClenachan
Captain James Robertson

Independent Companies, September-December 1774

Captain John Field
Captain George Mathews
Captain John Stewart
Captain John Lewis (son of Andrew Lewis)
Captain William Paul(lin)
Captain Matthew Arbuckle
Captain Alexander McClenachan
Captain Samuel McDowell
Captain Joseph Haynes
Captain James Ward
Captain Evan Shelby
Captain William Herbert
Captain William Russell

Captain John Stedman
Captain (John) Allen. Artificers.
Captain (?) Slaughter
Captain William McKee(?)

Virginia Troops in Gates's Army at Camden, August 1780

During the upsurge of British activity in North and South Carolina following the capitulation of Charleston in May 1780, large numbers of Virginia troops, mostly militia, were sent south. On August 14, 1780, seven hundred Virginia militia under General Edward Stevens joined Horatio Gates's force at Rugeley's Mills, South Carolina. Gates's southern army consisted of combined militia and regular units under Governor Richard Caswell, of North Carolina, and General Mordecai Gist, of Maryland, together with a detachment of volunteers under Colonel Charles Porterfield, of Virginia, and Armand's Legion. A detachment of Maryland and Delaware artillery and a small corps of militia light infantry completed the army. Baron de Kalb and his aide, Colonel Dubuyson, and Colonel John Christian Senf and his aide, Major Charles Magill, of Virginia, were present as observers.[3]

On August 15 the army marched to Camden, thirteen miles away. Armand's legionnaires, leading the column, were attacked by a unit of Cornwallis's cavalry. Porterfield's detachment managed to drive off the attackers, but Porterfield was mortally wounded and his men scattered. During a brief lull, Gates rallied his demoralized troops and arranged them in a formal line of battle: Gist's Maryland brigade on the right, Caswell's North Carolina militia in the center, and the Virginia militia, light infantry, and Porterfield's detachment on the left. The 1st Maryland Continental Regiment formed a reserve line, while Armand's troopers guarded the flanks and van.

Gates's hastily contrived strategy called for the militia to fire the first volley and then retire behind the Maryland line, but their movements were blocked on the right flank by a swamp. As the first wave of British infantry closed with the American line, the front-line militia panicked, threw away their guns, and gave way through the center. As the left flank also began to disintegrate, "confusion insued" among the Maryland troops, who endeavored to fire on the British without hitting their own milling militia. The 1st Maryland Regiment and Porterfield's volunteers held what was left of the line, while the militia "took to the woods in all directions," sustaining heavy casualties. During the rout, Baron de Kalb was wounded eight times, and his aide, Dubuyson, was wounded and taken prisoner. In the disorderly retreat, eight cannon and all the dead and wounded were abandoned.

Gates later reported to the Continental Congress that when the militiamen returned to their homes after a month or so of running and hiding, they met with frigid receptions from their neighbors. With more wisdom than he had displayed during the battle, Gates suggested that the men not be punished—their shame and remorse over their cowardice, he said, would be the best incentive to do better in the future.[4]

Militia Companies, August 1780
Captain William Craddock. Raised in Amelia.
Captain (?) Price. Raised in Amelia.
Captain Nathaniel Tate. Raised in Bedford.
Captain James Johnson. Raised in Caroline.
Captain Archibald Walthall. Raised in Chesterfield.
Captain John Price. Raised in Hanover.
Captain John Bias. Raised in Louisa (2d Regiment).
Captain Thomas Minor. Raised in Spotsylvania.

Virginia Militia at Kings Mountain

(Also designated as: Colonel William Campbell's Militia Regiment of 1780.)

Field Officers
Colonel William Campbell, 1777-1780
Major William Edmondson, 1780

The most spectacular conflict in which Virginia militia played a part was the battle of Kings Mountain, North Carolina, on October 7, 1780. The battle was unusual in many ways, not the least of which was the composition of the contending forces. Both armies were made up of militiamen—Patrick Ferguson's Provincial Rangers on the British side and William Campbell's combined force of Virginians and North Carolinians on the American.[5]

Patrick Ferguson, inventor of an advanced breech-loading rifle, had commanded a picked corps of riflemen at the battle of Brandywine in 1777. After losing the use of his right arm from a wound received in that engagement, he returned to England and trained himself to write, shoot, and fence with his left hand. He came back to America and won promotions to major and then to lieutenant colonel. Between late 1779 and early 1780 he organized the loyalist militia in the Carolinas into a corps of provincial rangers and marched them north from Savannah, Georgia, in March 1780 to join other British units. The combined force headed north to subdue whig centers in the Carolinas and Virginia and presumably to attack the Virginia lead mines in what is now Wythe County.

The North Carolina legislature raised a force of militia to meet the threat and requested assistance from Virginia. From present-day Tennessee came the "over-the-mountain men," under colonels Evan and Isaac Shelby and John Sevier; they were joined by militia regiments from the Carolinas under colonels Frederick Hambright, Charles McDowell, Joseph Winston, Benjamin Cleveland, William Lacey, and James Williams. About ten companies of

Virginia militiamen under Campbell arrived in September. These men included musketeers, riflemen, and some mounted troops.

On October 7 the two armies met at the British camp on Kings Mountain. Ferguson's command was completely surrounded by the nearly equal force of Virginia and North Carolina militia, who charged the hilltop position. In the thickest of the fighting Ferguson was hit simultaneously by several American bullets. British resistance ceased soon afterwards.

About four hundred Virginians participated in the battle.[6]

Companies, Campbell's Regiment, 1780

Captain David Beatie
   1st Lieutenant Robert Edmundson, Jr. Wounded.
   2d Lieutenant Nathaniel Dryden
   Ensign William Willoughby
Captain William Bowen
   1st Lieutenant Reece Bowen, commanding. Killed.
Captain Andrew Colville
   1st Lieutenant Samuel Newell. Wounded.
   2d Lieutenant William Davidson
   Ensign John Beatie. Killed.
Captain Robert Craig
   1st Lieutenant William Blackburn. Killed.
   2d Lieutenant William Bartlett
   Ensign Andrew Goff
Captain James Dysart. Horsemen.
   1st Lieutenant Andrew Kincannon
   2d Lieutenant James Roberts
   Ensign Robert Campbell
Captain William Edmondson
   1st Lieutenant Robert Edmundson, Sr. Killed.
   2d Lieutenant Patrick Campbell
   Ensign James Houston
Lieutenant Thomas McCullough
   2d Lieutenant Humbertson Lyon. Killed.
Captain William Neal
   1st Lieutenant William Russell, Jr.
Captain John Campbell
Captain James Elliott

The Virginia Militia at Cowpens, January 17, 1781, and at Guilford Court House, March 15, 1781

On December 4, 1780, Major General Nathanael Greene accepted command of the Southern Department, replacing Horatio Gates. Like his predecessor, Greene was allotted only a fraction of the troops needed to match Cornwallis's army; moreover, fully a third of them were raw militia. The Continental regulars at his disposal, however, nearly made up for the small size of his force. These were battle-hardened veterans under Daniel Morgan, William Washington, and Edward Carrington who had avoided capture at Charleston the year before. Thanks to Morgan's Maryland, Virginia, and Delaware troops, the British Legion under Tarleton suffered their first setback at Cowpens on January 16, 1781, but Cornwallis's main force was still nearly intact.

After two months of parrying and retreating over the North Carolina-Virginia border (maneuvers often sarcastically called "Cornwallis's Country Dance") Greene's army, augmented by large numbers of Virginia militia, returned to North Carolina to face the British.

The two armies met at Guilford Court House on March 15, and Greene barely escaped the same disaster that had cost Gates his command. His militia fired and withdrew according to plan and then kept running, leaving the regulars pinned down and forced to face the enemy unsupported. Greene's Continentals, however, held their positions as Gates's had not and were even able to launch several small counterattacks. These failed and Greene's men were finally forced to withdraw, but they did so in good order. Cornwallis was left in possession of the field, but the Americans still retained a fighting force.[7]

Companies, Virginia Militia at Cowpens

Captain Francis Triplett. Raised in Fauquier.
Captain James Winn. Raised in Fauquier.
Captain James Gilmore. Raised in Rockbridge.
Captain Robert Craven. Raised in Rockingham.

The militia were divided into two brigades commanded by brigadiers Robert Lawson and Edward Stevens, who received a leg wound at Guilford Court House. Two rifle regiments under Colonel Charles Lynch and Colonel William Campbell were also present.

Companies, Militia at Guilford Court House

Captain John Smith. Raised in Augusta.
Captain David Gwin. Raised in Augusta.
Captain James Tate. Raised in Augusta.
Captain (?) Sullivan. Raised in Berkeley.
Captain William McClanachan. Raised in Botetourt.
Captain (?) Hoyd. Raised in Botetourt.
Captain Francis Cowherd. Raised in Caroline.
Captain Stephen Pankey. Raised in Chesterfield.
Captain George Williamson. Raised in Goochland.
Captain John Wynn. Raised in Halifax.
Captain John Brown. Raised in Mecklenburg.

Captain (?) Overstreet. Raised in Nottoway.
Captain James Brewer. Raised in Pittsylvania.
Captain Robert Hughes. Raised in Powhatan.
Captain Nathaniel Cunningham. Raised in Prince Edward.

Crawford's Expedition Against the Wyandots, May-June 1782

Field Officers
Colonel William Crawford, May-June 1782
Major David Williamson
Major Thomas Gaddis
Major John McClelland
Major James Benton
Brigade Major Daniel Leet
Aide-de-Camp John Rose (pseudonym of Baron Gustavus Henri de Rosenthal, a Russian nobleman)
Surgeon (Dr.) John Knight
Guides: John Slover
        Jonathan Zane
        Thomas Nicholson

In March 1782 ninety-six Christianized Indians were murdered at Gnadenhutten, in present-day Ohio, by Colonel David Williamson, of the Pennsylvania forces. The so-called Moravian Massacre led to skirmishing between Indians and whites on the western frontier and threatened to set off a full-scale border war. Another village of Moravian converts at Sandusky became the target of a second punitive expedition on the part of the white settlers.

General James Irvine raised nearly five hundred volunteers to march on Sandusky in May 1782. These troops mustered at Fort Pitt. Since Irvine could not leave his duties as administrator of the Western Department, he chose Colonel William Crawford to lead the volunteer horsemen against the Indians. Crawford, the retired colonel of the 7th Virginia Continental Regiment, had served with Washington on Forbes's expedition against Fort Duquesne over twenty-four years earlier. Somewhat against his will he let himself be persuaded to march on Sandusky, although he bore no personal grudge against the Indians.

Only a small effort at secrecy was made, and the British at Detroit soon learned of Crawford's departure from Fort Pitt. A company of British rangers under Captain William Caldwell alerted the Shawnees, Wyandots, Mingoes, and Delawares in the vicinity of Sandusky. On June 5, 1782, Crawford's men were surprised and routed, and Crawford was captured. About fifty of his men were killed and many others wounded, but Major Williamson managed to lead most of the survivors to safety despite constant harassment along the line of retreat. In retaliation for the Moravian Massacre, in which he had had no part, Crawford was tortured to death with particular savagery.[8]

Companies

Captain William Crawford
Captain John Crawford
Captain John Biggs
Captain John Minter
Captain William Harrison
Captain William Harrod

 *The Virginia State Navy, 1775-1787*

10

Since the early seventeenth century, maritime commerce has been important to Virginia's economy. Merchantmen and armed vessels were a common sight in the Chesapeake Bay and other major Virginia waterways long before the outbreak of the Revolution. The first conflicts fought on Virginia soil in 1775 and 1776 involved naval operations as well as land actions, particularly the bombardment of Hampton and Norfolk by Lord Dunmore's fleet.

Virginia's leaders recognized the defenseless condition of the vital coastal areas, and they took early measures to provide for their safety. Late in 1775 construction began on two row galleys—half-decked, mastless gunboats, at first propelled by oars—for harbor defense. During the war years additional galleys, fitted with masts and sails, were commissioned. Other sailing vessels of all classes—sloops, brigs, brigantines, cutters, and flatboats—were eventually purchased or built by the state. At least seventy-seven commissioned vessels made up the state navy, augmented by about one hundred privateers. The state navy's war record was not as eventful as that of the embryonic United States Navy. Most of the Virginia vessels were smaller than those of the American navy, and their activities, with some exceptions, were usually confined to patrol duty at the mouths of rivers.[1]

Captain James Barron, of the state boat *Liberty*, was promoted to commodore in 1780, a post which he held until his death in 1787. As commodore of the state navy, Barron assumed the duties formerly held by the navy board, created in May 1776.[2] In February 1776 a state marine corps was created to man the gundecks and fighting tops of the state vessels. These men also served as auxiliary coastal gunners and shore patrolmen. In December 1776 the marine corps was abolished as a separate organization, and its personnel were incorporated into the State Garrison Regiment and Thomas Marshall's state artillery. Small parties of temporary marines were still attached to the larger state ships as late as 1781.[3]

Commissioned officers in the state navy held ranks corresponding to those in the British and American navies. These officers were: commodores, commanders (of squadrons), captains, lieutenants, and midshipmen (or cadets). Below them were the warrant officers, including the sailing masters, boatswains, gunners, pursers, carpenters, sailmakers, cooks, coopers, clerks, masters-at-arms, stewards, and chaplains. Next were the mates and their assistants and the able-bodied seamen. On the larger ships the common sailors were rated as topmen, anchormen (also known as fo'c's'le men), and waisters, indicating whether their posts were on the masts, in the forecastle, or in the midships, or waist.

Unless the ship was engaged by the enemy, the captain, first lieutenant, surgeon, purser, boatswain, and gunner stood no regular watch; nor did the idlers—the carpenter, sailmaker, cooper, clerk, steward, and chaplain. All other personnel were divided into the port and starboard watches, performing their duties for four-hour periods, marked by the ringing of the ship's bell each half-hour. This system of nautical timekeeping and duty assignment dates back to Elizabethan times and is still in use today.[4]

In the session of May 1776 the Virginia convention created a board of commissioners "particularly to superintend . . . the naval preparations of this colony." The board had charge of all shipbuilding, ropemaking, drydocks, naval stores, and "victualling" for the new state navy.[5]

Commissioners of the Navy (Navy Board) May 1776

1st Commissioner Thomas Whiting
Commissioner John Hutchings
Commissioner Champion Travis
Commissioner Thomas Newton, Jr.
Commissioner George Webb

New Appointments
Edward Archer, 1777
Warner Lewis, 1777
James Innes, 1778
Jacquelin Ambler, 1779
James Maxwell, 1780

The navy board managed all naval accounts and recommended officers for appointments. In July 1780 the board was abolished and its duties assumed by Commodore James Barron, formerly commander of the state boat *Liberty*. During the British invasion of Virginia a separate commission was hastily created to superintend the defense of the Chesapeake Bay. It continued to function until two years after Yorktown.

Commissioners for the Defense of the Chesapeake Bay, 1781-1783

Commissioner Paul Loyall
Commissioner Thomas Brown
Commissioner Thomas Newton, Jr.

Flag Officers

Commodore John Bowcher (Boucher), April 1776-November 26, 1776
Commodore Walter Brooke, April 8, 1777-September 30, 1778
Commodore James Barron, July 3, 1780-May 14, 1787

Shipyards of the Revolution

Two shipyards were operated by the commonwealth for the state navy. The first and most important was the Chickahominy shipyard near modern-day Toano, which remained in use from 1777 to 1781, when it was burned by the British. By the end of 1781, however, a major portion of the yard had been rebuilt. The second yard was at Gosport, located in what is now the city of Portsmouth, on the land of Andrew Sprowle. In July 1780 the state purchased the facility from Sprowle's heirs.

Other yards known to have supplied vessels and naval stores to the state navy were located at Alexandria, Carter's Ferry, Cumberland, Frazer's Ferry, Fredericksburg, Indian Creek, Minge's Ferry, Muddy Creek, Portsmouth, Richmond, and South Quay. There were others, but they have not as yet been identified.

Vessels and officers[6]

Boats

Boats were small, open vessels propelled by oars or sail. They were manned by small crews, had shallow drafts, and were easy to manuever. Boats used for military purposes in the eighteenth century included longboats, barges, pinnaces, cutters, yawls, pirogues, and shallops. Most of the Virginia State Navy's boats probably were either shallops, large two-masted boats rigged like schooners, or sloops (*see* page 162).

Dasher, 1780
(Officers not identified)
Dolphin, 1779
Captain James Maxwell
Captain John Cowper
Lieutenant Philip Chamberlayne

The *Dolphin* sank with all on board off Cape Henry in 1779, after a fight with three British tenders.

>*Eastern Shore*, 1776
>Captain Francis Bright

>*Eastern Shore Betsey*, 1781
>(Officers not identified)

>*Fly*, 1779-1783
>Captain (name unknown)
>Lieutenant George Chamberlayne

The *Fly*, a schooner-rigged boat, was sold in 1786.

>*Jenny*, 1777
>Captain George Ralls

The *Jenny*, captured in June 1777, may have been a privateer rather than a state-owned boat. However, it was fitted out and armed at public expense.

>*Liberty*, 1776-1787
>Captain James Barron
>1st Lieutenant Richard Servant. (Commanded after Barron's promotion.)
>2d Lieutenant Theophilus Field

The *Liberty* was the most distinguished vessel in the state navy. It participated in twenty known engagements and served as Commodore Barron's flagship. In 1776 it captured both the transport *Oxford*, carrying a full detachment of Highland troops for Lord Dunmore, and the British sloop *Dorothy*. In 1779 it captured the British tender *Fortunatus*. At various times, the *Liberty* was schooner rigged.

>*Nicholson*, 1777-1780[7]
>Captain John Sinclair
>Lieutenant Isaac Mercer
>Lieutenant James (or Joseph?) Speake

Essentially an armed trading vessel operating between Virginia and the Dutch port of St. Eustatius in the West Indies, the *Nicholson* captured a British schooner in April 1777.

>*Patriot*, 1776-1781
>Captain Richard Barron
>1st Lieutenant Charles Jones
>2d Lieutenant Benjamin Rust

Virginia State Navy

Next to the *Liberty*, the *Patriot*, which was commanded by James Barron's brother, had the longest career in state service. It assisted in the capture of the *Oxford* in 1776 and the brig *Fanny* in the same year. The *Patriot*'s pilot was the famous Negro slave, Caesar Tarrant. In 1781 the *Patriot* was captured by the British and later surrendered to the French navy. The French turned it into a government packet boat, carrying dispatches across the Atlantic.

Patriot, 1783-1787
Captain James Barron
Lieutenant Samuel Barron

After the loss of the first *Patriot*, another schooner-rigged boat was commissioned and remained in service until 1787. It was commanded at various times by Commodore Barron.

Washington, 1781
(Officers not identified)

Brigs

Brigs were two-masted vessels larger than boats and square rigged on both foremast and mainmast. The Virginia armed brigs were capable of transatlantic voyages; a typical brig had the following dimensions:

```
length of keel ......................... 51 feet, 6 inches
breadth of beam ....................... 22 feet, 6 inches
depth of hold ......................... 9 feet, 4 inches
rake forward ................................ 20 feet
rake aft ............................ 7 feet, 6 inches
```

American Fabius, 1778-1783[8]
Captain John Barrett

Although this brig was often entered on state naval accounts, it may have been a privateer. It was owned by Benjamin Harrison, Jr.

Dolphin[9]
Captain Thomas Lilly

Fanny, 1779[10]
Captain John Young

The *Fanny* was captured by two British ships off Cape Henry in the spring of 1779 and its crew confined aboard a New York prison ship for nine months until exchanged.

Jefferson, 1779-1780[11]
Captain Richard Barron

Captain George Chamberlayne
Captain Willis Wilson
1st Lieutenant George Chamberlayne

Built at the Chickahominy shipyard, the *Jefferson* was both a commissioned state vessel and a privateer. On its last voyage in January 1780 the *Jefferson* was brigantine rigged. It sank near Jamestown.

Liberty, 1776-1778[12]
Captain George Goosley
Captain Thomas Lilly
1st Lieutenant Thomas Herbert
2d Lieutenant George Rogers

Originally built in April 1776 for James River defense, the brig *Liberty* became almost as illustrious on the high seas as its namesake, the boat *Liberty*. It captured the ship *Jane* in November 1776 and the armed vessel *Ida and Ann* the next year. The latter, a merchant ship, had left Malaga when it encountered and was captured by the *Liberty* in the Bay of Biscay. The cargo was sold in Martinique and provided the state with needed credit for purchasing supplies in the West Indies.

In 1778 the *Liberty* captured the ship *Portland* and another British vessel from Ireland. Early in its career it carried an armament of two six-pounders and six four-pounders, later increased to eighteen pieces of various calibers. Lieutenant Herbert lost his left hand in battle and wore a silver device to replace it, hence his nickname, "Old Silverfist."

Mosquito, 1776-1777[13]
Captain Jacob Valentine
Captain Isaac Younghusband
Captain John Harris
1st Lieutenant George Rogers
1st Lieutenant Robert Bolling
1st Lieutenant Byrd Chamberlayne

The *Mosquito*, which was also rigged as a brigantine at various times, captured two British vessels, the snow *John* and the transport *Noble*, before it was taken by the armed sloop *Ariadne* in 1777. Its crew was imprisoned in Barbados and Jamaica and its officers in Forton Prison, Portsmouth, England.

Northampton, 1776-1780
Captain John Lurty
Captain Francis Bright
1st Lieutenant Michael James
2d Lieutenant Lewis Jones

The *Northampton* captured at least one British prize in February 1777. It was decommissioned and sold on November 5, 1780.

Raleigh, 1776-1777
Captain James Cocke
Captain Edward Travis
1st Lieutenant John (or Jonathan) Barrett
2d Lieutenant Joel Sturdivant
2d Lieutenant Robert Gray

The *Raleigh*, formerly the *Hope*, was captured by the frigate *Phoenix* in April 1777.

Brigantines

Brigantines were two-masted merchant vessels similar to brigs except that brigantines were fore-and-aft rigged on the mainmast and square rigged only on the foremast. By changing the sails on the mainmast, the same vessel might be rigged either as a brig or as a brigantine.

Betsey, 1778-1779
Captain John Archer
Captain John Young

The *Betsey* was built as a schooner.

Greyhound, 1776-1778
Captain Edward Woneycutt

The *Greyhound*, built at Minge's Ferry and designed as a cargo vessel, was lost at sea in 1778.

Hampton, 1777
(Officers not identified)

Industry, 1780
Captain John Rogers

Rochester, 1777
Captain (?) Bozeman
Mate Henry Stratton

Although carrying armament, the *Rochester* seems to have been used primarily as a cargo vessel. It transported military stores for both the army and the navy. In 1777 it was captured by the British and its crew imprisoned in Philadelphia. First Mate Henry Stratton escaped in 1778 and returned to Virginia.

Galleys

Galleys were low, flat vessels propelled by sails and oars. These broad-beamed, single-decked craft carried fairly heavy armament and were valuable for coastal and river defense. Many galleys were patterned after the vessels used by General Benedict Arnold on Lake Champlain in 1776. Galleys were the most numerous vessels in the Virginia State Navy. One such galley was described as follows:[14]

> 75 feet streight rabit (keel measurement)
> 27 feet beam
> 10 feet hold
> 26 inches dead rise
> A long Floor, good entrance, very clean abaft, a full harping, bottom 22 Inch plank. Floor heads 3 Inch plank, one Streak [Strake] 3 Inch under the Wales & above them—3 Wales—Waste [Waist] 22 Inch plank, scantling large—strongly built forward & abaft—
> Beams 14 Inches deep, well kneed, one horizontal & 1 dogger Knee—at each end. Slides fited at each end for 24 pound Cannon, two in the Bow & two in the Stern—
> Six parts of a side for 9 pounders—
> Waste 3 feet 10 Inches, to rise forward to five feet—
> A quarter deck, sufficient to hole the officers—
> A spar deck, below for the men—
> Long grating hatches—24 row ports of a side—
> The Rigg to be fixed hereafter, at present it is intended to rig after the Miditerranian Gallies.

> *Accomack*, 1777-1782
> Captain Ishmael Andrews
> Captain William Underhill
> 1st Lieutenant Robert Miller (Milliner)
> 2d Lieutenant Ishmael Andrews

The *Accomack* was built at the Eastern Shore shipyard at Muddy Creek. It captured a British vessel in 1779.

> *Caswell*, 1776-1779
> Captain Willis Wilson
> 1st Lieutenant Argyle Herbert
> 2d Lieutenant Robert Bland(?)
> 2d Lieutenant Charles Boush

The *Caswell*, intended for service off the North Carolina coast, was built at South Quay in September 1776. In September 1777 it sailed for Edenton and remained on guard in Okracoke Sound. Captain Hance Bond, of North Carolina, commanded its marine detachment. It was offered for sale to North Carolina in June 1779, but it rotted and sank at its berth and could not be repaired.

> *Dasher*, 1778
> Captain Willis Wilson
>
> *Diligence*, 1777-1781
> Captain Johannes Watson
> 1st Lieutenant Richard Parker
> 2d Lieutenant Jesse Cannon

The *Diligence*, built at Muddy Creek shipyard on the Eastern Shore, carried three masts and five sails in 1781.

> *Henry*, 1776-1779
> Captain Robert Tompkins
> Captain Joshua Singleton
> Captain Wright Westcott
> 1st Lieutenant Joshua Singleton
> 2d Lieutenant Christopher Tompkins

The *Henry*, named for Governor Patrick Henry, carried at least two masts. It was dismantled in 1779.

> *Hero*, 1776-1779
> Captain George Muter
> Captain Philip Chamberlayne
> Captain John Barrett
> 1st Lieutenant Benjamin Pollard
> 1st Lieutenant Richard Dale
> 2d Lieutenant Thomas Swallow
> 2d Lieutenant John V. Kautzman

The *Hero*, originally a row galley, was ninety feet long and carried two cannon—an eighteen-pounder and a twenty-four-pounder. It was constructed of oak with yellow pine decks. Including marines, the *Hero* had a crew of fifty. It was dismantled and sold at auction on July 7, 1779.

> *Lewis*, or *First Row Galley*, 1776-1781
> Captain Celey Saunders
> Captain John Stevens
> 1st Lieutenant Stafford Lightbourne
> 2d Lieutenant Jesse George
> 2d Lieutenant Samuel Healy

The first of the row galleys built in 1776, the *Lewis*, was ordered sold in

1779. The General Assembly revoked the order and had the *Lewis* converted into a schooner for state service. On March 27, 1781, it was sunk near the Chickahominy shipyard to avoid capture.

> *Manley,* 1776-1779
> Captain James Cocke
> Captain William Saunders
> 1st Lieutenant Joel Sturdivant
> 2d Lieutenant George Chamberlayne
> 2d Lieutenant Joshua Singleton

On September 6, 1776, the *Manley* encountered Lord Dunmore's flagship, the H.M.S. *Fowey,* but managed to escape after a chase. It was dismantled and sold in 1779. The vessel was named for John Manley, captain of the Boston privateer *Lee.*

> *Mattaponi,* 1776-1777
> Captain Fendall Sutherland

> *Norfolk Revenge,* 1776-1778
> Captain John Calvert
> Captain Wright Westcott
> 1st Lieutenant Argyle Herbert
> 1st Lieutenant Thomas Pollard
> 2d Lieutenant Robert Glenn
> 2d Lieutenant Charles Boush

The *Norfolk Revenge,* built after the burning of Norfolk on New Year's Day, 1776, was sunk in the Nansemond River on May 29, 1778.

> *Page,* or *Second Row Galley,* 1776-1779
> Captain James Markham
> 1st Lieutenant John Lurty
> 1st Lieutenant Lewis Jones
> 2d Lieutenant Henry Lightbourne

The *Page* was dismantled and sold in 1779.

> *Protector,* 1776-1779
> Captain Robert Conway
> 1st Lieutenant John Thomas
> 2d Lieutenant Jesse George
> 2d Lieutenant Lewis Jones

The *Protector* was stationed at Wicomico in February 1777. It burned in June 1779.

Revenge, 1776-1777
Captain William Deane
Captain Samuel Towles
1st Lieutenant Aaron Jeffries
1st Lieutenant Edward Morton
2d Lieutenant Samuel Towles

The *Revenge* was schooner-rigged and carried two eighteen-pounders.

Safeguard, 1777-1780
Captain George Elliott
1st Lieutenant Joseph Speake
2d Lieutenant Merryman Payne

The *Safeguard* was stationed at the mouth of the Potomac in February 1777. In August 1780 it was ordered sold.

Washington, 1779
Lieutenant Charles Boush

Like the *Caswell*, the *Washington* was built in Virginia for North Carolina service. Its officers and crew were all from North Carolina. It was offered for sale to North Carolina in June 1779.

Pilot Boats

Beginning in November 1762, Virginia pilots were required by law to maintain pilot boats measuring at least eighteen feet in the keel and rigged as light sloops.

Adventure, 1776
Captain John Calvert

This vessel patrolled the Rappahannock River.

Lee, 1777
(Officers not identified)

Molly, 1777-1778
Captain John Pasteur
Captain John Archer
Lieutenant Edward Lattimer

This schooner-rigged pilot boat from St. Eustatius was purchased by the state for £425 on January 20, 1777. It was used mostly as a packet boat and blockade-runner.

Schooners

Schooners were small vessels of two or more masts, rigged fore and aft. In 1782 a state schooner being built by John Nash was described as having:

fifty five & a half feet keel, twenty one and a half feet beam, and ten feet four inches hold. . . . The waist to be near . . . [?] foot high, and a roundhouse about fourteen foot long; the whole of the waist to be filled in with the heart of poplar timber, lined with inch & quarter, or inch & half plank, & caulked inside and out, with fourteen ports at least, for guns.

Adventure, 1776
Captain William Saunders
Lieutenant Richard Lightbourne

In April 1776 this vessel was purchased by the state from Maximilian Calvert.

Alliance, 1779-1780
Captain Henry Stratton

The *Alliance* was captured off the Virginia capes on July 16, 1779. (Captain Stratton, former mate of the brigantine *Rochester*, had recently escaped from captivity in British-held Philadelphia.)

Baker, 1781[15]
Captain Hezekiah Holliday

Experiment, 1778
Captain William Ham

Harrison, 1782-1783[16]
Captain Richard Barron

The *Harrison* may have been built by James Nash at Indian Creek in 1782. It was sold by the state in October 1783.

Hornet (formerly the *Liberty*), 1776-1777
Captain Richard Taylor
Lieutenant Edward Woneycutt(?)

Originally built as a sloop, the *Liberty* was refitted as a schooner and rechristened the *Hornet*. It captured the schooner *Speedwell* in 1776.

Mayflower, 1777
Captain Caleb Herbert

Peace and Plenty, 1776-1778
Captain Alexander Guthrie
Captain Pharaoh Fitzpatrick
Lieutenant Robert Bolling
Lieutenant John Williams

The *Peace and Plenty* was primarily a trading vessel.

Speedwell, 1776
Captain James Cocke

This schooner was originally a British ship. It was captured by the state schooner *Liberty* (later the *Hornet*) in 1776 and refitted as a state vessel.

Ships

Seamen referred to the first rank of ocean-going vessels as ships: square-rigged vessels of three or more masts. Inasmuch as eighteenth-century terminology was often inexact, some of the ships listed below may have been large brigs, brigantines, or schooners.

Cormorant, 1782-1783[17]
Captain James Maxwell
Lieutenant Edward Woneycutt

The *Cormorant* was a British ship captured by the French in 1781. David Ross, the Virginia state agent, purchased it for the state in 1782. It was sold at public auction in October 1783. Its bottom was copper sheathed.

Dragon, 1776-1779 (1781)[18]
Captain Eleazer Callender
Captain John Markham
1st Lieutenant John Lurty
1st Lieutenant Joshua Singleton
2d Lieutenant John Hamilton

This schooner-rigged vessel, built at the Fredericksburg shipyard, carried eight six-pounders, four four-pounders, and two swivel guns. It was stationed on the Rappahannock River until 1779. In 1780 it sank in its berth at the Chickahominy shipyard while undergoing repairs. It was raised and being refitted in February 1781 as a fireship during the British invasion when the project was halted on February 12 by General Thomas Nelson after the British learned of it. (See "2d Regiment, Virginia State Line.")

Gloucester, 1777-1779[19]
Captain Thomas Lilly
1st Lieutenant William Christian
2d Lieutenant John Archer

In 1780 the *Gloucester* was converted into a prison hulk.

Loyalist, 1782-1786
Captain John Hardyman

Oliver Cromwell, 1781-1782
Captain John Harris

Like the *Cormorant*, this was a British ship captured by the French and bought by David Ross.

>*Tartar*, 1776-1780[20]
>Captain Richard Taylor
>Captain John Lurty
>Captain William Saunders
>1st Lieutenant Merryman Payne
>1st Lieutenant William Parker
>2d Lieutenant William Richards

The ship *Tartar* was built at Frazer's Ferry on the Mattaponi River. With the boat *Patriot* it engaged the H.M.S. *Lord Howe* in 1778 but failed to capture it. In 1780 the *Tartar* was transferred to the Virginia Board of Trade. It was sold after August 1780.

>*Tempest*, 1777-1779[21]
>Captain Celey Saunders
>Captain John Markham
>Lieutenant Michael James
>Lieutenant William Steele
>Lieutenant William Harwar Parker

Also built at Frazer's Ferry, the *Tempest* captured a British brig off Hog Island in 1779. In 1781 it was captured by the enemy off Hood's (later Fort Powhatan) on the James River.

>*Thetis*, 1778-1781
>(Officers not identified)

The *Thetis* was built at Chickahominy shipyard.

>*Virginia*, 1778-1779
>Captain James Barron

This frigate was burned at Portsmouth in May 1779.

>*Washington*, 1777-1778
>Captain Goodrich Boush

The British transport *Oxford*, captured in 1776, was considered a part of the state navy. It may have been rechristened subsequently.

Sloops

Sloops were small, single-masted vessels rigged fore and aft.

>*(American) Congress*, 1776-1780[22]
>Captain William Skinner
>1st Lieutenant Absalom Cabell

The *Congress*, of 110 tons burden, mounting fourteen four- and six-pounders and two nine-pounders, was the flagship of Commodore Boucher's Potomac River squadron. It carried ninety-six sailors and marines.

Defiance, 1776-1778[23]
Captain Eleazer Callender
Captain William Greene
1st Lieutenant William Greene
1st Lieutenant John Crew
2d Lieutenant Lewis Jones

Although built as a sloop, the *Defiance* was schooner rigged when it was captured in May 1778.

Dolly Henry, 1778
Captain Samuel Healy

Eminence, 1781
(Officers not identified)

This sloop, mounting one howitzer, was impressed into state service after Benedict Arnold's invasion in 1781.

Liberty, 1776[24]

While still rigged as a sloop the *Liberty* captured four enemy vessels: the *Oliver*, the *Lark*, the *Susannah*, and the sloop *Speedwell*.

Scorpion, 1776-1781
Captain Wright Westcott
1st Lieutenant Laban Goffigon
2d Lieutenant William Ivy
2d Lieutenant John Archer

The *Scorpion* was captured by H.M.S. *Cerberus* in 1781.

Shore, 1777[25]
Captain Robert Elam

Virginia, (date unknown)
(Officers not identified)

Cruisers and Privateers[26]

These constituted a class of privately owned armed vessels, carrying from one to three masts, which were used for patrolling, blockade-running, and raiding merchant ships. Approximately one hundred privateers from Virginia were given letters of marque during the war, but only about sixty-five can be positively identified.

Brig ———, 1781
Owned by   Richard Baker, Richard Blow, and Company
Captain   Christopher Clark
Armament   14 carriage guns
Crew   65 men

Brig ———, 1781
Owned by   James Hunter, John Banks, and Company
Captain   Esek Brown
Armament   12 carriage guns
Crew   75 men

Brig *American Fabius*, 1781-1783
Owned by   Benjamin Harrison, Jr., and Company
Captain   John Barrett
Armament   12 carriage guns
Crew   45 men

Ship *Annette*, 1782
Owned by   (name unknown)
Captain   John Audobon
Armament   12 carriage guns
Crew   45 men

Ship *Buckskin*, 1782
Owned by   Hunter, Banks, and Company
Captain   William Lewis
Armament   20 carriage guns
Crew   150 men

Boat *Capitol Landing's Revenge*, 1781
Owned by   Thomas Mathews and William Roane
Captain   William Roane
Armament   20 carriage guns
Crew   40 men

Sloop *Catharine*, 1781
Owned by   James Byrne and Company
Captain   Thomas McNally
Armament   20 carriage guns
Crew   40 men

Brigantine *Cornet*, 1782
Owned by   Thomas Shore, McConnico, and Company
Captain   William Thompson
Armament   14 carriage guns
Crew   40 men

Schooner *Count de Grass*, 1781
Owned by   Baker and Blow
Captain   Alexander Stockdale
Armament   14 carriage guns
Crew   80 men

Brigantine *Courtney*, 1782
Owned by   James Hunter and Francis Bright
Captain   Francis Bright
Armament   12 carriage guns
Crew   25 men

Brig *Dolphin*, 1781
Owned by   Henry Banks
Captain   Madett Engs
Armament   10 carriage guns
Crew   40 men

Galley *Dreadnaught*, 1782
Owned by   James Nelson of Petersburg
Captain   William Bellamy
Armament   6 carriage guns
Crew   50 men

Brig *Engilbert*, 1781
Owned by   Fine, Lott, and Company
Captain   John Gale
Armament   14 carriage guns
Crew   55 men

Schooner *Ferret*, 1779
Owned by   Francis Lewis, Jr.
Captain   James Robertson
Armament   8 carriage guns
Crew   24 men

Ship *Friendship*, 1781
Owned by   James Byrne and Company
Captain   John McCabe
Armament   20 carriage guns
Crew   40 men

Game Cock, 1781
Owned by   (name unknown)
Captain   John Cox
Armament   (information unknown)
Crew   (information unknown)

Brig *Goldfinger*, 1782
Owned by   Anderson and Company
Captain   Nicholas Brown Seabrook
Armament   8 carriage guns
Crew   25 men

Brigantine *Governor Nelson*, 1781
Owned by   Josiah Parker and John S. Wells
Captain   Nathaniel Parker
Captain   Byrd Chamberlayne
Armament   12 carriage guns
Crew   40 men

Brigantine *Grand Turk*, 1781
Owned by   Thomas Walker, James Brade, and Richard Baker
Captain   Cornelius Schermerhorn
Armament   14 carriage guns
Crew   60 men

This vessel captured the *Three Friends*, which was thought to be British but was actually a North Carolina schooner.

Schooner *Hannah*, 1781
Owned by   James Smith, Bowdoin Hunter, and John Banks
Captain   Christopher Gardiner
Captain   George Cross
Captain   John Cooper
Armament   14 carriage guns
Crew   75 men

Schooner *Hazard*, 1782
Owned by   Hunter, Banks, and Company and George Winn and Company
Captain   Daniel Connant
Armament   16 carriage guns
Crew   75 men

Schooner *Hope*, 1781
Owned by   Richard Conway, Robert Conway, and William Hunter
Captain   Robert Conway
Armament   6 carriage guns
Crew   21 men

Schooner *Hopewell*, 1782
Owned by   Richard Conway
Captain   Richard Conway
Armament   4 swivel guns
Crew   12 men

Schooner *Hunter*, 1781
Owned by   John Banks and Company
Captain   John McClure
Armament   10 carriage guns
Crew   50 men

Whaleboat *Intrepid*, 1781
Owned by   Josiah Parker and Thomas Brown
Captain   Nathaniel Parker
Armament   1 carriage gun and 6 swivel guns
Crew   35 men

Brigantine *Jolly Tarr*, 1781
Owned by   John Banks and Company
Captain   George Cross
Captain   Philip Turner
Armament   14 carriage guns
Crew   90 men

Whaleboat *Liberty*, 1781
Owned by   John Young and (?) Webb
Captain   John Young
Armament   1 swivel gun
Crew   20 "musket men"

Cutter *Lincoln*, 1781
Owned by   Hamilton and Wootton
Captain   William Wootton
Armament   2 carriage guns
Crew   22 men

Boat *Lizard*, 1778
Owned by   John Campbell, John Harvie, and Company
Captain   (name unknown)
Armament   (information unknown)
Crew   (information unknown)

Ship *Marquis la Fayette*, 1781
Owned by   Willis, Cowper, and Company of Norfolk
Captain   Joseph Meredith
Armament   18 carriage guns
Crew   120 men

Brigantine *Morningstar*, 1781
Owned by   John Banks and Company
Captain   George Batty

Captain   Henry Stratton
Armament 10 to 12 carriage guns
Crew   45 to 60 men

Ship *Nancy*, 1782
Owned by John King and Company
Captain   Hillary Moseley
Armament 12 carriage guns
Crew   45 men

Ship *Nancy*, 1782
Owned by David Ross and Company
Captain   William Hill Serjeant
Armament 14 carriage guns
Crew   30 men

Brig *Nestor*, 1782
Owned by Stephen Lacosté, Brumfield, and Company
Captain   Elisha Smith/Gabriel Lallement
Armament 8 carriage guns
Crew   30 men

Schooner *Non-Pareil*, 1781
Owned by Baker and Blow
Captain   John Addison
Captain   James Coffin
Armament 14 carriage guns
Crew   80 men

Boat *Otter*, 1778
Owned by John Campbell and John Harvie
Captain   (name unknown)
Armament (information unknown)
Crew   (information unknown)

Ship *Patty*, 1782
Owned by George Nicholson (Virginia) and Joseph Carson (Pennsylvania)
Captain   John Willett
Armament 12 carriage guns
Crew   35 men

Brig *Peggy*, 1782
Owned by Peter Lafargue, Michie, and Company
Captain   Michael James
Armament 8 carriage guns
Crew   18 men

Schooner *Peggy*, 1782
Owned by John Harmon and Company
Captain   William Moore
Armament 6 carriage guns
Crew   10 men

Brig *Perseverance*, 1782
Owned by William Pennock and Company
Captain   Robert Harris
Armament 10 carriage guns
Crew   30 men

Brig *Pilgrim*, 1782
Owned by John Harmanson
Captain   James Starr
Armament 8 carriage guns
Crew   18 men

Brig *Prosperity*, 1781
Owned by Hugh Young and Company
Captain   Alexander Murray
Armament 14 carriage guns
Crew   40 men

Schooner *Protector*, 1782
Owned by Baker, Blow, and Company
Captain   John Anderson
Armament 14 carriage guns
Crew   30 men

Boat *Revenge*, 1781
Owned by Sir John Peyton, James Proby, and James Earlwood
Captain   Nicholas Lawrence
Armament 2 swivel guns
Crew   45 men

Schooner *Revenge*, 1782
Owned by Joseph Granberry and James Hunter
Captain   John Mercier
Armament 6 carriage guns
Crew   25 men

Sloop *Richardson*, 1778
Owned by Thomas Russell, Thomas Noel, Edward Noel, Thomas Dawson, James L. Chamberlayne, William Perry, and William Hindman

Captain   Nathaniel Cooper
Armament 2 three-pounders, 4 swivels
Crew   10 men

Schooner *Richmond*, 1782
Owned by Nicholas Low, Job Peay, and Company
Captain   Job Peay
Armament 12 carriage guns
Crew   20 men

Brig *Rising States*, 1781
Owned by Baker and Blow
Captain   James Pasteur
Armament 14 carriage guns
Crew   70 men

Brig *Ross*, 1782
Owned by David Ross and Company
Captain   James Chambers
Armament 12 carriage guns
Crew   25 men

Sally Norton, 1781
Owned by (name unknown)
Captain   John Cox
Armament (information unknown)
Crew   (information unknown)

The *Sally Norton* was captured by the brig *Eagle*.

"*Sanders' Cruizer*," 1776
Owned by (?) Sanders
Captain   (name unknown)
Armament (information unknown)
Crew   (information unknown)

Ship *Saucy Jack*, 1782
Owned by Hunter, Banks, and Company
Captain   John Cooper
Armament 72 carriage guns
Crew   140 men

Sloop *Saint Patrick*, 1781
Owned by Richard Conway and Company
Captain   John Sanford
Armament 6 carriage guns
Crew   8 men

Cutter *Sincola*, 1781
Owned by (name unknown)
Captain W. Wooder
Armament 2 carriage guns
Crew 22 men

Whaleboat *The Swift*, 1781
Owned by Josiah Parker and Thomas Brown
Captain John Brown
Armament 1 carriage gun
Crew 30 men

Schooner *Taming*, ca.1781
Owned by (name unknown)
Captain S. Hooke
Armament 12 carriage guns
Crew 20 men

Brig *Tartar*, 1782
Owned by Baker, Blow, and Company
Captain William Gibbons
Armament 18 carriage guns
Crew 120 men

Galley *Tartar*, 1781
Owned by Baker, Blow, and Company
Captain Levin Trippe
Armament 5 carriage guns
Crew 30 men

Brig *Thoroughgood*, 1782
Owned by Hunter, Banks, and Company
Captain William Thomas
Armament 11 carriage guns
Crew 40 men

Schooner *Turn of the Times*, 1782
Owned by Joseph Williams and Company
Captain William Read
Armament 4 carriage guns
Crew 25 men

Brig *Two Brothers*, 1783
Owned by Burk, Wilson, and Company
Captain Thomas Osborne (?)
Armament 14 carriage guns
Crew 75 men

Schooner *Venus*, 1782
Owned by   Baker, Blow, and Company
Captain   John Cunningham
Armament   18 carriage guns
Crew   75 men

Brigantine *Virginia*, 1780
Owned by   Hooe and Harrison of Alexandria
Captain   Joseph Greenway
Armament   8 carriage guns and 24 swivels
Crew   24 men

Brigantine *Wilkes*, 1781
Owned by   Samuel B. Cunningham
Captain   William Cunningham
Armament   14 carriage guns
Crew   50 men

Brigantine *Willing Lass*, 1781
Owned by   Hunter, Banks, and Company
Captain   Thomas Williams
Armament   16 carriage guns
Crew   95 men

Ship *Wolf*, 1782
Owned by   Baker, Blow, and Company
Captain   Samuel Butler
Armament   16 carriage guns
Crew   60 men

Schooner *York*, 1782
Owned by   Willis, Cowper, and Company
Captain   Isaiah Keel
Armament   14 carriage guns
Crew   40 men

Miscellaneous[27]

The vessels *Rattlesnake*, *America*, and *Pocahontas* are occasionally mentioned in documents relating to the state navy; they were probably privateers. In addition to the usual type of sailing vessels in the state navy, a number of scows, barges, and flatboats also were employed in emergencies as fighting craft. Sometimes these had masts and sails, but often they were poled or rowed.

Barges and Flatboats

Buckskin, 1779-1781
Captain John Bowers

Protector, 1782
Captain John Cropper

Richmond, 1783
Captain John Herbert

Victory, 1780
Captain (name unknown)

York, 1783
Captain Thomas Herbert

The Emergency Fleet, March-April 1781

In the winter and spring of 1780-1781 a combined British raiding force under generals William Phillips and Benedict Arnold nearly succeeded in knocking Virginia out of the war. Large quantities of military stores, public tobacco, civilian property, and boats were burned or otherwise ruined. In a vain attempt to gain time, Governor Jefferson pressed a number of private vessels into emergency service and placed them under the command of Captain James Maxwell at Hood's, in Prince George County. By the time the creaky flotilla was ready, the British had already sailed up the James River and into the Appomattox. After occupying Petersburg the force under Arnold recrossed the Appomattox and marched to Coxendale, or Osbornes, where a small quantity of military supplies was stored. On April 27 Arnold's infantry and artillery encountered the emergency fleet and a body of militiamen on the left bank. After a request for the Americans to surrender was refused, Arnold's cannon and musketry annihilated the fleet. When the smoke cleared, twelve of the disabled vessels were still afloat and easily captured. All the rest had been sunk.[28]

Various flats, barges, and row boats served as tenders.

Commander James Maxwell

Ships

Renown
Captain William Lewis
Dutch-owned merchantman
Armament 16 six-pounders

Tempest
Captain John Markham

Willing Lass
Captain Thomas Williams
Armament 12 four-pounders

Brigs

Alert (flag vessel)
Captain Edward Woneycutt

American Fabius
Captain Robert Mitchell
Armament 18 guns

Jefferson
Captain Willis Wilson (?)

Mars
Captain (?) Thomas
Armament 8 four-pounders

Morning-Star
Captain (?) Beaty
Armament 12 guns

Wilkes
Captain William Cunningham
Armament 14 guns

Galleys

Lewis
Captain B. Edgar Joel
Captain Celey Saunders

Safeguard
Captain George Elliott

Schooners

Heron
Captain (?) Howell
Armament 3 swivel guns

Sloops

Eminence
Captain Wright (?) Westcott
Armament 1 howitzer

Miscellaneous

Apollo
Captain (name unknown)
Armament 18 six-pounders

The Virginia Marine Corps, February-December 1776

In February 1776 a force of amphibious troops was raised for service aboard the state's armed vessels. They were to assist the naval gunners, act as shore patrolmen, form landing parties, and provide sharpshooters during engagements. Two rifle guns were purchased for the marines of the galley *Hero* in September 1776. At least twelve, and possibly as many as sixteen, marine companies were raised before the corps was abolished in December 1776. The marines were subsequently incorporated into the State Artillery and State Garrison regiments.[29]

Companies, February-December 1776
Captain Alexander Dick (first to be raised)
Captain John Allison
Captain William Mitchell
Captain Valentine Peers
Captain Thomas Meriwether
Captain Gabriel Madison
Captain John Arell
Captain Thomas Hamilton
Captain John Lurty
Captain Gabriel Jones
Captain James Foster
Captain John Lee
Captain John Catesby Cocke
Captain Samuel Carr
Captain Benjamin Pollard
Captain Samuel Hanway
Lieutenant John Shields
Lieutenant Robert Windsor Brown

In 1780 a new force of temporary marines was raised for coastal defense. Captain John Catesby Cocke raised at least one company for this purpose.

Colonel John Cropper's "Accomack Gentlemen Volunteers," 1782

Officers
Colonel John Cropper
Major Smith Snead

On November 28, 1782, Colonel John Cropper, formerly of the 9th Virginia Continental Regiment, was persuaded to come out of retirement and join an expedition against British-paid pirates who were raiding the Eastern

Shore. On November 29, Zedekiah Walley's Maryland squadron of armed barges picked up Cropper and twenty-five "gentlemen volunteers" from Accomack and set out after a notorious marauder known as Captain Kidd. Cropper's detachment, aboard the barge *Protector*, encountered Kidd's fleet near Smith's Island in Chesapeake Bay, and a furious battle ensued. Walley was killed, Cropper wounded, and most of the Marylanders and Virginians were captured and later paroled.[30]

Companies, November 1782

Captain Thomas Parker
Captain William Snead
Captain George Christian

Virginia Troops at Charleston, South Carolina, 1779-1780

Appendix A

BY 1777 most of the Virginia regiments could scarcely muster enough men fit for duty to fill two companies. The problem of high attrition was overcome by several means, principally by consolidating two or more units into a detachment. Some of these reshufflings were made permanent by the White Plains arrangement of September 14, 1778, but the steady dwindling continued, and new detachments had to be created for the southern campaigns of 1779-1781.[1]

In July 1778 the 3d and 7th Virginia Continental regiments were temporarily consolidated under Colonel William Heth and Major Charles West of the 3d and Lieutenant Colonel Holt Richeson of the 7th. The White Plains arrangement merged the 5th Virginia Continental Regiment with the 3d and renumbered the combined unit the 3d Virginia Regiment. By the spring of 1779, however, the 3d Virginia Regiment had shrunk again and had to be combined with the 4th Virginia Regiment. At the same time, the depleted 5th and 11th Virginia regiments were also combined, as were the 1st, 6th, and 10th Virginia regiments. This last consolidation was placed under Colonel Nathaniel Gist and incorporated with his additional Continental regiment.[2]

In May 1779 Virginia's Continental units were rearranged again, this time by a board of field officers meeting at Middlebrook, New Jersey. Three Virginia detachments were created out of the remnants of the numbered Continental regiments and formed into a brigade under General Charles Scott. Even this consolidation proved insufficient to fill the state quota, and a separate detachment of troops from the Virginia State Line was created to serve under Lieutenant Colonel Charles Porterfield, of the State Garrison Regiment. Eventually, several hundred militiamen were formed into two brigades under generals Robert Lawson and Edward Stevens. All the Virginia detachments ultimately served in the Carolinas, and most of them were captured at the fall of Charleston in May 1780.[3]

The three official detachments that made up Scott's Virginia brigade were organized by the summer of 1779, with the officers chosen by ballot. As Lieutenant Colonel Gustavus Brown Wallace reported to Colonel John Cropper, the officers for these units were:[4]

1st Battalion
Colonel Richard Parker, 1st Virginia Regiment
Lieutenant Colonel Samuel Hopkins, 10th Virginia Regiment
Major Richard Clough Anderson, 1st Virginia Regiment

2d Battalion
Colonel William Heth, 3d Virginia Regiment
Lieutenant Colonel Gustavus Brown Wallace, 11th Virginia Regiment
Major James Lucas, 3d Virginia Regiment

3d Battalion
Colonel Abraham Buford, 11th Virginia Regiment
Lieutenant Colonel Robert Ballard, 4th Virginia Regiment
Major Thomas Ridley, 6th Virginia Regiment

Major Lucas resigned from the service on May 16, 1779, and Lieutenant Colonel Ballard did likewise on July 4, 1779. The first two battalions or detachments managed to recruit their men by December 1779 and were soon on their way south, but Buford's detachment (the 3d Battalion) encountered difficulties in raising men and was unable to march to the Carolinas until May.

The battalions commanded by Parker and Heth were sent to Charleston (or Charles Town, as it was called in contemporary accounts), which in 1779 became a principal objective of British strategy. With eight thousand men, Sir Henry Clinton moved against the South Carolina port. To oppose him General Benjamin Lincoln assembled a force of five thousand Virginia and Carolina Continentals, to which militia reinforcements were added.[5]

Lincoln was not convinced that the fortified city could hold out against Clinton's British-Hessian armies and Admiral Arbuthnot's supporting fleet, but he yielded to the civilian authorities and decided to defend Charleston. On April 8 Lincoln's evacuation route across the Cooper River was cut off, and the city was completely surrounded. The American positions at Haddrel's Point and Fort Moultrie surrendered on April 24 and May 7, respectively, and Lincoln saw that all was lost.[6]

By then life inside the besieged city had become desperate. Food supplies were reduced to almost nothing, and all dogs were ordered shot in order to conserve the available rations for the soldiers. Fuel was saved by burning barrels of turpentine instead of bonfires on guard posts at night. One

Virginia officer noted in his diary that the night of May 12 was the first time in fifty-five days that he had been able to remove his clothing to sleep.[7]

The Virginia garrison at Charleston was organized as follows:[8]

1st Virginia Brigade (Woodford's)

1st Virginia Continental Regiment
Colonel William Russell
Lieutenant Colonel Burgess Ball (?)
Major (name unknown)
Captain Callohill Minnis, 1st Virginia Regiment
Captain Tarleton Payne, 1st Virginia Regiment
Captain Custis Kendall, 1st Virginia Regiment
Captain Thomas Holt, 1st Virginia Regiment
Captain Holman Minnis, 1st Virginia Regiment
Captain Thomas Buckner, 5th Virginia Regiment
Captain Mayo Carrington, 5th Virginia Regiment
Captain William Moseley, 5th Virginia Regiment
Captain William Bentley, 5th Virginia Regiment
Captain William Johnston, 7th Virginia Regiment
Captain James Wright, 7th Virginia Regiment
Captain Thomas Hunt, 10th Virginia Regiment
Captain Lawrence Butler, 11th Virginia Regiment
Captain Philip Mallory, 11th Virginia Regiment

2d Virginia Continental Regiment
Colonel John Neville
Lieutenant Colonel Nicholas Cabell(?)
Major David Stephenson(?)
Captain Benjamin Taliaferro, 2d Virginia Regiment
Captain Alexander Parker, 2d Virginia Regiment
Captain John Blackwell, 3d Virginia Regiment
Captain LeRoy Edwards, 3d Virginia Regiment
Captain Robert Beale, 3d Virginia Regiment
Captain James Curry, 4th Virginia Regiment
Captain John Stith, 4th Virginia Regiment

3d Virginia Continental Regiment (Gist's)
Colonel Nathaniel Gist
Captain Joseph Blackwell, 6th Virginia Regiment
Captain John Gillison, 6th Virginia Regiment
Captain Clough Shelton, 6th Virginia Regiment
Captain Abraham Hite, 8th Virginia Regiment
Captain Alexander Breckinridge, Gist's Regiment
Captain Francis Muir, Gist's Regiment

2d Virginia Brigade (Scott's)[9]

1st Virginia Detachment
Colonel Richard Parker
Lieutenant Colonel Samuel Hopkins
Major Richard Clough Anderson

There is some evidence that the last nine captains listed under the 1st Virginia Regiment were parcelled among the two detachments in Scott's brigade after the Charleston garrison was set up.

2d Virginia Detachment
Colonel William Heth
Lieutenant Colonel Gustavus Brown Wallace

The third detachment, commanded by Colonel Abraham Buford, which had been slower in recruiting men than the other two, was on its way into Carolina. Soon after three-hundred-man unit arrived in South Carolina, Buford learned of the surrender of Charleston and decided to turn back. But on May 29, 1780, Banastre Tarleton's British Legion caught up with the Virginians near The Waxhaws. Tarleton issued an ultimatum, calling on Buford to surrender or be cut to pieces. His wagons and supplies were far ahead, as were his artillery crews, but Buford was determined to fight. The engagement was short and deadly. Tarleton's cavalry rode over Buford's position and sabered his men. Those who were still on their feet were cut down by bayonets of the legion infantry. The pitiful few who survived averaged seventeen wounds apiece. Over half the detachment were killed outright, and many of the wounded died that night. Miraculously, Buford himself was unhurt. Under the mistaken impression that he had defeated the veteran 11th Virginia Continental Regiment, Tarleton sent a glowing report to Cornwallis: "I have cut 170 officers and men to pieces. 2 six pounders 2 pair culverin 2 royals and all their baggage have fallen into my hands." The exact composition of Buford's detachment has long been a minor mystery, since most later chroniclers tended to repeat Tarleton's error and assume that the 11th Virginia Regiment was involved. For this reason, the organization in full is given below:[10]

3d Virginia Detachment
Colonel Abraham Buford
Major Thomas Ridley
Surgeon Mace Clements
Captain Adam Wallace
Captain John Stokes
Captain Andrew Wallace
Captain Claiborne W. Lawson
Captain Robert Woodson

Captain Thomas Catlett
Captain John Champe Carter (artillery)
Adjutant Lieutenant Henry Bowyer (dragoons)
Lieutenant Thomas Hord
Lieutenant William Epes
Lieutenant George Holland
Lieutenant Tarpley White
Lieutenant (James?) Morton
Lieutenant Isaiah Marks
Lieutenant (William?) Porter
Lieutenant (Thomas?) Pearson
Lieutenant Francis Minnis
Lieutenant Robert Dewit
Lieutenant (John?) Bowen
Lieutenant (Thomas?) Miller
Lieutenant (Robert?) Jouett
Lieutenant (?) Jones
Ensign Willis Wilson
Ensign Charles Erskine
Ensign John Crute

In addition to the Virginia infantry regiments and detachments, portions of Colonel Charles Harrison's 1st Regiment of Continental Artillery were present at Charleston. Captain-Lieutenant William Meredith, lieutenants Samuel Coleman, William B. Wallace, William Stevenson, and William McGuire were all captured.

Lieutenant Colonel William Washington commanded the combined 1st and 3d regiments of Continental Light Dragoons (Bland's and Baylor's) at Charleston. Most of his troopers escaped, but Captain Robert Yancey and 331 men were captured in the city.

The legion, or partizan corps, under Charles Armand Tuffin, marquis de la Rouerie, was also at Charleston. Three captains and a lieutenant were captured. The other legion, under Henry Lee, assisted in moving military stores from the city before it fell. Major Henry Peyton, of Lee's Legion, was mortally wounded.

Surgeon John Brownlee, of the 1st Virginia Continental Regiment, was captured. Either he was the only Virginia surgeon in the garrison, or else the others escaped.[11]

Virginia Troops at Yorktown, 1781

Appendix B

FOLLOWING the Charleston surrender in May 1780, Virginia's Continental forces in the field were reduced to the 9th Virginia Continental Regiment stationed at Fort Pitt, a temporary Virginia Battalion of short-term recruits, and the remnants of the artillery and cavalry still operating in the Carolinas. By the late summer of 1781 Captain Alexander Parker and about one hundred Continental regulars who had escaped from the British returned home. These and the other remnants of the Continental and state lines were amalgamated into Washington's main army when the scene of operations shifted to Virginia.[12]

After commencing siege operations against Cornwallis at Yorktown, the combined American-French army was arranged into a formal line of battle according to the best European traditions. American troops formed the advance guard, the right wing (post of honor) of the front line, the right and left flanks of the intermediate line, the entire second (or reserve) line, and the rear guard. The French army under Rochambeau formed the left wing of the front line and engineered the fortifications. At Gloucester Point the duc de Lauzun's marine regiment and a combined Virginia force of state line regulars and militia took up positions to prevent Cornwallis from escaping across the York River.

The Virginians who took part in the siege of Yorktown were scattered throughout Washington's divisions and brigades. From the often contradictory evidence of eyewitness memoirs, pay vouchers, and audited accounts it appears that the following Virginia units—composed of approximately 3,925 men—were engaged in the battle and siege:[13]

Advance Guard
Moylan's 4th Regiment of Continental Light Dragoons (about 60 troopers)

Armand's Legion, or 2d Partizan Corps (about 40 troopers and infantry)

183

Front Line—Right Flank

Major General Benjamin Lincoln's division
Brigadier General Anthony Wayne's brigade
    Colonel Thomas Gaskin's detachment of the Virginia Battalion
    Major John Poulson's detachment of the Virginia Battalion
    Captain Alexander Parker's company of Charleston refugees
(In Lafayette's brigade, one company of Virginians was in Hazen's Regiment)

Intermediate Line—Right

Lieutenant Colonel Edward Carrington and Captain Whitehead Coleman's company of the 1st Regiment of Continental Artillery (about 25 gunners and matrosses)

Intermediate Line—Left

Colonel George Gibson's 1st Virginia State Regiment (about 150 men)

2d or Reserve Line—Right Flank

Nelson's Division
    Brigadier General Robert Lawson's militia brigade (750 men)

At Gloucester Point

Duc de Lauzun's French and American division
    Brigadier General George Weedon's militia detachment (about 1500 men)
    Lieutenant Colonel Charles Dabney's 2d Virginia State Regiment, with militia reinforcements (about 200 men)

Loyalist Organizations, 1775-1776

Appendix C

BANDS of tories, some of them sincere royalists and others merely opportunists, harrassed Virginians throughout the war. Usually they were mobs or small gangs of raiders operating independently of the royal government. However, Governor Dunmore authorized three units: the Queen's Own Loyal Virginia Regiment, the Loyal Foresters, and the Royal Ethiopian Regiment. Despite their lofty designations these units were small, poorly organized, and short-lived. The remnants that accompanied Dunmore to New York after his defeat at Gwynn's Island on July 9, 1776, were incorporated into the Queen's Rangers. Under the command of Lieutenant Colonel John Graves Simcoe, this unit headed Benedict Arnold's invasion of Virginia in 1781.

The Queen's Own Loyal Virginia Regiment, 1775-1776

Colonel Jacob Ellegood

The nucleus of Dunmore's force in the tidewater area, this unit was composed of Norfolk merchants, runaway indentured servants, unemployed sailors and vagabonds, and a few professional soldiers and captured militiamen. Ellegood was captured soon after receiving his commission and ceased to play an active part in the loyalist opposition.[14]

Companies, 1775-1776
Captain John Saunders
Captain Stair Agnew
Captain George Blair
Ensign (Dr.) Thomas Hall

The Royal Ethiopian Regiment, 1775-1776

Captain John Collett
Captain John McKay
Sergeant Anthony Parmore

The deed that solidified Virginia's opposition to Governor Dunmore was his proclamation of November 7, 1775, which offered freedom to any slave who joined his forces. John Collett, the former commandant at Fort Johnston, North Carolina, was offered a noncommissioned post in the Queen's Own Loyal Virginia Regiment but declined in favor of a commission in the Royal Ethiopians. Some of his black soldiers fought at Great Bridge on December 10, 1775, but most of his company was at that time transporting provisions across Chesapeake Bay for Dunmore's fleet. While encamped at Gwynn's Island the Royal Ethiopians were ravaged by smallpox and fevers. After Dunmore was finally driven from the Chesapeake the black volunteers were disbanded; some of them remained with the British forces in New York, and others dispersed.[15]

The Loyal Foresters, 1775-1776

Colonel John Connolly
Lieutenant Colonel Alexander McKee
Surgeon John F. D. Smyth
Lieutenant Allen Cameron

In 1775 Dr. John Connolly, who had been a major in the Virginia militia in 1774 during Dunmore's War, became the governor's agent in the area of Fort Pitt, which in 1774 had been rechristened Fort Dunmore. Situated in the disputed Virginia-Pennsylvania frontier region, Fort Dunmore was garrisoned by Captain George Aston's company. After the British had abandoned the fort and as relations between the governor and citizenry worsened in August 1775, the Virginia convention sent Captain John Neville to hold the fort.[16]

Acting under Dunmore's instructions Connolly had traveled extensively in the frontier regions and invited Indian tribal leaders to a congress at the fort. The invitation was consistent with Dunmore's earlier Indian policies, but the congress also was planned to insure that if the governor failed to maintain his power in the east, the Indians' continuing friendship would discourage them from an alliance with the rebels.

In autumn 1775 Connolly traveled to Boston, where he procured a royal commission from General Gage and laid Dunmore's plan before the British command. On November 5 Connolly was appointed a lieutenant colonel with full power to raise a loyalist battalion. His plans came to a halt on November 19, when, en route to Fort Pitt with Cameron and Smyth, he was arrested near Hagerstown, Maryland. On the basis of documents in his possession, Connolly was imprisoned as an enemy to America. He spent the next five years in confinement, his personal estate confiscated and his health broken. Exchanged in 1780, Connolly recuperated and was reinstated in his old commission by Sir Henry Clinton, who sent him to join Cornwallis. In September 1781 he was recaptured near Newport News and placed under Lafayette's authority until the surrender of Cornwallis's army. His Loyal Foresters, recruited from New York, Virginia, and North Carolina tories, were among those who laid down their arms at Yorktown.[17]

A Calendar of Unit Names and Variants

Appendix D

BOTH historians of and participants in the American Revolution have referred to military units by descriptive names (such as Grayson's Regiment, or the Virginia Riflemen), and during the war as units were consolidated or reorganized their numbered designations sometimes changed. The researcher who seeks a path through this tangle of nomenclature will find assistance in this calendar of unit names and variants, entries in which are arranged first in numerical and then in alphabetical order. For example, the researcher looking for either the "16th Virginia Regiment" or "Grayson's Regiment" will find references to the main entry "Colonel William Grayson's Additional Continental Regiment of Infantry, 1777-1779," which is printed in boldface type at its appropriate place in the calendar, followed by page references to the text of the guide.

1st and 2d Virginia State Legions, 1781-1783, 134
1st Battalion, Virginia Forces on Provincial Establishment.
    See 1st Virginia Regiment of Foot, 1775-1783
1st Legionary Corps.
    See 1st Regiment of Continental Light Dragoons, 1776-1783
1st Partizan Corps.
    See Armand's Legion, 1777-1783
1st Regiment, Virginia State Line, 1776-1782, 110-111
1st Regiment of Continental Artillery, 1776-1783, 97-100
1st Regiment of Continental Light Dragoons, 1776-1783, 101-104
1st Virginia Battalion.
    See 1st Virginia Regiment of Foot, 1775-1783; Colonel Thomas Posey's Virginia Battalion, 1782-1783

189

1st Virginia Battalion of Foot in the Service of the United States.
: *See* 1st Virginia Regiment of Foot, 1775-1783
1st Virginia Brigade (Woodford's), 179
1st Virginia Continental Regiment, 1779, 32-34
1st Virginia Regiment of Foot, 1775-1783, 29-32
1st Virginia Regiment on Continental Establishment.
: *See* 1st Virginia Regiment of Foot, 1775-1783
2d Battalion, Virginia Forces on Provincial Establishment.
: *See* 2d Virginia Regiment of Foot, 1775-1783
2d Canadian Regiment, 1776-1783, 82
2d Georgia Battalion of Foot, 1776-1780, 83-84
2d Partizan Corps.
: *See* Lee's Legion, 1778-1781
2d Regiment, Virginia State Line, 1776-1782, 112-113
2d Virginia Battalion.
: *See* 2d Virginia Regiment of Foot, 1775-1783
2d Virginia Battalion of Foot in the Service of the United States.
: *See* 2d Virginia Regiment of Foot, 1775-1783
2d Virginia Brigade (Scott's), 180-181
2d Virginia Continental Regiment, 179
2d Virginia Detachment.
: *See* 2d Virginia Regiment of Foot, 1775-1783
2d Virginia Regiment of Foot, 1775-1783, 34-38
2d Virginia Regiment on Continental Establishment.
: *See* 2d Virginia Regiment of Foot, 1775-1783
3d Georgia Battalion of Foot, 1776-1780, 85
3d Legionary Corps.
: *See* 3d Regiment of Continental Light Dragoons, 1777-1783
3d Regiment, Virginia State Line, 1776-1778, 113
3d Regiment of Continental Light Dragoons, 1777-1783, 104-106
3d Virginia Battalion of Foot in the Service of the United Colonies.
: *See* 3d Virginia Regiment of Foot, 1776-1782
3d Virginia Continental Regiment (Gist's), 179
3d Virginia Regiment of Foot, 1776-1782, 38-41
3d Virginia Regiment on Continental Establishment.
: *See* 3d Virginia Regiment of Foot, 1776-1782
4th Georgia Battalion of Foot, 1776-1780, 85
4th Regiment of Continental Light Dragoons, 1777-1782, 106-107
4th Virginia Battalion of Foot in the Service of the United States.
: *See* 4th Virginia Regiment of Foot, 1776-1783
4th Virginia Regiment of Foot, 1776-1783, 41-44
4th Virginia Regiment on Continental Establishment.
: *See* 4th Virginia Regiment of Foot, 1776-1783
5th Battalion of the New Raised Virginia Continental Regulars.
: *See* 14th Virginia Regiment of Foot, 1776-1778

5th Virginia Battalion of Foot in the Service of the United States.
   See 5th Virginia Regiment of Foot, 1778-1782
5th Virginia Regiment of Foot, 1778-1782, 45-48
5th Virginia Regiment on Continental Establishment.
   See 5th Virginia Regiment of Foot, 1778-1782
6th Virginia Battalion of Foot in the Service of the United States.
   See 6th Virginia Regiment of Foot, 1776-1778, 1778-1782
6th Virginia Regiment of Foot, 1776-1778, 1778-1782, 48-51
6th Virginia Regiment on Continental Establishment.
   See 6th Virginia Regiment of Foot, 1776-1778, 1778-1782
7th Virginia Battalion of Foot in the Service of the United States.
   See 7th Virginia Regiment of Foot, 1776-1778, 1778-1782
7th Virginia Regiment of Foot, 1776-1778, 1778-1782, 51-54
7th Virginia Regiment on Continental Establishment.
   See 7th Virginia Regiment of Foot, 1776-1778, 1778-1782
8th Battalion of Foot on Continental Establishment.
   See 8th Virginia Regiment of Foot, 1776-1778, 1778-1782
8th Virginia Regiment of Foot, 1776-1778, 1778-1782, 54-58
8th Virginia Regiment of Foot in the Service of the United Colonies.
   See 8th Virginia Regiment of Foot, 1776-1778, 1778-1782
9th Virginia Battalion of Foot in the Service of the United States.
   See 9th Virginia Regiment of Foot, 1776-1778, 1779-1781
9th Virginia Regiment of Foot, 1776-1778, 1779-1781, 58-61
9th Virginia Regiment on Continental Establishment.
   See 9th Virginia Regiment of Foot, 1776-1778, 1779-1781
10th Continental Virginia Regiment.
   See 10th Virginia Regiment of Foot, 1776-1778, 1778-1781
10th Virginia Battalion of Foot in the Service of the United States.
   See 10th Virginia Regiment of Foot, 1776-1778, 1778-1781
10th Virginia Regiment of Foot, 1776-1778, 1778-1781, 61-64
10th Virginia Regiment on Continental Establishment.
   See 10th Virginia Regiment of Foot, 1776-1778, 1778-1781
11th Virginia Battalion of Foot in the Service of the United States.
   See 11th Virginia Regiment of Foot, 1776-1778, 1778-1781
11th Virginia Regiment of Foot, 1776-1778, 1778-1781, 64-66
11th Virginia Regiment on Continental Establishment.
   See 11th Virginia Regiment of Foot, 1776-1778, 1778-1781
12th Virginia Battalion of Foot in the Service of the United States.
   See 12th Virginia Regiment of Foot, 1776-1778
12th Virginia Regiment of Foot, 1776-1778, 67-68
12th Virginia Regiment on Continental Establishment.
   See 12th Virginia Regiment of Foot, 1776-1778
13th Virginia Battalion in the Service of the United States.
   See 13th Virginia Regiment of Foot, 1776-1778
13th Virginia Regiment of Foot, 1776-1778, 68-70

13th Virginia Regiment on Continental Establishment.
  See 13th Virginia Regiment of Foot, 1776-1778
14th Virginia Battalion of Foot in the Service of the United States.
  See 14th Virginia Regiment of Foot, 1776-1778
14th Virginia Regiment of Foot, 1776-1778, 70-71
14th Virginia Regiment on Continental Establishment.
  See 14th Virginia Regiment of Foot, 1776-1778
15th Virginia Battalion in the Service of the United States.
  See 15th Virginia Regiment of Foot, 1776-1778
15th Virginia Regiment of Foot, 1776-1778, 71-72
15th Virginia Regiment on Continental Establishment.
  See 15th Virginia Regiment of Foot, 1776-1778
16th Virginia Regiment.
  See Colonel William Grayson's Additional Continental Regiment of Infantry, 1777-1779
Albemarle County Battalion.
  See Convention Army Guard Regiment, 1779-1781
Armand's Legion, 1777-1783, 93-95
Armand's Partizan Corps.
  See Armand's Legion, 1777-1783
Baylor's Dragoons.
  See 3d Regiment of Continental Light Dragoons, 1777-1783
Baylor's Regiment.
  See 3d Regiment of Continental Light Dragoons, 1777-1783
Bland's Horse.
  See 1st Regiment of Continental Light Dragoons, 1776-1783
Captain Decrome de la Porte's French Company, 1777-1778, 115-116
Colonel Charles Dabney's Virginia State Legion, 1782-1783, 135-136
Colonel Charles Mynn Thruston's Additional Continental Regiment, 1777-1779, 75-77
Colonel Christian Febiger's Light Infantry, 1779, 90-91
Colonel Daniel Morgan's Battalion of Riflemen, 1777-1778, 88-89
Colonel Francis Taylor's Guard Regiment.
  See Convention Army Guard Regiment, 1779-1781
Colonel Hugh Stephenson's Virginia and Maryland Rifle Battalion, 1775-1776, 86-88
Colonel John Cropper's "Accomack Gentlemen Volunteers," 1782, 175-176
Colonel Moses Rawlings's Additional Continental Regiment, 1779-1780, 77-78
Colonel Nathaniel Gist's Additional Continental Regiment of Infantry, 1777-1781, 74-75
Colonel Thomas Gaskins's Virginia Regiment, 1781, 91
Colonel Thomas Posey's Virginia Battalion, 1782-1783, 92-93

Colonel William Grayson's Additional Continental Regiment of Infantry, 1777-1779, 73-74
Commander in Chief's Guard.
>*See* Washington's Life Guard, 1776-1783

Continental Corps of Invalids, 1777-1783, 86
Convention Army Guard Regiment, 1779-1781, 117-122
Convention Guard Regiment.
>*See* Convention Army Guard Regiment, 1779-1781

Eastern Shore Regiment.
>*See* 9th Virginia Regiment of Foot, 1776-1778, 1779-1781

Edmunds's Corps.
>*See* Virginia State Artillery Regiment, 1777-1782

Febiger's Battalion.
>*See* Colonel Thomas Posey's Virginia Battalion, 1782-1783

Free and Independent Chasseurs.
>*See* Armand's Legion, 1777-1783

General Charles Lee's Life Guard, 1776, 80-81
George Rogers Clark's Illinois Regiment, Virginia State Forces, 1778-1783, 127-133
German Regiment.
>*See* 8th Virginia Regiment of Foot, 1776-1778, 1778-1782

Gist's Rangers.
>*See* Colonel Nathaniel Gist's Additional Continental Regiment of Infantry, 1777-1781

Gist's Regiment.
>*See* Colonel Nathaniel Gist's Additional Continental Regiment of Infantry, 1777-1781

Grayson's Regiment.
>*See* Colonel William Grayson's Additional Continental Regiment of Infantry, 1777-1779

Harrison's Regiment.
>*See* 1st Regiment of Continental Artillery, 1776-1783

Harrison's Train of Artillery.
>*See* 1st Regiment of Continental Artillery, 1776-1783

Independent Virginia Frontier Companies, 1775-1778, 81-82
Independent Volunteer Companies, 1774-1776, 7-11
Lady Washington Dragoons.
>*See* 3d Regiment of Continental Light Dragoons, 1777-1783

Lee's Legion, 1778-1781, 95-96
Lee's Partizan Corps.
>*See* Lee's Legion, 1778-1781

Lieutenant Colonel Charles Porterfield's State Detachment, 1780, 123-124
Lieutenant Colonel James Monroe's Regiment, Virginia State Line, July-December 1779, 116-117
Lieutenant Colonel Joseph Crockett's Western Battalion, Virginia State Forces, 1779-1782, 133-134

194 *Virginia Military Organizations*

Light Horse Harry Lee's Legion.
See Lee's Legion, 1778-1781
Loyal Foresters, 1775-1776, 186-187
Major John Nelson's Regiment of Virginia State Cavalry, 1779-1782, 126-127
Marshall's Artillery.
See Virginia State Artillery Regiment, 1777-1782
Militia Regiments on the Frontier, 1774-1775, 138-142
Minute Service, 1775-1776, 11-25
Morgan's Rifle Corps.
See Colonel Daniel Morgan's Battalion of Riflemen, 1777-1778
Morgan's Riflemen.
See Colonel Daniel Morgan's Battalion of Riflemen, 1777-1778
Moylan's Dragoons, Moylan's Regiment.
See 4th Regiment of Continental Light Dragoons, 1777-1782
Posey's Virginia Battalion.
See 1st Virginia Regiment of Foot, 1775-1783
Queen's Own Loyal Virginia Regiment, 1775-1776, 185
Royal Ethiopian Regiment, 1775-1776, 186
St. François de Loyeauté's Corps of State Artillery Cadets, 1777-1778, 125-126
Spotswood's Legions.
See 1st and 2d Virginia State Legions, 1781-1783
State Guard Regiment.
See Convention Army Guard Regiment, 1779-1781
Taylor's State Regiment.
See Convention Army Guard Regiment, 1779-1781
Thruston's Regiment.
See Colonel Charles Mynn Thruston's Additional Continental Regiment, 1777-1779
Virginia Marine Corps, 1776, 175
Virginia Riflemen.
See Colonel Daniel Morgan's Battalion of Riflemen, 1777-1778
Virginia State Artillery Regiment, 1777-1782, 124-125
Virginia State Engineer Department, 1775-1781, 113-115
Virginia State Garrison Regiment, 1777-1782, 122-123
Volunteer Battalions for the Grand Army, June-August 1778, 89-90
Washington's Bodyguard.
See Washington's Life Guard, 1776-1783
Washington's Dragoons.
See 3d Regiment of Continental Light Dragoons, 1777-1783
Washington's Life Guard, 1776-1783, 80
West Augusta Regiment.
See 13th Virginia Regiment of Foot, 1776-1778

Short Titles

Appendix **E**

THE following list includes titles of works cited frequently. Full citations have not been made elsewhere.

I. Manuscript Sources

Bounty Warrant.   Bounty Warrants, Governor's Office, Executive Department, Archives Division, VSL. (Filed alphabetically by applicant.)

Captain Robert Gamble's Memorandum Book.   Memorandum Book of Captain Robert Gamble, War Office, Governor's Office, Executive Department, Archives Division, VSL.

Cont. Congress Papers.   Papers of the Continental Congress, 1774-1789, National Archives Microfilm Publications no. 247 (Washington, D.C.), 204 rolls.

Convention Papers, 1775 and 1776.   Papers of the Conventions of 1775 and 1776, Archives Division, VSL.

List of Officers Entitled to Half-Pay.   List of Officers of the State Line that are Entitled to Half-Pay, Miscellaneous Revolutionary War Records, Governor's Office, Executive Department, Archives Division, VSL.

Misc. Legislative Petitions.   Miscellaneous Legislative Petitions, 1776-1800, General Assembly, Archives Division, VSL.

II. Printed Sources

Berg, *Army Units*.   Fred Anderson Berg, *Encyclopedia of Continental Army Units* (Harrisburg, Pa., 1972).

Clark, *Papers*.   George Rogers Clark, *George Rogers Clark Papers*, ed.

James Alton James, *Collections of the Illinois State Historical Library* (Springfield, Ill., 1912, 1926), vol. 8, *1771-1781*, vol. 19, *1781-1784*.

Cont. Congress Journals.   Worthington Chauncey Ford et al., eds., *Journals of the Continental Congress, 1774-1789*, 34 vols. (Washington, D.C., 1904-1937).

Council Journals.   H. R. McIlwaine et al., eds., *Journals of the Council of State of Virginia* (Richmond, 1931-).

Governors' Letters.   H. R. McIlwaine, ed., *Official Letters of the Governors of the State of Virginia* [July 1, 1776-February 27, 1783], 3 vols. (Richmond, 1926-1929).

Hening, ed., *Statutes*.   William Waller Hening, ed., *The Statutes at Large; Being a Collection of all the Laws of Virginia, from the First Session of the Legislature in the Year 1619* . . ., 13 vols. (Richmond, Philadelphia, and New York, 1809-1823).

Jefferson, *Papers*.   Thomas Jefferson, *The Papers of Thomas Jefferson*, ed. Julian P. Boyd et al. (Princeton, N.J., 1950-).

McAllister, *Virginia Militia*.   Joseph Thompson McAllister, *Virginia Militia in the Revolutionary War* (Hot Springs, Va., 1913).

Mag. Am. Hist.   *Magazine of American History with Notes and Queries*, 30 vols. (1877-1893).

Muhlenburg, *Life of Muhlenburg*.   Henry A. Muhlenburg, *The Life of Major General Peter Muhlenburg of the Revolutionary Army* (Philadelphia, 1849).

Saffell, *Records*.   William Thomas Roberts Saffell, *Records of the Revolutionary War* (New York, 1858).

State Papers.   William P. Palmer et al., eds., *Calendar of Virginia State Papers and Other Manuscripts*, 11 vols. (Richmond, 1875-1893).

Tyler's Quarterly.   *Tyler's Quarterly Historical and Geneological Magazine*, 33 vols. (1919-1952).

Va. Gaz.   *Virginia Gazette* (identified in specific citations by publisher and place of publication).

VMHB.   *Virginia Magazine of History and Biography*

Washington, *Writings*.   George Washington, *The Writings of George Washington from the Original Manuscript Sources, 1745-1799*, ed. John C. Fitzpatrick, 39 vols. (Washington, D.C., 1931-1944).

WMQ.   *William and Mary Quarterly*

Notes

CHAPTER TWO

The Provincial Forces

1. Ivor Noël-Hume, *1775: Another Part of the Field* (New York, 1966), 219.
2. Bounty Warrant: Henry Nicholson.
3. Stanislaus Murray Hamilton, ed., *Letters to Washington, and Accompanying Papers*, 5 vols. (Boston, 1898-1900), 5:162; James Spottswood Keene, "Hugh Mercer," *John P. Branch Historical Papers of Randolph-Macon College* 2(1905-1908):204-205; Account Book of George Weedon, 1765, 1773-1785, 1791 (microfilm, Archives Division, VSL), 151.
4. Hamilton, ed., *Letters to Washington*, 5:68, 163; Washington, *Writings*, 3:265-266.
5. Purdie's *Va. Gaz.* (Williamsburg), Aug. 11, 1775.
6. "Papers, Military and Political, 1775-1778, of George Gilmer, M.D., of 'Pen Park,' Albemarle County, Va.," *Collections of the Virginia Historical Society*, n.s. 6(1886): 71-140.
7. Pinckney's *Va. Gaz.* (Williamsburg), Oct. 27, 1774.
8. Robert Douthat Meade, *Patrick Henry*, 2 vols. (Philadelphia, 1957-1969), 2:50; Douglas Southall Freeman, *George Washington*, vol. 3, *Planter and Patriot* (New York, 1951), 422; Noël-Hume, *Another Part of the Field*, 153; William Wirt, *Sketches of the Life and Character of Patrick Henry* (Philadelphia, 1817), 140.
9. The companies and officers listed in the following sketches were gleaned largely from the account books kept by the Virginia Committee of Safety in 1775 and 1776. These books record payments in cash, tobacco, and subsistence to the first volunteers of the Revolution. A printed version of the account books manuscript appears in volume 8 of the *Calendar of Virginia State Papers* and is indexed in Earl G. Swem's *Virginia Historical Index* (2 vols. [Roanoke, 1934-1936]). The second major source of information on Virginia's minutemen is the manuscript collection of journals, daybooks, and loose papers of the public stores at Williamsburg, Richmond, and Philadelphia, preserved in the Archives Division of the Virginia State Library. Throughout the remainder of this chapter citations are made only to sources other than those described here or in the preface. For the legislation establishing the Virginia minute service, see Hening, ed., *Statutes*, 9:16.
10. "Virginia Legislative Papers: Accomack Committee to the Convention, November 30, 1775," *VMHB* 14 (1906-1907): 257-259.
11. E. M. Sanchez-Saavedra, " 'All Fine Fellows and Well-Armed': The Culpeper Minute Battalion, 1775-1776," *Virginia Cavalcade* 24 (1974-1975):4-11.
12. Receipt Book, Sept. 1775-Apr. 1776, 139, Treasurer's Office, Executive Department, Archives Division, VSL.

CHAPTER THREE
The Virginia Continental Infantry

1. Information about one or more of Virginia's 15 Continental regiments may be found in the following sources: Charles A. Flagg and W. O. Waters, "Virginia's Soldiers in the Revolution," *VMHB*, 20:66-67, 181-194, 270-287; Peter Force, comp., *American Archives*, 5th ser., 2 vols. (Washington, D.C., 1848-1851), 2:319-320; *Cont. Congress Journals*, 3:463; 4:131-132; R. A. Brock, ed., "Orderly Book of Captain Robert Gamble, 1779," *Collections of the Virginia Historical Society*, n.s. 11(1892):264-272; *State Papers*, 1:302, 319, 326, 410-411; 2:582-584; 8:105; D. Eggleston, "Officers of Virginia Line at Winchester, 1783," *WMQ*, 2d ser. 7(1927):61; *Council Journals*, 1:399; Hening, ed., *Statutes*, 9:9-11, 75-92, 179-184; Virginia Muster Rolls, 1776-1783, nos. 1-58, 60-80, 102-132, 189, 190, 193, 194, 197, 262, 290; Captain Robert Gamble's Memorandum Book; Arrangement of the Continental Line, 1781, acc. no. 42 (copy acc. no. 13657); Miscellaneous Revolutionary War Records, Governor's Office, Executive Department, Archives Division, VSL; List of American Officers taken in the Southern Department by the British Army previous to Nov. 26, 1782, enclosed with Robert Morris to the president of Congress, Feb. 17, 1783, Cont. Congress Papers, roll 149, item 137. Further citations to these sources have not been made in this chapter.
2. David J. Mays, *Edmund Pendleton, 1721-1803: A Biography*, 2 vols. (Cambridge, Mass., 1952), 2:62; William Woodford to the Convention, Dec. 10, 1775, Convention Papers, 1775 and 1776.
3. *The Orderly Book of That Portion of the American Army Stationed at or Near Williamsburg, Va. . . .* (Richmond, 1860), passim; George Weedon, *Valley Forge Orderly Book of George Weedon* (New York, 1902), 62, 95; and in the serial printings: "Orderly Book of Gen. John Peter Gabriel Muhlenberg, March 26-December 20, 1777," *Pennsylvania Magazine of History and Biography* 33-35(1909-1911), and "Revolutionary Army Orders for the Main Army under Washington, 1778," *VMHB* 13-17(1906-1910).
4. Purdie and Dixon's *Va. Gaz.* (Williamsburg), Dec. 15, 1775; Force, comp., *American Archives*, 5th ser., 2:319.
5. "Woodford, Howe, and Lee Letters," *Richmond College Historical Papers* 1(1915):96-163; Noël-Hume, *Another Part of the Field*, 443-445.
6. Dixon and Hunter's *Va. Gaz.* (Williamsburg), Feb. 21, 1777.
7. Bounty Warrant: Alexander Parker; Harry E. Wildes, *Anthony Wayne: Trouble Shooter of the American Revolution* (New York, 1941), 268-289. See App. A.
8. Andrew Lewis to John Hancock, Aug. 22, 1776, Cont. Congress Papers, roll 178, item 159, no. 3.
9. Bounty Warrants: John Ashby, John Chilton, Richard Francis Lee, Hugh Mercer, John Peyton, Robert Slaughter, John Thornton, William Washington, and George Weedon.
10. Adam Stephen to Congress, Oct. 17, 1776, Cont. Congress Papers, roll 179, item 161, no. 3.
11. Purdie's *Va. Gaz.* (Williamsburg), Sept. 27, 1776.
12. Leonard Cooper's leg was amputated after his 1779 duel with Abraham Kirkpatrick, and Cooper subsequently served in the Continental Corps of Invalids.
13. Andrew Lewis to John Hancock, Sept. 20, 1776, Cont. Congress Papers, roll 178, item 159, no. 3.
14. Ibid.
15. Washington, *Writings*, 7:66, 76, 105, 122, 146, 152; Richard Graham to Levin Powell, Feb. 20, 1777, Powell Family Correspondence, Earl Gregg Swem Library, College of

William and Mary, Williamsburg, Va.; Lyon G. Tyler, "The Old Virginia Line in the Middle States during the American Revolution," *Tyler's Quarterly* 12(1930-1931):90-141.
16. Andrew Lewis to John Hancock, Sept. 20, 1776, Dec. 21, 1776, and Jan. 10, 1777, Cont. Congress Papers, roll 178, item 159, no. 3.
17. Captain George George, of the 11th Virginia Regiment, was omitted from the official arrangement made at Ramapo, N.J.
18. Muhlenburg, *Life of Muhlenburg*, 338-339; *The Proceedings of the Convention of Delegates . . . on the 20th of March, 1775* (1775; reprint ed., Richmond, 1816), 3.
19. Don Higginbotham, *The War of American Independence: Military Attitudes, Policies, and Practice, 1763-1789* (New York, 1971), 135-137; Muhlenburg, *Life of Muhlenburg*, 57-59; "Woodford, Howe, and Lee Letters," *Richmond College Historical Papers* 1(1915):156-158; Andrew Lewis to John Hancock, June 18, 1776, Cont. Congress Papers, roll 178, item 159.
20. Muhlenburg, *Life of Muhlenburg*, 64-69.
21. "Return of the 8th Virginia Regiment of Foot in the service of the United Colonies Com[mande]d by Abra[ham] Bowman, Esq. April 11th, 1777," William H. Cabell Papers, Executive Papers, Executive Department, Archives Division, VSL.
22. "Virginia Legislative Papers: Accomack Committee to the Convention, November 30, 1775," *VMHB* 14(1906-1907):257-258; *Cont. Congress Journals*, 3:403; 4:40-41.
23. *Cont. Congress Journals*, 5:466.
24. *Governors' Letters*, 1:44; Higginbotham, *War of Independence*, 186-187; Muhlenburg, *Life of Muhlenburg*, 106-109.
25. Higginbotham, *War of Independence*, 162.
26. On one occasion Gibson and Brodhead had each other arrested. Pennsylvania Indian Forts Commission, *Report of the Commission to Locate the Site of the Frontier Forts of Pennsylvania*, 2d ed., 2 vols. (Harrisburg, Pa., 1916), 2:137; David I. Bushnell, Jr., "The Virginia Frontier in History, 1778," *VMHB* 23(1915):113, 257, 357.
27. William H. English, *Conquest of the Northwest*, 2 vols. (Indianapolis, 1896), 2:710-720; *State Papers*, 2:108, 116. Clark's letters to Washington and to the governor of Virginia, dated May 23, 1781, stated that von Steuben had given him permission to take Gibson's detachment on his planned expedition against Detroit. However, Brodhead, the ranking officer, forbade Gibson to leave, and in late July Clark sailed without him. Illinois Papers, George Rogers Clark Papers, Auditor of Public Accounts, Executive Department, Archives Division, VSL.
28. Continental Congress resolution, Sept. 16, 1776, Governor's Office, Letters Received, Executive Department, Archives Division, VSL. (This item was calendared as "Resolutions. Re: revolutionary army" in Claudia B. Grundman, comp., *Calendar of Continental Congress Papers* [Richmond, 1973], 1). *See also* Dixon and Hunter's *Va. Gaz.* (Williamsburg), Feb. 28, 1777.
29. "A General Return of the 10th Continental Virg[ini]a Regiment, Commanded by Colo. Edward Stevens, April the 10th 1777," folder 13, William H. Cabell Papers, Executive Papers, Executive Department, Archives Division, VSL.
30. "Diary of a Prisoner of War at Quebec, 1776," *VMHB*, 9(1902):144; William Fletcher Boogher, *Gleanings of Virginia History: An Historical and Genealogical Collection . . .* (Washington, D.C., 1903), 171.
31. Saffell, *Records*, 269.
32. Bushnell, "Virginia Frontier," *VMHB* 23(1915):113, 257, 357.
33. Bounty Warrant: Joseph Michaux.
34. *Council Journals*, 1:381.

CHAPTER FOUR

The Additional Continental Regiments

1. Tyler, "Old Virginia Line," *Tyler's Quarterly* 12 (1930-1931):109; Bounty Warrant: William Grayson.
2. Bounty Warrants: Nathaniel Gist and John Gist; Berg, *Army Units*, 48; *Archives of Maryland*, vol. 18, *Muster Rolls and Other Records of Service of Maryland Troops in the American Revolution* (Baltimore, 1900), 596; Purdie's *Va. Gaz.* (Williamsburg), Feb. 14, 1777; List of American Officers taken in the Southern Department by the British Army previous to Nov. 26, 1782, enclosed with Robert Morris to the president of Congress, Feb. 17, 1783, Cont. Congress Papers, roll 149, item 137; Saffell, *Records*, 285.
3. Bounty Warrant: Nathaniel Gist.
4. Tyler, "Old Virginia Line," *Tyler's Quarterly* 12(1930-1931), 115; Bounty Warrants: John Thornton and Charles M. Thruston; "Revolutionary Letters," *Tyler's Quarterly* 9(1928):245-248.
5. Danske B. Dandridge, *Historic Shepherdstown* (Charlottesville, 1910), 154-155; *Cont. Congress Journals*, 6:1045; Washington, *Writings*, 14:180,347.
6. *State Papers*, 1:395.

CHAPTER FIVE

Miscellaneous and Special Units and the Partizan Legions

1. Washington, *Writings*, 4:388.
2. John Blair Linn and William Henry Egle, *Pennsylvania in the War of the Revolution, Battalions and Line, 1775-1783*, 2 vols. (Harrisburg, Pa., 1880), 2:367-368. See also Carlos E. Godfrey, *The Commander in Chief's Guard, Revolutionary War* (Washington, D.C., 1904).
3. Charles Lee to John Hancock, Cont. Congress Papers, roll 177, item 158.
4. Public Store, Williamsburg, Day Book, Oct. 1775-Oct. 1776, 132; Public Store, Williamsburg, Journal, Oct. 1775-Oct. 1776, 116, State Agent, Governor's Office, Executive Department, Archives Division, VSL; Invoice of goods "Delivered to Charles Diele, Esq. for the use of a soldier of General Lee's Party . . .," Apr. 26, 1776, acc. no. 20624d, item 1, James Hunter Papers, Personal Papers, Archives Division, VSL.
5. *Cont. Congress Journals*, 7:21-22; *Council Journals*, 1:337-338; Bushnell, "Virginia Frontier," *VMHB* 23 (1915):113-123, 256-268, 337-351; 24(1916):44-55, 168-179; Henry Howe, *Historical Collections of Virginia* . . . (Charleston, S.C., 1846), 200-201; Frederick B. Kegley, *Kegley's Virginia Frontier: The Beginning of the Southwest* . . . (Roanoke, 1938), 634; Petition of certificer William Arbuckle, Nov. 5, 1788, Misc. Legislative Petitions.
6. Saffell, *Records*, 113; *Cont. Congress Journals*, 4:75; Washington, *Writings*, 20:277-281; 24:352; 25:466; 26:497; *Archives of Maryland*, vol. 18, *Muster Rolls of Maryland Troops*, 596; "Memorial of Moses Hazen, 1779," *Pennsylvania Archives*, 1st ser. 8(1859):17.
7. *Cont. Congress Journals*, 5:521; *Council Journals*, 1:122, 270, 332; Continental Congress resolution, Sept. 16, 1776, Governor's Office, Letters Received, Executive Department, Archives Division, VSL; *Governors' Letters*, 1:55, 74, 131.
8. Berg, *Army Units*, 46; Wymberley Jones DeRenne, ed., "Order Book of Samuel Elbert, . . . October 1776, to November 1778," *Collections of the Georgia Historical Society*, 5, pt. 2 (1902): 6-8, 23, 31, 40.

9. Berg, *Army Units*, 46; Georgia State Papers, 1777-1788, Cont. Congress Papers, roll 87, item 73.
10. Purdie's *Va. Gaz.* (Williamsburg), Aug. 23, 1776; Dec. 6, 1776; June 15, 1776; Jan. 3, 1777; Jan. 10, 1777; Feb. 14, 1777; Mar. 21, 1777; Apr. 4, 1777; May 9, 1777; June 13, 1777; June 20, 1777; June 27, 1777; Dec. 12, 1777; Dixon and Hunter's, *Va. Gaz.* (Williamsburg), June 15, 1776; Sept. 27, 1776; Dec. 13, 1776; Jan. 24, 1777; Dec. 12, 1777; Dec. 19, 1777.
11. Bounty Warrant: John W. Nash and others; Petition of James Cooper, Oct. 28, 1791, Misc. Legislative Petitions.
12. Purdie's *Va. Gaz.* (Williamsburg), June 13, 1777; Dixon and Hunter's *Va. Gaz.* (Williamsburg), Dec. 19, 1777.
13. Berg, *Army Units*, 46-47; Purdie's *Va. Gaz.* (Williamsburg), Nov. 28, 1777.
14. Berg, *Army Units*, 54-55.
15. Saffell, *Records*, 116-117, 222; Hening, ed., *Statutes*, 10:346.
16. Dandridge, *Historic Shepherdstown*, 154-155; Purdie and Dixon's *Va. Gaz.* (Williamsburg), Aug. 4, 1776.
17. John R. Sellers, "The Virginia Continental Line, 1775-1780," (Ph.D. diss., Tulane University, 1968); *Cont. Congress Journals*, 2:89.
18. Dixon and Hunter's *Va. Gaz.* (Williamsburg), Nov. 15, 1776; William Louis Calver and Reginald P. Bolton, *History Written with Pick and Shovel* . . . (New York, 1950), 47; Saffell, *Records*, 298-301; Bounty Warrant: Moses Rawlings; Dandridge, *Historic Shepherdstown*, 150-151.
19. Don Higginbotham, *Daniel Morgan, Revolutionary Rifleman* (Chapel Hill, 1961), 55, 96; Berg, *Army Units*, 77; Captain Robert Gamble's Memorandum Book; Saffell, *Records*, 268.
20. *Council Journals*, 2:154, 174; Hening, ed., *Statutes*, 9:445-456.
21. Henry P. Johnston, "Christian Febiger: Colonel of the Virginia Line of the Continental Army," *Mag. Am. Hist.* 6(1881):188-203; Christian Febiger Correspondence, Orderly Books, Etc., 1777-1782 (microfilm, Archives Division, VSL).
22. Virginia Muster Rolls, 40, 56, 57, 58; Bounty Warrants: Alexander McDonald and William Spencer; Johnston, "Christian Febiger," *Mag. Am. Hist.* 6(1881):188-203.
23. Boogher, *Gleanings of Virginia History*, 227; Henry Phelps Johnston, *The Yorktown Campaign and the Surrender of Cornwallis, 1781* (New York, 1881), 112; Wildes, *Anthony Wayne*, 268-289; *State Papers*, 2:582-584.
24. Berg, *Army Units*, 124; Army Register, War Office, Governor's Office, Executive Department, Archives Division, VSL.
25. *State Papers*, 1:410.
26. Ibid., 1:603; 371, 354; Wildes, *Anthony Wayne*, 268-289.
27. Berg, *Army Units*, 9-10, 92, 107; *Cont. Congress Journals*, 19:xix, 76-77; 24:xxiv, 344-345; Albert W. Haarmann, "General Armand and his Partisan Corps, 1777-1783," *Military Collector and Historian* 12 (1960):97-98.
28. Washington, *Writings*, 10:147-148; Harrmann, "General Armand," *Military Collector and Historian* 12(1960):98; *Cont. Congress Journals*, 11:642.
29. *State Papers*, 2:647-649.
30. Ibid., 2:649, 663; 3:31-32, 37, 38, 79, 129-130, 293; Bounty Warrants: Matthew Shan, Frederick Shafer, and Thomas Davis.
31. Louis Alexander Burgess, *Virginia Soldiers of 1776* . . ., 3 vols. (Richmond, 1927-1929), 3:1253; "A List . . . of Officers and Soldiers," *Journal of the House of Delegates . . . 1833-1834*, doc. no. 34, no. 6, 2-16.
32. Bounty Warrant: Matthew Irvine; Berg, *Army Units*, 60-61.
33. *Cont. Congress Journals*, 14:822; 16:164.
34. A photograph of the medal may be found in John Richard Alden, *The American Revolution* (New York, 1954), following page 140.

35. Harold L. Peterson, *Book of the Continental Soldier* (Harrisburg, Pa., 1968), 270.
36. Berg, *Army Units*, 61.
37. Henry Lee, *Memoirs of the War in the Southern Department of the United States*, 2 vols. (Philadelphia and New York, 1812).

CHAPTER SIX
The Continental Artillery

1. *Cont. Congress Journals*, 4:111, 120; 6:981; Hening, ed., *Statutes*, 9:83.
2. Dixon and Hunter's *Va. Gaz.* (Williamsburg), Mar. 30, 1776; Charles Lee to John Hancock, Apr. 19, 1776, Charles Lee Papers, Cont. Congress Papers, roll 177, item 158; Purdie's *Va. Gaz.* (Williamsburg), Apr. 26, 1776, supp.; Accounts of the Committee of Safety, Convention Papers, 1775 and 1776, 68; Bounty Warrant: Samuel Denny; *Cont. Congress Journals*, 4:364.
3. Purdie's *Va. Gaz.* (Williamsburg), Feb. 16, 1776. According to the Public Store, Williamsburg, Daybook entry for May 8, 1776, Isaac Deane was a lieutenant in the artillery company. He officially became a 3d lieutenant on Jan. 13, 1777.
4. Purdie's *Va. Gaz.* (Williamsburg), July 19, 1776.
5. Peterson, *Continental Soldier*, 261-263; *Cont. Congress Journals*, 6:981, 995.
6. *Council Journals*, 1:312-313; Peterson, *Continental Soldier*, 261-262.
7. Saffell, *Records*, 229-232, 255.
8. Peterson, *Continental Soldier*, 263; List of American Officers taken in the Southern Department by the British Army previous to Nov. 26, 1782, enclosed with Robert Morris to the president of Congress, Feb. 17, 1783, Cont. Congress Papers, roll 149, item 137; Captain Robert Gamble's Memorandum Book.

CHAPTER SEVEN
The Continental Light Dragoons

1. Purdie's *Va. Gaz.* (Williamsburg), Apr. 26, 1776, June 28, 1776; Hening, ed., *Statutes*, 9:137-138; *Proceedings of the Convention... May, 1776* (1776; reprint ed., Richmond, 1816), 45-48.
2. Purdie's *Va. Gaz.* (Williamsburg), July 5, 1776; *Proceedings of the Convention, May, 1776*, 45-48.
3. The chevalier de St. Aubin, a French officer left behind by Lord Dunmore, was appointed a cadet in Bland's troop on Aug. 23, 1776, and made adjutant on Nov. 7, 1776. *Governors' Letters*, 1:34, 61.
4. Peterson, *Continental Soldier*, 266; *Cont. Congress Journals*, 7:34; Theodorick Bland, *The Bland Papers* . . ., ed. Charles Campbell, 2 vols. (Petersburg, 1840-1843), 1:45-46.
5. Washington, *Writings*, 9:311; Burt Garfield Loescher, "Bland's Virginia Horse: The Story of the First Continental Light Dragoons," *Military Collector and Historian* 6(1954):[3].
6. *Council Journals*, 2:251; Lee, *Memoirs of the War in the Southern Department*.
7. A. M. W. Woodhull, comp., "Memoirs of Brig. Gen. Anthony Walton White," *Proceedings of the New Jersey Historical Society*, 2d ser. 7(1882):106-115; Edward McCrady, *The History of South Carolina in the Revolution, 1775-1780* (New York, 1901), 493-495.

8. Berg, *Army Units*, 29, 31; *Cont. Congress Journals*, 18:896. Eventually, William Washington's light dragoons became the nucleus of a temporary 3d legionary corps.
9. Loescher, "Bland's Virginia Horse," *Military Collector and Historian* 6(1954): 5-6.
10. Saffell, *Records*, 92-93. *See* "3d Regiment of Continental Light Dragoons"; Petition of Noncommissioned Officers and Privates of Baylor's Regiment, May 22, 1783, Misc. Letters, N-P, Cont. Congress Papers, roll 100, item 78.
11. *Cont. Congress Journals*, 6:1045; 7:7; Godfrey, *The Commander in Chief's Guard*, 21:205-206.
12. Berg, *Army Units*, 30-31; Dixon and Hunter's *Va. Gaz.* (Williamsburg), Nov. 1778; List of American Officers taken in the Southern Department by the British Army previous to Nov. 26, 1782, enclosed with Robert Morris to the president of Congress, Feb. 17, 1783, Cont. Congress Papers, roll 149, item 137.
13. Petition of Noncommissioned Officers and Privates of Baylor's Regiment, May 22, 1783, Misc. Letters, N-P, Cont. Congress Papers, roll 100, item 78.
14. Berg, *Army Units*, 28-31.
15. Ibid., 13; Washington, *Writings*, 25:466.

CHAPTER EIGHT

The Virginia State Line

1. Hening, ed., *Statutes*, 9:192-201; *Council Journals*, 1:23, 307, 308, 437, 439, 443.
2. Petition, May 17, 1777, Misc. Legislative Petitions; *Council Journals*, 1:437-443; Muhlenburg to Board of War, Apr. 15, 1780, Cont. Congress Papers, roll 161, item 148; Jefferson, *Papers*, 4:529; Hening, ed., *Statutes*, 9:337; List of Officers Entitled to Half-Pay.
3. Virginia Muster Rolls, nos. 19, 20.
4. Ibid., nos. 47, 48, 49, 55; *Council Journals*, 1:437, 443; Muster Roll of the Field, Staff, Warrant, and Noncommissioned Officers of the 2d Va. State Regiment of Foot, 1779, Returns of Military Units, War Office, Executive Department, Archives Division, VSL; List of Officers Entitled to Half-Pay.
5. Muster Roll of the Field, Staff, Warrant, and Noncommissioned Officers of the 2d Va. State Regiment of Foot, 1779, Returns of Military Units, War Office, Executive Department, Archives Division, VSL. Beesly Edgar Joel, a British defector, joined Brent's Corps in Apr. or May 1781 and was given the rank of major; he served as a recruiter and spy before and during the siege of Yorktown. Jefferson, *Papers*, 4:382, 553-554, 569, 602, 608, 640; *State Papers*, 2:112, 155, 177-179, 196.
6. Hening, ed., *Statutes*, 9:192; *Council Journals*, 1:437-443; 2:105.
7. *The Proceedings of the Convention of Delegates . . . on Monday the 17th of July, 1775* (1775; reprint ed., Richmond, 1816), 19; Bounty Warrant: Thomas Bullitt; "The Journal of Ebenezer Hazard in Virginia, 1777," ed. Fred Shelley, *VMHB* 62 (1954): 410.
8. Charles Lee to John Hancock, May 7, 1776, Charles Lee Papers, item 158, 47-57; Cont. Congress Papers, roll 177, item 158; *Cont. Congress Journals*, 4:241.
9. *State Papers*, 3:96; Jefferson, *Papers*, 4:474, 480, 582, 644; *Council Journals*, 1:302; 2:502.
10. Perkins Library at Duke University has an undated printed commission appointing Joseph Louis de Beaulieu a lieutenant in the company. Pierre Dubar and Pierre du Chatelier may have been names for the same man.
11. *Council Journals*, 1:389, 473, 499; 2:116. De la Porte apparently served temporarily with Marshall's State Artillery Regiment.
12. Ibid., 2:209; Purdie's *Va. Gaz.* (Williamsburg), May 1, 1778; Public Store, Wil-

liamsburg, Daybook, Aug. 8, 1778, State Agent, Governor's Office, Executive Department, Archives Division, VSL; Clarkson and Davis's *Va. Gaz.* (Williamsburg), Oct. 30, 1779.

13. Bounty Warrant: James Monroe; Muhlenburg, *Life of Muhlenburg*, 210; Petition of J. F. Mercer, Oct. 15, 1792, and Petition of Charles de Klaumann, Nov. 20, 1783, Misc. Legislative Petitions; War Office Letter Book, 1779-1780, 37, Governor's Office, Executive Department, Archives Division, VSL.
14. Jefferson, *Papers*, 3:229-230, 236, 464-467; Petition of Edward Digges, Nov. 28, 1785, Misc. Legislative Petitions. The men in his company apparently joined Porterfield's detachment in 1779.
15. *Council Journals*, 2:251; *Governors' Letters*, 1:349; 2:83; Jefferson, *Papers*, 3:155-156; Alden, *American Revolution*, 129-149; William M. Dabney, *After Saratoga: The Story of the Convention Army* (Albuquerque, N.M., 1954), 24-26, 56-57, 81-82.
16. *Governors' Letters*, 1:348-349.
17. Jefferson, *Papers*, 3:155-156; McAllister, *Virginia Militia*, 15, 18, 28, 29, 31, 32.
18. *Governors' Letters*, 1:335. Friedrike C. L. von Riedesel, *Letters and Journals, Relating to the War of the American Revolution*, 2 vols. (Albany, N.Y., 1867), 2:71; Gilbert Chinard, ed., *The Letters of Lafayette and Jefferson* (Baltimore, 1929), 110.
19. *Governors' Letters*, 2:67; Dabney, *After Saratoga*, 66; Dixon and Nicholson's *Va. Gaz.* (Williamsburg), Sept. 11, 1779.
20. Jefferson, *Papers*, 3:155-156; Bounty Warrants: James Burton and William Abney.
21. McAllister, *Virginia Militia*, 17, 215, 220; Return of Taylor's Regiment of Guards, Oct. 4, 1779, Albemarle Barracks Returns, 1779-1780, James Wood Papers, War Office, Executive Department, Archives Division, VSL.
22. Hawkins to Bland, June 3, 1779, Campbell Papers, Virginia Historical Society; Dabney, *After Saratoga*, 62-63; Albemarle Barracks Returns, Apr. 8, 1780, and July 1, 1780, James Wood Papers, War Office, Executive Department, Archives Division, VSL.
23. McAllister, *Virginia Militia*, 15, 31, 41; Albemarle Barracks Returns, 1779-1780, James Wood Papers, War Office, Executive Department, Archives Division, VSL.
24. Dabney, *After Saratoga*, 67-68; *State Papers*, 2:141.
25. *State Papers*, 1:490, 496.
26. Ibid., 529, 556; *Governors' Letters*, 2:11, 229, 409.
27. *State Papers*, 2:29, 37; *Council Journals*, 2:312.
28. *State Papers*, 2:146-147, 578-579; 3:7, 9, 12, 173.
29. Hening, ed., *Statutes*, 9:452-453; Public Store, Williamsburg, Journal, 1777-1778, State Agent, Governor's Office, Executive Department, Archives Division, VSL; Jefferson, *Papers*, 2:179-180; *Council Journals*, 2:153, 287; Public Store, Richmond, Journal, 1779-1780, State Agent, Governor's Office, Executive Department, Archives Division, VSL.
30. Bounty Warrant: Thomas Upshaw; List of Officers Entitled to Half-Pay; *Council Journals*, 2:287.
31. Jefferson, *Papers*, 4:214; [Charles Porterfield], "Diary of a Prisoner of War at Quebec," ed. J. A. Waddell, *VMHB* 9 (1902):144.
32. Jefferson, *Papers*, 3:340; Captain Robert Gamble's Memorandum Book; Petition of Edward Digges, 1785, Misc. Legislative Petitions.
33. Petition of State Artillery Officers, n.d., Executive Communications, General Assembly, Archives Division, VSL; *Council Journals*, 1:459-461; 2:1, 156; Hening, ed., *Statutes*, 9:278-279; Petitions, Nov. 15, 1777, and Oct. 23, 1778, Misc. Legislative Petitions.
34. Jefferson, *Papers*, 4:536.
35. Return of the Officers of the Regiment of artillery . . . under . . . Col. Thomas Marshall, 1780, Returns of Military Units, War Office, Executive Department, Archives Division, VSL.

36. De Klaumann, a Danish officer in the service of King Christian VII, of Norway, was given leave of absence in Mar. 1777 to enlist in the American army. From Jan. 1778 to July 1779 he served with Marshall's artillery but entered recruiting service for a proposed regiment under Lt. Col. James Monroe. He resigned in Dec. 1779, when he was refused a major's commission in the State Garrison Regiment. Credentials of Charles de Klaumann, 1777-1778, Letters Received, Governor's Office, Executive Department, Archives Division, VSL; Petition of Charles de Klaumann, Nov. 20, 1783, Misc. Legislative Petitions; War Office Letter Book, 1779-1780, 37, Governor's Office, Executive Department, Archives Division, VSL.
37. André Lasseray, *Les Français Sous Les Treize Etoiles, 1775-1783*, 2 vols. (Paris, 1935), 1:288-299; Rough Bills and Resolutions, House of Delegates, General Assembly, Archives Division, VSL; Letters from Lafayette and Coudray, 1777-1787, Cont. Congress Papers, roll 176, item 156; Jefferson, *Papers*, 2:178; 4:344, 346, 632; *Council Journals*, 2:75.
38. Robert B. Munford, Jr., "Military Recommendations to the Governor and Council, May 15, 1778," *VMHB* 30 (1922): 286, *Council Journals*, 2:75; *Governors' Letters*, 1:203-204, 219, 234, 238, 250-251, 270-273, 276-277, 278, 283; *State Papers*, 1:174-175, 295.
39. Bounty Warrant: Major Nelson; List of Officers Entitled to Half-Pay; Hening, ed., *Statutes*, 10:28, 215. John Hastings Gwathmey, *Historical Register of Virginians in the Revolution: Soldiers, Sailors, Marines, 1775-1783* (Richmond, 1938), and McAllister, *Virginia Militia*, 129, 214, list a number of volunteer cavalry organizations commanded by captains Henry Holcombe, Thomas Watkins, Robert Bolling, Littleberry Mosby, White, and Webber. There were, however, others.
40. Jefferson, *Papers*, 4:397; *State Papers*, 2:219. Ensign Charles Fierer (or Fuhrer) of the Hessian Regiment von Knyphausen was captured at Trenton in 1776 and defected to the American side. In 1779 Jefferson appointed him a captain in the Virginia State Line. At some point in the southern campaign he was injured seriously and was prevented from rejoining Nelson's cavalry. After the war he settled in Dumfries, where he printed *The Virginia Gazette and Agricultural Repository* until his death in 1794. Alice H. Terch, "A Printer Soldier of Fortune," *Papers of the Bibliographical Society of America* 30 (1936): 91-103.
41. See n. 1, above. Bounty Warrants: Nathaniel Savage and Edmund Read; Roll of Vogluson's Troop, Clothing Returns, Auditor's Office, Archives Division, VSL; Burgess, *Virginia Soldiers of 1776*, 3:1277-1278.
42. List of Officers Entitled to Half-Pay; Clark, *Papers*, 8:78-82.
43. Clark, *Papers*, 8:174; William H. Gaines, Jr., "A Few Men Well Conducted," *Virginia Cavalcade*, 2, no. 3 (1952-1953):34-39.
44. Clark, *Papers*, 8:90-91, 265-266, 305.
45. Muster and Payrolls, 1779-1783, Illinois Papers, George Rogers Clark Papers, Auditor of Public Accounts, Executive Department, Archives Division, VSL.
46. The following lists were compiled from: George Rogers Clark Papers, Auditor of Public Accounts, Executive Department, Archives Division, VSL; Western Commissioners Papers, 1782-1783, Governor's Office, Executive Department, Archives Division, VSL; Clark, *Papers*, 8:326, 353-355, 363; 19:419-424.
47. Hening, ed., *Statutes*, 10:32, 215.
48. Albermarle Barracks Returns, Apr. 8 and Nov. 1, 1780, James Wood Papers, War Office, Executive Department, Archives Division, VSL; Jefferson, *Papers*, 3:302, 506; 4:12; Clark, *Papers*, 8:570, 594.
49. McAllister, *Virginia Militia*, 96; Bounty Warrants: Cole Digges and John Nicholas; E. Meade to the Governor, Dec. 20, 1794, Letters Received, Governor's Office, Executive Department, Archives Division, VSL; Hening, ed., *Statutes*, 10:391-393; Flagg and

Waters, "Virginia's Soldiers," *VMHB* 21 (1913):345-346; Marko Zlatich, "The 1st and 2nd Virginia State Legions, 1781-1783," *Military Collector and Historian* 17 (1965):35-37; *State Papers*, 2:175, 415, 519, 592; Pension Papers of Alexander Spotswood, acc. no. 12, John K. Martin Papers, Personal Papers, Archives Division, VSL; Hayes's *The Virginia Gazette, or, the American Advertiser* (Richmond), Nov. 8, 1783.

50. Muster Rolls of Dabney's Legion, Returns of Military Units, War Office, Executive Department, Archives Division, VSL; *Council Journals*, 3:29-30, 223; "Notes and Queries: Officers of the State Legion," *VMHB* 29 (1921):505; *State Papers*, 3:408; Letters for Feb. through Apr. 1783, Governor's Office Letter Book, 1782-1783, Executive Department, Archives Division, VSL; Payroll of Staff Officers of the Legion, doc. E-5, Revolutionary War Payrolls, Auditor of Public Accounts, Executive Department, Archives Division, VSL. Woodson's Company was formerly Capt. John Rogers's Illinois Petitions; Petition of the Officers of Dabney's Legion, Dec. 6, 1786, Misc. Legislative Petitions; Hayes's *Va. Gaz.* (Richmond), Jan. 26, 1783.
51. [John Blair Dabney], *The John Blair Dabney Manuscript, 1795-1868* . . . (n.p., 1942), 12; List of Officers Entitled to Half-Pay.
52. *State Papers*, 3:30, 83, 88, 196.
53. Ibid., 3:408; Papers of the Commissary, Quartermasters, and State Guards at Point of Fork and Richmond City, 1783-1788, Governor's Office, Executive Department, Archives Division, VSL; Rolls of the men under captains Vogluson, Roane, Crump, and Brown, item 279, Clothing Returns, Auditor's Office, Executive Department, Archives Division, VSL; "A Return of all the Men absent and present belonging to the Cavalry of Lieut. Col. Dabney's Legion, April 26, 1782," acc. no. 24816, Dabney Family Papers, Dabney-Jackson Collection, 1754-1867; Muster and Payrolls, doc. 99, Illinois Papers, George Rogers Clark Papers, Auditor of Public Accounts, Executive Department, Archives Division, VSL. Woodson's Company was formerly Capt. John Rogers's Illinois Dragoons; Rolls of men under captains Crump, Brown, and Roane, Miscellaneous Revolutionary War Records, Governor's Office, Executive Department, Archives Division, VSL; *Council Journal*, 3:279, 300, 344, 349, 356, 366, 368, 389, 391, 396, 403, 441, 491, 496, 503, 534; 4:163, 274.

CHAPTER NINE

The Virginia Militia

1. Louise Phelps Kellogg, with R. G. Thwaites, *Dunmore's War* (Madison, Wis., 1905), xvii-xxiii, 341-344, 368-395; Peter Force, ed., *American Archives*, 4th ser., 6 vols. (Washington, D.C., 1837-1853), 2:1016; J. T. McAllister, "The Battle of Point Pleasant," *VMHB* 9(1902):395-407; 10(1902):75-83; William H. B. Thomas and Howard McKnight Wilson, "The Battle of Point Pleasant, 1774," *Virginia Cavalcade* 24(1974-1975):100-107; Virgil A. Lewis, *History of the Battle of Point Pleasant* . . . (Charleston, W.Va., 1909), 22-23.
2. The following lists were derived from Dunmore's War Records, Archives Division, VSL; "Orderly Book and Journal of James Newell," *VMHB* 11(1904):242; and from these sources in the Revolutionary War Payrolls, Auditor of Public Accounts, Executive Department, Archives Division, VSL: Pittsburg Payrolls, Romney Payrolls, and Winchester Payrolls.
3. Correspondence of General Horatio Gates, 1775-1782, Cont. Congress Papers, roll 174, item 154.
4. Ibid.; Dixon and Nicholson's *Va. Gaz.* (Richmond), Sept. 6, 1780; McAllister, *Virginia Militia*, 16, 23, 26, 27, 35, 36, 45.

5. The most complete treatment of the strategy and personalities involved at Kings Mountain is Lyman C. Draper, *King's Mountain and Its Heroes* (Cincinnati, 1881).
6. Ibid., 402; Roster of Virginia Militia Troops at the Battle of King's Mountain, 1780, acc. no. 26081, Personal Papers, Archives Division, VSL.
7. Benson J. Lossing, *The Pictorial Field Book of the Revolution. . .* , 2 vols. (New York, 1850), 2:430; Charles Stedman, *The History of the Origin, Progress, and Termination of the American War*, 2 vols. (London, 1792), 2:324; McAllister, *Virginia Militia*, 31, 42, 43; Dixon and Nicholson's *Va. Gaz.* (Richmond), Apr. 14, 1781.
8. Lyman C. Draper Manuscript Collection, Pittsburg and Northwest Virginia Papers, 1NN:63, Border Forays, 5D: 134-156, State Historical Society of Wisconsin, Madison (microfilm, Archives Division, VSL); *State Papers*, 3:232, 235, 286.

CHAPTER TEN

The Virginia State Navy

1. Hening, ed., *Statutes*, 9:151, 290-292.
2. Accounts of the Committee of Safety, 1775-1776, Convention Papers, 1775 and 1776; Hening, ed., *Statutes*, 9:83, 195.
3. Jack Coggins, *Ships and Seamen of the American Revolution: Vessels, Crews, Weapons, Gear, Naval Tactics, and Actions of the War of Independence* (Harrisburg, Pa., 1969), 169-184; Howard I. Chapelle, *The History of the American Sailing Navy: The Ships and Their Development* (New York, 1949).
4. Hening, ed., *Statutes*, 9:149. Changes in board membership are reflected in the manuscript journals, letters, and books of the navy commissioners, Executive Department, Archives Division, VSL.
5. Hening, ed., *Statutes*, 9:42.
6. Basic data on most of these vessels, officers, crews, dates of service, etc., was found in one or more of the following sources in the Archives Division, VSL: Navy Account Book, 1775-1781, Auditor of Public Accounts, Executive Department; Papers Relating to Various Ships, State Navy, Governor's Office, Executive Department; Papers Relating to Various Ships, State Agent Papers, 1775-May 1779, 1788, Records, ca. 1776-1787, State Navy, Governor's Office, Executive Department; and Officers and Seamen of the State Navy and Marines, 1776-1779, State Navy, Governor's Office, Executive Department. Information was also found in Robert Armistead Stewart, *History of Virginia's Navy of the Revolution* (Richmond, 1933). Further citations to these sources have not been made in this chapter. Definitions of vessels were derived from William Falconer, *An Universal Dictionary of the Marine* (London, 1789), and Peter Kemp, ed., *The Oxford Companion to Ships and the Sea* (Oxford and London, 1976).
7. Jefferson, *Papers*, 3:following 254.
8. Bond for *American Fabius*, Jan. 29, 1783, Executive Papers, Executive Department, Archives Division, VSL.
9. Bounty Warrant: J. Godwin.
10. Petition of William Holliday, Nov. 7, 1791, Misc. Legislative Petitions.
11. Jefferson, *Papers*, 3:38.
12. Petition of Capt. Thomas Herbert, Nov. 13, 1794, Misc. Legislative Petitions.
13. Walter Drew McCaw, "Captain John Harris of the Virginia Navy," *VMHB* 22(1914):160, 163.
14. Miscellaneous papers of the convention of May 1776, Convention Papers, 1775 and 1776.
15. The *Baker* may have been a privateer.

16. Hayes's *Va. Gaz.* (Richmond), Oct. 11, 1783.
17. Ibid., Oct. 4, 1783.
18. Bounty Warrant: James Jennings; Jefferson, *Papers*, 4:382, 553-554, 569, 602, 608, 640.
19. Payroll of the *Gloucester*, 1780, Papers of the State Navy, Governor's Office, Executive Department, Archives Division, VSL.
20. Hening, ed., *Statutes*, 10:217.
21. Ibid.
22. Oct. 8, 1776, Executive Communications, General Assembly, Archives Division, VSL.
23. Ibid.
24. Ibid.
25. Ibid.
26. Ships' Bonds required for Letters of Marque and Reprisal, 1776-1783, Cont. Congress Papers, rolls 202-204, item 196; George F. Emmons, *The Navy of the United States . . .* (Washington, D.C., 1853), 127-169.
27. *State Papers*, 2:74.
28. Jefferson, *Papers*, 5:143, 181, 182.
29. Accounts of the Committee of Safety, 1776, Convention Papers, 1775 and 1776.
30. *State Papers*, 3:391-392.

APPENDIXES

1. Captain Robert Gamble's Memorandum Book.
2. "Letters to Thomas Adams," *VMHB* 5(1897-1898):297; Washington, *Writings*, 15:ii, 46, 147; Sellers, "Virginia Continental Line," 328.
3. William Moultrie, *Memoirs of the American Revolution . . .*, 2 vols. (New York, 1802), 2:app. See n. 2, chap. 3,
4. *State Papers*, 1:318.
5. Alden, *American Revolution*, 230-231.
6. "From the Diary of a Revolutionary Officer," *Southern Literary Messenger* 1(1835):341-342.
7. *Original Papers Relating to the Siege of Charleston, 1780 . . .* (Charleston, 1898), 79-87.
8. Captured American "returns" from Charleston, 1780, Sir Henry Clinton Papers, 1750-1812, Division of Manuscripts, William L. Clements Library, University of Michigan, Ann Arbor; Captain Robert Gamble's Memorandum Book.
9. Captain Robert Gamble's Memorandum Book; "Genealogy: The Parker Family," *VMHB* 6(1898):88.
10. Robert D. Bass, *The Green Dragoon: The Lives of Banastre Tarleton and Mary Robinson* (New York, 1957), 80-82; Banastre Tarleton, *A History of the Campaigns of 1780 and 1781, in the Southern Provinces of North America* (Dublin and London, 1787), 77-79, 83-84; Captain Robert Gamble's Memorandum Book.
11. *Original Papers Relating to the Siege of Charleston*, 79-87.
12. Arrangement of the Virginia Line for 1781, Feb. 10, 1781, Arrangement of the Continental Line, acc. no. 42 (copy acc. no. 13647), Governor's Office, Executive Department, Archives Division, VSL; *State Papers,* 2:582; Boogher, *Gleanings of Virginia History*, 227.
13. Asa Bird Gardner, comp., "Disposition and Order of Battle of the Allied Armies on the March from Williamsburgh, to the Siege of York, 27th September 1781," *Mag. Am. Hist.* 7(1881):267-268; Henry Phelps Johnston, *The Yorktown Campaign and the Surrender of Cornwallis, 1781* (New York, 1881), 112.
14. Philip Katcher, *Encyclopedia of British, Provincial, and German Army Units, 1775-1783*

(Harrisburg, Pa., 1973), 98; *Council Journals,* 1:63, 291, 439; 2:45, 147, 431, 464, 512; [John Graves Simcoe], *Simcoe's Military Journal* (New York, 1844); *Proceedings of the Convention . . . March, 1775* ([1776]; reprint ed., Richmond, 1816), 99.
15. Benjamin Quarles, "Lord Dunmore as Liberator," *WMQ,* 3d ser. 15(1958):494-507; John Collett to Lord Dunmore, Jan. 15, 1776, Convention Papers, 1775 and 1776, Archives Division, VSL; Purdie's *Va. Gaz.* (Williamsburg), Dec. 22, 1775, Apr. 5, 1776, Apr. 12, 1776; *Proceedings of the Convention . . . March, 1775,* 99.
16. Katcher, *Encyclopedia,* 91; "A Narrative of the Transactions, Imprisonment, and Sufferings of John Connolly, an American Loyalist and Lieut. Col. in His Majesty's Service," *PMHB* 12 (1888):310-324, 407-420; 13(1889):61-70, 153-167, 281-291; Pittsburg Payrolls, Revolutionary War Payrolls, Auditor of Public Accounts, Executive Department, Archives Division, VSL; *Proceedings of the Convention . . . March, 1775,* 69.
17. Skelton Jones and Louis Hue Giradin, "Examination of Connelly and His Companions," John Burk, *The History of Virginia* (Petersburg, 1816), 4:app. 4.

Index

THE military units listed in Appendix D, "A Calendar of Unit Names and Variants," are not indexed below. The researcher seeking information about a particular unit should consult Appendix D on pages 189-194.

A

Accomack, 156
Adams, George, 132
Addison, John, 168
Adventure, 159, 160
Alert, 174
Alexander, James, 139
Alexander, Morgan, 35, 36, 55
Allan, John, 125
Allen, Charles, 20, 24
Allen, David, 10
Allen, (John), 142
Allery, Joseph, 130
Alliance, 160
Allison, John, 110, 175
Ambler, Jacquelin, 150
America, 172
American Fabius, 153, 164, 174
Ancram, George, 124
Anderson, Andrew, 17
Anderson, Clough, 180
Anderson, James, 20, 24
Anderson, John, 34, 41, 44, 46, 169
Anderson, Richard, 20
Anderson, Richard Clough, 30, 38, 46, 49, 180
Anderson, Robert, 17
Anderson and Company, 166
Andrews, Ishmael, 156
Annette, 164
Antil, Edward, 82
Apollo, 174
Arbuckle, Matthew, 21, 23, 67, 81, 141
Arbuthnot, Marriot, 178
Archer, Edward, 150
Archer, John, 155, 159, 161, 163
Arell, David, 40
Arell, John, 175
Arendt, Baron de, 77
Ariadne, 154
Armistead, Thomas, 111, 113, 127, 136
Armistead, William, 103
Armstrong, James, 96
Arnold, Benedict, 87, 90, 92, 114, 121, 156, 163, 173
Arnold, Thomas, 86
Arundel, O'hickey d', 98
Ashby, John, 39, 40
Ashby, Stephen, 67
Ashmead, Jacob, 91
Asturgus, James, 133
Asturgus, Peter, 132
Audobon, John, 164
Avery, William Haley, 50, 90

B

Bailey, John, 128, 129
Baker, Richard, 166
Baker, Thomas, 141
Baker, 160
Baker, Blow, and Company, 164, 165, 169, 170, 171, 172
Ball, Burgess, 29, 32, 45, 58, 179
Ballard, Bland, 130
Ballard, John, 20, 24
Ballard, Robert, 29, 31, 42, 178
Ballinger, Richard, 118
Banks, Henry, 165
Banks, John, 166
Baptisti, John (viscount de Lomagne), 93
Barbee, Thomas, 50, 51
Bard, John, 84
Barett, William, 105
Barnett, Robert, 133
Barrett, Chiswell, 105
Barrett, John, 153, 155, 157, 164
Barrett, Robert, 118, 119
Barron, James, 149, 150, 152, 162
Barron, Richard, 152, 153, 160
Barron, Samuel, 153
Bartlett, William, 144
Batty, George, 167
Baud, Audré le, 115
Baugh, Alexander, 84
Baylor, George, 80, 104, 181
Baylor, John, 105
Baylor, Walker, 105
Baytop, James, 47
Baytop, Thomas, 100
Beale, Robert, 40, 41, 179
Beale, William, 19
Beall, Isaac, 42, 43
Beall, Robert, 54, 61, 69, 130
Beatie, David, 144
Beatie, John, 144
Beaty, ———, 174
Beaulieu, Joseph Louis de, 115
Belfield, John, 103
Bell, Henry, 14
Bell, John, 139
Bell, Thomas, 74, 75
Bellamy, William, 165
Bellecoeur, Le Brun de, 94
Bellini, Charles, 116
Benjamin, Peter, 65
Benjamin Harrison, Jr., and Company, 164
Bennett, Walker, 24
Bentley, William, 33, 41, 44, 179
Benton, James, 146

Bernard, Peter, 112, 120
Bernard, Richard, 19, 46
Berry, George, 54, 61, 130
Berry, Thomas, 55
Berryman, John, 19
Bert, Claudius de, 94
Betsey, 155
Bias, John, 143
Biggs, Benjamin, 54, 61, 130
Biggs, John, 147
Bird, Benjamin, 104
Blackburn, Thomas, 112
Blackburn, William, 144
Blackwell, John, 179
Blackwell, John E., 40, 41, 44
Blackwell, John, Jr., 16
Blackwell, Joseph, 50, 179
Blackwell, Samuel, 125
Blackwell, Thomas, 63
Blackwell, William, 65, 77
Blair, John, 60
Bland, Richard, Jr., 22
Bland, Robert, 156
Bland, Theodorick, 101, 102, 117, 118, 119, 181
Blankenburg, Frederick de, 123
Bledsoe, Anthony, 139
Bohannon, Ambrose, 34, 100
Bolling, Robert, 154, 160
Bond, Hance, 157
Booker, Richard, 125
Booker, Samuel, 38, 44, 66, 72
Boone, Daniel, 131
Boone, Hawkins, 89
Boone, Squire, 131
Bosseron, François, 128, 129
Boswell, Machen, 112
Boucher, Commodore, 163
Boush, Charles, 156, 158, 159
Boush, Goodrich, 162
Boush, Robert, 123
Bowcher, John, 249
Bowen, John, 181
Bowen, Reece, 144
Bowen, William, 144
Bowers, John, 173
Bowman, Abraham, 54
Bowman, John, 131
Bowman, Joseph, 127, 128, 129
Bowne, Thomas, 33, 51
Bowyer, Henry, 181
Bowyer, Michael, 57, 67
Bowyer, Thomas, 58, 68
Boyd, Samuel, 16
Boykin, Francis, 31

Index 213

Boyle, John, 133
Brade, James, 166
Bradley, James, 125
Brady, Samuel, 82
Brady, William, 65, 77, 87
Brant, Joseph, 129
Brashear, Richard, 129
Breckinridge, Alexander, 75
Brent, John, 42, 43
Brent, William, 112
Bressie, Thomas, 21, 113
Brewer, James, 146
Briffault, Augustine, 94
Bright, Francis, 152, 154, 165
Briscoe, Parmenas, 132
Briscoe, Reuben, 40
Brodhead, Daniel, 61, 70
Brooke, Walter, 151
Brown, Esek, 164
Brown, James, 23, 132
Brown, John, 145, 171
Brown, Robert Windsor, 111, 175
Brown, Thomas, 93, 151, 167, 171
Brown, William, 98, 100
Brown, Windsor, 135, 136
Brownlee, John, 181
Bruin, Peter Bryan, 53, 65
Buchanan, Andrew, 15, 25
Buckner, Mordecai, 15, 48
Buckner, Thomas, 33, 47, 58, 179
Buckskin, 164, 173
Buford, Abraham, 16, 28, 37, 38, 45, 48, 66, 70, 178, 180
Bull, Epaphras, 101
Bullitt, Thomas, 113, 114
Burford (Buford), Thomas, 141
Burgoyne, John, 117
Burk, Wilson, and Company, 171
Burnley, Garland, 118, 119
Burton, James, 119
Burwell, Lewis, 90
Burwell, Nathaniel, 99
Butler, Lawrence, 33, 44, 66, 179
Butler, Richard, 88
Butler, Samuel, 172
Byrd, William, 76, 138
Byrn, John, 76

C

Cabell, Absalom, 162
Cabell, Nicholas, 14, 24, 90, 179
Cabell, Samuel Jordan, 42, 46, 49, 53, 57, 63, 70, 89
Calderwood, James, 65
Caldwell, William, 146

Call, Richard, 102, 104
Callender, Eleazer, 161, 163
Calmes, Marquis, 36, 37
Calvert, John, 158, 159
Calvert, Maximilian, 160
Camp, John, 111
Campbell, David, 140
Campbell, John, 144, 168
Campbell, Patrick, 144
Campbell, Richard, 42, 54, 55, 56, 60, 68
Campbell, Robert, 82, 144
Campbell, William, 31, 111, 130, 140, 143, 145
Cannon, Jesse, 157
Capitol Landing's Revenge, 164
Carlivan, Joseph André, 115
Carnes, Patrick, 96
Carr, Samuel, 21, 175
Carrington, Edward, 13, 97, 98, 99, 145, 184
Carrington, Joseph, 13
Carrington, Mayo, 33, 47, 51, 179
Carson, Joseph, 168
Carter, John Champe, 100, 181
Cary, Archibald, 13
Cary, John, 17
Cary, Richard, 17
Cary, Robert, 21
Casey, Benjamin, 57, 67
Casey, William, 130, 133
Caswell, Richard, 142
Caswell, 156, 159
Catharine, 164
Catlett, Thomas, 37, 181
Catt, Michael, 131
Cerberus, 163
Chamberlayne, Byrd, 154, 166
Chamberlayne, George, 152, 154, 158
Chamberlayne, James L., 169
Chamberlayne, Philip, 151, 157
Chambers, James, 170
Chapline, Abraham, 134
Chapline, James, 76
Chapman, John, 120
Charleville, François, 128, 129
Chatelier, Pierre du, 115
Chenowith, Richard, 133
Cherry, William, 43, 120, 134
Chew, James, 131
Chilton, John, 16, 40
Chisholm, Thomas, 85
Christian, George, 176
Christian, Henry, 14
Christian, William, 29, 161
Claiborne, Buller, 36, 99

Clark, Christopher, 164
Clark, Edmund, 115
Clark, George Rogers, 47, 61, 76, 110, 116, 120, 127-129, 141
Clark, Jonathan, 55, 57, 67
Clark, Richard, 134
Clarke, John, 58, 84
Clary, Elisha, 132
Clay, Thomas, 125
Clements, Mace, 180
Cleveland, Benjamin, 143
Clinton, Henry, 28, 32, 37, 55, 187
Clough, Alexander, 104, 105
Cloyd, Joseph, 140
Cock, William, 140
Cocke, Colin, 37
Cocke, James, 155, 158, 161
Cocke, John Catesby, 175
Cocke, Nathaniel, 52, 110
Coffin, James, 168
Coleman, Samuel, 181
Coleman, Whitehead, 100, 184
Colfax, William, 80
Collier, Thomas, 20, 24
Colston, Samuel, 46
Colville, Andrew, 144
Congress, 162
Connant, Daniel, 166
Conner, Charles, 21
Connolly, John, 140
Constant, John, 132
Conway, Henry, 63, 71
Conway, Richard, 166
Conway, Robert, 158, 166
Cook, David, 132
Cook, Isham, 84
Cooke, James, 139
Cooke, Richard, 22
Cooper, John, 166, 170
Cooper, Leonard, 44, 86
Cooper, Nathaniel, 170
Cormorant, 161
Cornet, 164
Cornstalk (Shawnee chief), 7, 139
Cornwallis, Charles, 183
Coudray, Phillippe Charles Baptiste Trenson de, 126
Count de Grass, 165
Courtney, 165
Cox, John, 165, 170
Cowan, Edward, 139
Cowan, John, 132
Cowherd, Francis, 37, 145
Cowper, John, 151
Craddock, William, 143

Craig, Alexander, 130
Craig, Isaac, 134
Craig, Robert, 144
Crane, John, 99
Craven, Robert, 145
Crawford, John, 147
Crawford, William, 45, 51, 140, 146-147
Crawley, Samuel, 125
Cresap, Daniel, 140
Cresap, Michael, 87
Cresap, Michael, Jr., 140
Cresap, Michael, Sr., 138, 139, 140
Crew, John, 163
Crockett, Hugh, 140
Crockett, Joseph, 47, 52, 66, 110, 120, 129, 133
Crockett, Walter, 140
Croghan, William, 42, 44, 55
Crooks, Thomas, 131
Cropper, John, 13, 51, 53, 59, 64, 173, 175-176, 178
Cross, George, 166, 167
Cross, William, 131
Crump, Abner, 11, 135, 136
Crump, Goodrich, 31
Crute, John, 181
Culbertson, James, 31, 48
Cummins, Alexander, 31
Cunningham, John, 84, 172
Cunningham, Nathaniel, 146
Cunningham, Samuel B., 172
Cunningham, William, 31, 172, 174
Curry, James, 43, 44, 179
Cuthbert, Seth John, 83

D

Dabney, Charles, 19, 24, 35, 110, 112, 113, 123, 127, 135-136, 184
Dabney, James, 19, 24
Daingerfield, William, 51, 104
Dale, Richard, 157
Dale, Thomas, 137
Dandridge, Alexander Spotswood, 99, 102
Dandridge, John, 100
Daniel, Walker, 128
Darke, William, 54, 55, 56
Dasher, 151, 157
Davenport, Obadiah (Opie), 123
David Ross and Company, 168, 170
Davidson, William, 144
Davies, William, 29, 30, 51, 63, 70
Davis, James, 133
Davis, Jesse, 53
Davis, Robert, 139
Davis, Thomas, 9, 59

Index

Dawson, Henry, 120
Dawson, Thomas, 169
Deane, William, 159
Defiance, 163
Denholm, Archibald, 92
Denny, Samuel, 98, 99
Dewit, Robert, 181
Dick, Alexander, 112, 122, 123, 135, 175
Dickenson, John, 141
Dickinson, Edmund B., 29, 31
Dictorn, Joseph, 139
Diener, Jacob, 114
Dietrich, Nicholas (baron von Ottendorff), 93
Digges, Cole, 134
Digges, Edward, 117, 122, 124
Diligence, 157
Dillard, Thomas, 21, 24, 25
Dixon, Anthony Tucker, 123
Dixon, Robert, 20, 24, 25
Dixon, Walter, 85
Doak, Robert, 140
Dolly Henry, 163
Dolphin, 151, 152, 153, 165
Donovan, Matthew, 58, 98
Dorothy, 152
Dorsey, Richard, 100
Dougherty, John, 132
Downing, James, 132
Dragon, 161
Drayton, Stephen, 83
Dreadnaught, 165
Drew, Thomas H., 123
Dryden, Nathaniel, 144
Dubar, Pierre, 115
Dudley, Harry, 112
Dudley, John, 112
Duncanson, James, 112
Dunmore, earl of (John Murray), 7, 8, 19, 20, 140, 149
Dunn, ———, 23
Dunn, Peter, 49
Duval, Daniel, 84
Duval, William, 19
Dysart, James, 144

E

Eagle, 170
Earlwood, James, 169
Eastern Shore, 152
Eastern Shore Betsey, 152
Eddins, Samuel, 100
Edmonds, Elias, 16
Edmondson, William, 140, 143, 144
Edmunds, Elias, 124
Edmunds, Thomas, 34, 41, 66, 72
Edmundson, Robert, Jr., 144
Edmundson, Robert, Sr., 144
Edwards, Leroy, 40, 41, 179
Eggleston, Joseph, 95, 96
Elam, Robert, 163
Elbert, Samuel, 83
Ellegood, Jacob, 114
Elliott, George, 159, 174
Elliott, James, 144
Elliott, Thomas, 17, 41, 48
Eminence, 163, 174
Engilbert, 165
Engs, Madett, 165
Epes, William, 181
Eppes, Francis, 29
Erskine, Charles, 181
Estill, James, 132
Eustace, John, 31
Eustace, John Skey, 85
Evans, Elijah, 77
Evans, Jesse, 129, 130
Evans, John, 130
Ewell, Charles, 111
Ewell, Thomas Winder, 111
Ewing, Alexander, 64
Ewing, James, 139
Experiment, 160

F

Fanny, 153
Faulcon, Nicholas, 21
Faulkner, Ralph, 13, 35, 46
Fauntleroy, Henry, 46
Febiger, Christian, 34, 64, 88, 90-91, 92
Ferguson, Patrick, 143
Ferret, 165
Field, Henry, 16
Field, John, 141
Field, Theophilus, 152
Fields, Benjamin, 130
Fields, Reuben, 44
Fierer, Charles, 124, 127
Fine, Lott, and Company, 165
Finley, Samuel, 33, 42, 44, 65, 77, 87
Finn, Thomas, 100
First Row Galley. See Lewis
Fitzgerald, John, 10, 22, 39
Fitzgerald, John Henry, 41, 51
Fitzhugh, Peregrine, 105
Fitzpatrick, Patrick, 85
Fitzpatrick, Pharaoh, 160
Fleming, Charles, 13, 38, 42, 52, 57
Fleming, John, 31
Fleming, Thomas, 58

Fleming, William, 151
Fleury, François Louis de, 90, 91
Floyd, John, 133, 140
Fly, 152
Fog, William, 24
Fontaine, William, 36, 117, 118
Forsyth, Robert, 95, 134
Fortunatus, 152
Foster, James, 72, 175
Fournier, J. F., 114
Fowey, 158
Fowler, William, 40, 46
Fox, Nathaniel, 49
Fox, Thomas, 50
Franklin, James, 62
Friend, Jonas, 139
Friendship, 165

G

Gaddis, Thomas, 131, 146
Gaines, Daniel, 14
Gale, John, 165
Gallahue, Charles, 65
Gamble, Robert, 58, 68
Game Cock, 165
Gardiner, Christopher, 166
Garland, David, 20
Garland, Edward, 71, 90
Garland, James, 118
Garland, Samuel, 20, 24
Garnett, Henry, 123
Gaskins, Thomas, 28, 38, 42, 44, 45, 91, 184
Gass, David, 131
Gates, Horatio, 88, 117, 142-143
Gatliffe, Charles, 130, 131
George, Jesse, 157, 158
George, Robert, 128, 130
George, William, 65, 77
George Winn and Company, 166
Georges, Jean-Baptiste (chevalier de Fontvieux), 94
Gerault, John, 130
Gibbons, William, 161
Gibbs, Caleb, 80
Gibson, George, 31, 42, 110, 112, 113, 184
Gibson, John, 48, 53, 60, 68, 129, 130, 139, 141
Gilchrist, George, 59
Gill, Samuel, 43
Gillespie, William, 130
Gillison, John, 33, 50, 62, 179
Gilmer, George, 10
Gilmore, James, 145
Gilmore, John, 139

Gilpin, George, 10
Girty, Simon, 141
Gist, John, 75
Gist, Mordecai, 142
Gist, Nathaniel, 73, 74, 75, 76, 177, 179
Glenn, John, 20, 24
Glenn, Robert, 158
Gloucester, 161
Goff, Andrew, 144
Goffigon, Laban, 163
Goldfinger, 166
Goodall, Parke, 11
Goode, Francis, 13
Goosley, George, 154
Goosley, William, 17
Governor Nelson, 166
Granberry, Joseph, 169
Grand Turk, 166
Grant, Peter, 74, 122
Gray, James, 66, 72
Gray, Robert, 155
Gray, William, 103
Grayson, William, 9, 22, 73-74, 110
Greathouse, Daniel, 138
Green, Berryman, 103
Green, John, 17, 29, 30, 50, 62
Greene, Nathanael, 64, 92, 93, 96, 144-145
Greene, William, 163
Greenway, Joseph, 172
Gregory, John, 66, 72
Gregory, William, 17, 49
Greyhound, 155
Griffith(s), David, 22
Griffith, Philemon, 87
Grymes, William, 72
Gunn, James, 93, 103
Guthrie, Alexander, 160
Gwin, David, 145

H

Hall, Daniel, 131
Ham, William, 160
Hambright, Frederick, 143
Hamilton, Henry, 128
Hamilton, John, 161
Hamilton, Thomas, 111, 175
Hamilton and Wootton, 167
Hammer, Nicholas, 121
Hampton, 155
Hancock, George, 84
Hancock, John, 98
Handy, George, 96
Hannah, 166
Hanway, Samuel, 175
Hardyman, John, 161

Index

Harlan, William, 130
Harmanson, John, 169
Harmon, John, 169
Harris, James, 72
Harris, John, 92, 154, 161
Harris, Robert, 169
Harrison, Benjamin, 15, 69, 93, 94, 135, 141
Harrison, Benjamin (of Pennsylvania), 61
Harrison, Benjamin, Jr., 153
Harrison, Charles, 97, 98, 181
Harrison, Cuthbert, 22, 102
Harrison, John Peyton, 36, 37
Harrison, Peyton, 36
Harrison, Richard, 129
Harrison, Robert Hanson, 10
Harrison, Valentine, 37
Harrison, William, 147
Harrison, 160
Harrod, James, 140
Harrod, William, 128, 129, 131, 147
Hart, Nathaniel, 132
Hartley, Thomas, 76
Harvie, John, 118, 168
Harwood, Samuel, 17
Hawes, Samuel, 29, 34, 36, 50, 62
Hawkins, John, 41, 84
Hawkins, Moses, 71
Hayden, Joseph, 119
Haynes, Joseph, 141
Hays, John, 39, 59
Hays, William, 132
Hazard, 166
Hazen, Moses, 82
Hazlerigg, Charles, 132
Healy, Samuel, 157, 163
Heer, Bartholomew von, 80
Helm, Leonard, 128, 129
Helphenstine, Peter, 54
Henderson, Anthony, 121
Henderson, James, 140
Henderson, William, 60, 89
Hendricks, James, 10, 22, 29, 48
Henry, John, 100
Henry, Patrick, 7, 11, 16, 29, 30, 102, 116, 118, 128, 157
Henry, William, 13
Henry, 157
Herbert, Argyle, 156, 158
Herbert, Caleb, 160
Herbert, John, 173
Herbert, Thomas, 154, 173
Herbert, William, 141
Herndon, Edward, 119
Hero, 157, 175

Heron, 174
Heth, Henry, 81, 82
Heth, William, 38, 64, 177, 178, 179, 180
Hicks, Isaac, 85
Higgins, James, 56
Higgins, Robert, 37, 56
Hill, Baylor, 103
Hill, Hardy, 131
Hill, Thomas, 47, 52
Hills, Ebenezer, 86
Hinchman, Lewis, 133
Hindman, William, 169
Hite, Abraham, 57-58, 179
Hite, Matthias, 56
Hoagland, ———, 140
Hoard, Thomas, 51
Hobson, Nicholas, 49
Hoffler, William, 21, 111
Hogan, William, 131
Hogg, Samuel, 34
Holcombe, John, 43
Holder, John, 131
Holland, George, 181
Holland, John, 81
Holland, Richard, 121
Holliday, Hezekiah, 160
Holmer, Christian, 98, 99
Holmes (Hoomes), Benjamin, 36
Holmes, Joseph, 122
Holt, John Hunter, 111
Holt, Thomas, 33, 63, 92, 179
Hooe and Harrison, 172
Hook(e), James, 69
Hooke, S., 171
Hope, 155, 166
Hopewell, 166
Hopkins, John, 139
Hopkins, Samuel, 29, 49, 63, 70, 178, 180
Hopkins, Walter, 17
Hord, John, 95
Hord, Thomas, 181
Hornet, 160, 161. See also *Liberty*
House, Lawrence, 125
Houston, James, 144
Hovenden, Thomas, 85
Howe, Bezaleel, 80
Howe, Robert, 35
Howell, ———, 174
Hoyd, ———, 145
Hudson, John, 113
Hugh Young and Company, 169
Hughes, John, 103
Hughes, Pratt, 136
Hughes, Robert, 146
Hull, Edwin, 66, 72

Humble, Michael, 131
Hunt, Thomas, 33, 179
Hunter, Bowdoin, 166
Hunter, James, 165, 169
Hunter, William, 166
Hunter, 167
Hunter, Banks, and Company, 164, 166, 171, 172
Huston, Nathan, 132
Hutchings, John, 150
Hutchings, Joseph, 21
Hutchings, Thomas, 40, 49
Hynes, Andrew, 133

I

Ida and Ann, 154
Industry, 155
Inglis (Ingles), William, 141
Innes, James, 8, 58, 71, 98, 150
Intrepid, 167
Irvine, James, 146
Irvine, John, 132
Irvine, William, 61
Israel, Isaac, 44, 56
Ivy, William, 163

J

Jacob, ———, 118
James Byrne and Company, 164, 165
James Hunter, John Banks, and Company, 164
James, Michael, 154, 162, 168
James, Richard, 13, 23
Jameson, David, 90
Jameson, John, 16, 101, 102, 103
Jane, 154
Jefferson, Thomas, 121, 137, 173
Jefferson, 153-154, 174
Jeffries, Aaron, 159
Jenkins, Thomas, 24
Jenny, 152
Jeter, Andrew, 85
Joel, B. Edgar, 174
John, 154
John Banks and Company, 167
John Campbell, John Harvie, and Company, 167
John Harmon and Company, 169
John King and Company, 168
Jones, Peter, 32, 64
Johnson, Gideon, 123
Johnson, James, 49, 143
Johnson, Richard, 15
Johnson, Robert, 120, 132
Johnson, Thomas, Jr., 39

Johnson, William, 22, 65
Johnston, George, 16, 36, 45
Johnston, Gideon, 123
Johnston, James, 48
Johnston, John Boswell, 92
Johnston, William, 33, 41, 53, 72, 179
Jolly Tarr, 167
Jones, ———, 181
Jones, Abraham, 84
Jones, Cadwallader, 105
Jones, Charles, 152
Jones, Churchill, 105
Jones, Gabriel, 111, 175
Jones, John, 49
Jones, Lewellin, 13
Jones, Lewis, 154, 158, 163
Jones, Llewellin, 102
Jones, Peters, 32, 64
Jones, Strother, 74, 75
Jones, Thomas, 19
Jones, Thomas, Jr., 114, 126
Jones, Wood, 36
Jordan, John, 37
Joseph Williams and Company, 171
Jouett, Matthew, 52
Jouett, Robert, 181
Joynes, Levin, 59, 67

K

Kalb, Johann, baron de, 142
Kautzman, John V., 157
Kearney, John, 120, 134
Keel, Isaiah, 172
Kellar, Abraham, 129
Kemp, Peter, 125
Kendall, Custis, 32, 33, 48, 60, 179
Kennedy, James, 121, 123
Kennedy, John, 131
Kenton, Simon, 132, 141
Kidd, Joseph, 122
Kilty, John, 105
Kincannon, Andrew, 144
King, Miles, 17
Kinkead, Andrew, 132
Kinkead, Joseph, 132
Kinley, Benjamin, 120, 134
Kirkham, Samuel, 132
Kirkpatrick, Abraham, 34, 44, 56, 91
Kirkwood, Robert H., 107
Kirtley, William, 119
Klaumann, Charles de, 116, 125
Knight, John, 146
Knott, Elvington, 21
Knox, Henry, 99
Knox, James, 55, 59, 89

Index

L

Lacey, William, 143
Lafayette, marquis de, 184
Laird, David, 62, 63
Lallement, Gabriel, 168
Lamb, John, 99
Lambert, George, 71
Lammé, Nathan, 41, 50, 51, 63
Lane, Anna Maria, 127
Lane, Joseph, 85
Lane, William, Jr., 84
Langdon, Jonathan, 68
Lapsley, Samuel, 57, 68, 75
Lark, 163
Lattimer, Edward, 159
Laurens, John, 96
Lauzun, duc le, 183, 184
Lawrence, Nicholas, 169
Lawson, Anthony, 21
Lawson, Benjamin, 91
Lawson, Claiborne, W., 32, 180
Lawson, John, 19
Lawson, Robert, 42, 138, 145, 177, 184
Lee, Charles, 56, 79, 80-81, 98, 102, 114
Lee, Hancock, 140
Lee, Henry, 22, 79, 95-96, 102, 103, 181
Lee, John, 111, 112, 175
Lee, Philip Richard Francis, 9, 39
Lee, Richard, 133
Lee, Richard Henry, 126
Lee, William, 19
Lee, 158, 159
Leet, Daniel, 246
Leftwich, William, 139
Legrace, J. M. P., 128, 130
Leitch, Andrew, 22, 29, 39
Lemon, John, 69
Lewis, Addison, 103
Lewis, Andrew, 7, 91, 98, 139, 141
Lewis, Charles, 10, 14, 24, 70, 117, 118, 141
Lewis, Francis, Jr., 165
Lewis, George, 80, 105
Lewis, James, 124
Lewis, John, 113, 141
Lewis, Nicholas, 14, 24
Lewis, Thomas, 141
Lewis, Warner, 150
Lewis, Warner, Jr., 18
Lewis, William, 31, 32, 39, 63, 164, 173
Lewis, William Terrill, 10
Lewis, 157-158, 174
Lewis, or *First Row Galley*, 157
Liberty, 149, 150, 152, 153, 154, 160, 161, 163, 167. *See also Hornet*

Liebert, Philip, 86
Lightbourne, Henry, 158
Lightbourne, Richard, 160
Lightbourne, Stafford, 157
Lilly, Thomas, 153, 154, 161
Lincoln, Benjamin, 32, 103, 178, 184
Lincoln, 167
Lindsay, William, 95, 134
Lingan, James McCubbin, 77
Linitot, Godfrey, 130
Lipscomb, Reuben, 52
Livingston, Henry Philip, 80
Livingston, Joseph, 82
Lizard, 167
Lloyd, James, 134
Lochry, Archibald, 129, 130
Lockridge, Andrew, 141
Long, Alexander, 14, 139
Long, Gabriel, 53, 65, 89
Long, William, 113
Looney, David, 140
Lord Howe, 162
Love, Philip, 113, 141
Lovely, William Lewis, 44, 91
Loving, ———, 120
Lowe, Philip, 85
Lowther, William, 139
Loyalist, 161
Loyall, Paul, 151
Loyeauté, St. François A. M. D. de, 114, 125-126
Lucas, James, 39, 43, 178
Lucas, Nathaniel, 43
Lurty, John, 154, 158, 161, 162, 175
Lynch, Charles, 21, 145
Lyne, George, 18, 58, 68
Lynn, William, 127
Lyon, Humbertson, 144

M

Mabin (Maybone), James, 37
McAdams, John, 46
McAfee, Robert, 140
McAfee, Samuel, 132
McAfee, William, 131
McBride, William, 132
McCabe, John, 165
McCarty, Richard, 128, 129
McClanachan (McClenachan), Alexander, 51, 141
McClanachan, William, 16, 141
McClelland, John, 146
McClenachan, Robert, 141
McClure, John, 167
McClure, William, 133

McConnell, William, 132
McCormick, George, 69
McCracken, William, 130
McCullough, Thomas, 144
McDonald, Angus, 75, 140
McDonnal, Francis, 132
McDowell, Charles, 143
McDowell, Samuel, 141
McElhaney, John, 113
McFarland, Moses, 86
McFarlin, Daniel, 131
McGary, Hugh, 128
McGillivray, Alexander, 93
McGowan, John, 86
McGuire, James, 74
McGuire, John, 74
McGuire, William, 181
McHatton, William, 86
McIlhaney, James, 63
McIntosh, John, 85
McKay, John, 19, 186
McKee, Alexander, 186
McKee, William, 23, 67, 81, 142
McKenny, James, 85
McLane, Allen, 95
McMurtry, John, 133
McNally, Thomas, 164
McWilliams, William, 39
Madison, Ambrose, 118, 119
Madison, Gabriel, 132, 175
Madison, Rowland, 68
Magaw, Robert, 87
Magill, Charles, 122, 142
Mallory, Philip, 33, 66, 179
Manley, John, 158
Manley, 158
Mann, David, 123, 136
Markham, James, 158
Markham, John, 13, 30, 35, 54, 161, 162, 173
Markle, Charles, 94
Marks, Isaiah, 37, 53, 181
Marks, John, 10
Marquis la Fayette, 167
Mars, 174
Marshall, Humphrey, 125
Marshall, John, 16, 53, 72
Marshall, Thomas, 10, 16, 38, 40, 109, 124, 125, 149
Marshall, Thomas, Jr., 125
Martin, John, 10, 132
Martin, Thomas, 48
Martin, Thomas, Jr., 10
Mason, David, 22, 66, 71
Mason, James, 23, 24, 72

Mason, Nathaniel, 43
Mason, William, 22
Massie, Thomas, 17, 35, 49, 64
Mathews, George, 14, 58, 114, 141
Mathews, Richard, 18
Mathews, Thomas, 21, 43, 123, 124, 164
Mattaponi, 158
Maxwell, James, 150, 151, 161, 173
Mayflower, 160
Mazarett, John, 124, 125
Meade, Everard, 36, 134
Meade, Richard Kidder, 36, 70
Mercer, Hugh, 8, 9, 15, 38
Mercer, Isaac, 152
Mercer, John Francis, 15, 40, 116
Mercier, John, 169
Meredith, Joseph, 167
Meredith, Samuel, 11
Meredith, William, 24, 100, 181
Meriwether, James, 131
Meriwether, Nicholas, 121
Meriwether, Thomas, 110, 111, 175
Michaux, Joseph, 71
Middleton, William, 19
Millen, John, 120
Miller, David, 41
Miller, Elisha, 84
Miller, Robert, 120, 156
Miller, Thomas, 181
Miller, William, 23
Minnis, Callohill, 31, 32, 54, 179
Minnis, Francis, 92, 181
Minnis, Holman, 32, 33, 54, 179
Minor, Garrett, 19
Minor, Peter, 46
Minor, Thomas, 15, 112, 143
Minor, Vivion, 15, 25
Minter, John, 147
Mitchell, Joseph, 68
Mitchell, Nathaniel, 74, 75
Mitchell, Robert, 174
Mitchell, William, 175
Moëballé, Nicholas George, 122, 124
Moffatt, George, 139
Molly, 159
Monroe, James, 39, 76-77, 109, 116-117
Montgomery, John, 128, 129
Montgomery, Thomas, 130
Moody, Edward, 124
Moody, James, 113
Moore, Charles, 14
Moore, Cleon, 74
Moore, Francis, 83, 84
Moore, Peter, 134
Moore, Thomas, 61, 69, 132

Index

Moore, William, 169
Morgan, Daniel, 53, 64, 77, 87, 88-89, 90, 140, 145
Morgan, Haynes, 24, 110
Morgan, Simon, 54, 56, 61, 69
Morgan, Zachquill, 131
Morningstar, 167-168, 174
Morris, Joseph, 88
Morris, Nathaniel G., 60
Morrison, John, 84
Morton, Edward, 159
Morton, Hezekiah, 58
Morton, James, 181
Morton, John, 43
Mosby, John, 84
Mosby, Littleberry, 13, 84
Mosby, William, 46
Moseley, Hillary, 168
Moseley, William, 33, 47, 52, 179
Mosquito, 154
Moss, Henry, 37
Moss, John, 31
Mossom, David, 125
Mountjoy, John, 15, 25, 63
Moylan, Stephen, 106-107, 183
Muhlenburg, John Peter Gabriel, 54-56, 76
Muir, Francis, 75, 179
Murdagh, James, 21
Murray, Alexander, 169
Murray, John. *See* Dunmore, earl of
Murray, William, 99
Muter, George, 122, 124, 125, 157
Myer, Christopher, 44

N

Nalle, William, 139
Nancy, 168
Napier, Pat[rick], 10
Nash, James, 160
Nash, John, 159
Neal, James, 61, 69
Neal, William, 144
Nelson, Hugh, 17
Nelson, James, 165
Nelson, John, 47, 51, 52, 102, 109, 124, 126-127
Nelson, Thomas, 161
Nelson, Thomas, Jr., 31
Nelson, William, 19, 51, 54
Nestor, 168
Neville, James, 67
Neville, John, 42, 44, 54, 81, 179
Neville, Presley, 57
Newell, James, 141
Newell, Samuel, 144

Newton, Thomas, Jr., 150, 151
Nicholas, ———, 17
Nicholas, George, 36, 62, 64
Nicholas, John, 111, 134
Nicholas Low, Job Peay, and Company, 170
Nicholson, George, 168
Nicholson, Henry, 8
Nicholson, Thomas, 146
Nicholson, 152
Nicola, Lewis, 86
Nixon, Andrew, 103
Noble, 154
Noel, Edward, 169
Noel, Thomas, 169
Non-Pareil, 168
Norfolk Revenge, 158
Northampton, 154-155

O

O'Hara, James, 81, 82
Oldham, Conway, 58
Oldham, William, 131
Oliver, Drury, 71
Oliver, 163
Oliver Cromwell, 161
Olivia, Lawrence, 82
O'Neal, Ferdinand, 96
Orr, Robert, 130
Osborne, Thomas, 171
Otter, 168
Overstreet, ———, 146
Overton, John, 24, 32, 64, 70, 91, 92
Owens, George, 131
Oxford, 25, 152, 153, 162

P

Page, Carter, 105
Page, or *Second Row Galley*, 158
Pamplin, Richard, 118
Pankey, Stephen, 145
Pannill, Joseph, 83, 85
Parker, Alexander, 36, 37, 38, 91, 179, 183, 184
Parker, Josiah, 21, 45, 166, 167, 171
Parker, Nathaniel, 166, 167
Parker, Peter, 55
Parker, Richard, 29, 35, 36, 48, 157, 178, 180
Parker, Thomas, 34, 38, 48, 60, 176
Parker, William, 162
Parker, William Harwar, 162
Parr, James, 89
Parramore, Thomas, 59
Parrish, Humphrey, 120
Parsons, James, 141

Parsons, William, 105
Pasteur, James, 170
Pasteur, John, 159
Patriot, 152-153, 162
Patterson, Robert, 131, 132
Patterson, Thomas, 14, 49
Patton, Henry, 140
Patton, James, 133
Patty, 168
Paty, Bernard, 85
Paul(lin), William, 141
Paulling, Henry, 139
Payne, Merryman, 159, 162
Payne, Tarleton, 31, 32, 54, 179
Payne, Thomas, 61
Payne, William, 16, 111
Peace and Plenty, 160
Peachey, William, 19, 45
Pearson, Thomas, 181
Peay, Job, 170
Peers, Valentine, 175
Peggy, 168, 169
Pelham, Charles, 31, 32, 35, 53
Pelham, Peter, 24
Pemberton, Thomas, 103
Pendleton, Edmund, 9
Pendleton, James, 100
Pendleton, Nathaniel, 33, 41, 65
Penn, Abraham, 14, 24
Penn, Gabriel, 14, 24
Penn, William, 102
Pennell, David, 125
Perkins, Peter, 21, 24, 25
Perrault, Michael, 130
Perry, William, 169
Perseverance, 169
Peter Lafargue, Michie, and Company, 168
Pettot, Benjamin, 132
Pettus, John, 99
Pettus, Thomas, 121
Peyton, Francis, 22
Peyton, Henry, 95, 181
Peyton, John, 40
Peyton, Sir John, 169
Peyton, Thomas, 18
Peyton, Valentine, 40, 41, 44
Phillips, William, 119, 121, 173
Phoenix, 155
Pickett, William, 16
Pierre, Guillaume, 125
Pierce, William, 100
Pierce, William L., Jr., 99
Pilgrim, 169
Pleak, John, 132
Pleasants, John, 18, 45

Pocahontas, 172
Pollard, Benjamin, 157, 175
Pollard, Thomas, 125, 158
Polly, 83
Polk, Charles, 131, 132
Port, Griffin, 124
Porte, Decrome de la, 115-116, 125, 126
Porter, Benjamin, 83, 84
Porter, Thomas, 119, 121
Porter, William, 181
Porterfield, Charles, 53, 65, 66, 88, 122, 123-124, 127, 142, 177
Porterfield, Robert, 37, 53
Portland, 154
Posey, Thomas, 30, 33, 35, 53, 89, 91, 92-93, 141
Poulson, John, 57, 59, 91, 184
Powell, Levin, 22, 74
Powell, Robert, Sr., 40
Prather, Henry, 131
Price, ———, 143
Price, John, 143
Price, Thomas, 87
Proby, James, 169
Prosperity, 169
Protector, 158, 169, 173, 176
Purvis, James, 119
Pyeatt, John, 130

Q

Quarles, Harry, 124
Quarles, James, 112
Quarles, John, 18, 22, 112
Quarles, Thomas, 113
Quirk, Thomas, 127, 129

R

Rae, Robert, 85
Ragsdale, Drury, 18, 100
Rakestraw, Robert, 24
Raleigh, 155
Ralls, George, 152
Ramsey, William, 10
Randolph, Peter, 134
Randolph, Thomas, 13
Randolph, William, 13
Ransdell, Thomas, 41, 53
Rastel, Philippe de (sieur de Rocheblave), 128
Rattlesnake, 172
Ravenscroft, Thomas, 130
Rawlings, Moses, 65, 73, 77-78, 86, 87, 88, 117
Read, Edmund, 121, 127
Read, Isaac, 29, 42

Index

Read, William, 171
Reeves, George, 23, 24
Reid, James R., 82
Reid, John K., 24
Reid, Nathan, 32, 33, 63, 71, 92
Renown, 173
Revenge, 158, 169
Rice, Frederick William, 94
Rice, George, 65, 119
Rice, Holman, 119
Richards, William, 18, 162
Richardson, Samuel, 119
Richardson, Turner, 124
Richardson, 169
Richeson, Holt, 46, 51, 71, 177
Richmond, 170, 173
Riddick, Jason, 43, 44
Ridley, Thomas, 180
Ridley, William, 23
Riedesel, Baron, 119
Riedesel, Baroness, 119
Riely, John, 86
Rising States, 170
Roane, Christopher, 125, 136
Roane, William, 164
Roberts, Benjamin, 129, 130
Roberts, Cyrus L., 71
Roberts, Daniel, 83, 85
Roberts, James, 144
Roberts, John, 117, 118, 119
Robertson, James, 141, 165
Robertson, Tully, 113
Robinson, John, 82
Robinson, William, 21, 140
Rochambeau, Donatien Marie Joseph de Vimeur, viscount de, 183
Rochester, 155, 160
Rogers, George, 154
Rogers, James, 133
Rogers, John, 128, 130, 131, 155
Rogers, William, 43, 48
Rose, Alexander, 50
Rose, John. *See* Rosenthal, Gustavus Henri, baron de
Rosenthal, Gustavus Henri, baron de, 146
Ross, David, 74, 161, 162
Ross, 170
Rucker, Angus, 111
Ruddell, Isaac, 129
Rudder, Epaphroditus, 24
Rudolph, Michael, 96
Ruffin, John, 22, 23
Ruffin, Thomas, 49
Russell, Andrew, 46
Russell, Thomas, 169
Russell, William, 32, 46, 68, 141, 179
Russell, William, Jr., 144
Rust, Benjamin, 152

S

Safeguard, 159, 174
St. Clair, Arthur, 92
Saint Patrick, 170
Sale, John, 118
Sally Norton, 170
Samuels, James, 133
Sanders, ———, 170
"Sanders' Cruizer," 170
Sanford, John, 170
Sanford, William, 36
Saunders, Celey, 157, 162, 174
Saunders, William, 158, 160, 162
Sansum, Philip, 34
Saucy Jack, 170
Sayres, John, 18, 30, 42, 58
Sayres, Robert, 47, 52
Schaffner, George, 94
Schermerhorn, Cornelius, 166
Schuyler, Philip, 98
Sclater, William Sheldon, 17
Scorpion, 163
Scott, Charles, 35, 45, 74, 177, 178, 180
Scott, David, 69
Scott, George, 76
Scott, James, 16
Scott, Joseph, 99
Scott, Joseph, Jr., 92
Scott, Joseph, Sr., 31, 32, 48
Scott, Samuel, 84, 132
Scott, Thomas, 85
Scott, Thomas, Jr., 84
Scott, William, 76, 85
Screven, James, 85
Scruggs, Gross, 46
Seabrook, Nicholas Brown, 166
Second Row Galley, or *Page. See Page*
Selin, Anthony, 82
Senf, John Christian, 114, 142
Serjeant, William Hill, 168
Servant, Richard, 152
Sevier, John, 143
Shannon, Samuel, 131
Shannon, William, 129
Sharp, John, 94
Shelby, Evan, 24, 141
Shelby, James, 129
Shelby, Isaac, 143
Sheldon, Elisha, 104
Shelton, ———, 118
Shelton, Clough, 33, 50, 51, 63, 91, 179

Shepherd, Abraham, 53, 65, 77, 87
Shepherd, Solomon, 21
Sherwin, Samuel, 13, 24
Shields, John, 111, 175
Shore, 163
Sigonnier, Louis de, 94
Simms, Charles, 35, 48, 67, 141
Simpson, Michael, 89
Simpson, Southey, 12
Sinclair, John, 152
Sincola, 171
Singleton, Anthony, 100
Singleton, Joshua, 157, 161
Skeggs, Henry, 140
Skinner, William, 162
Slate, James, 20
Slaughter, ———, 142
Slaughter, George, 55, 67, 90, 128, 133
Slaughter, James, 16
Slaughter, John, 16
Slaughter, Philip, 53, 65, 89
Slaughter, Robert, 40
Slover, John, 146
Smallwood, Hebard, 74
Smith, Alexander Lawson, 65, 77, 87
Smith, Arthur, 43
Smith, David, 140
Smith, Elisha, 168
Smith, Granville, 74
Smith, Gregory, 18, 52, 113
Smith, James, 139, 166
Smith, John, 122, 132, 145
Smith, Joseph, 75, 91
Smith, Matthew, 99
Smith, Samuel, 66, 72
Smith, William, 28, 65
Snead, Charles, 48, 57
Snead, Smith, 38, 60, 175
Snead, Thomas, 59, 64
Snead, William, 176
Snickers, S. William, 76
Snoddy, John, 132
South, John, 132, 135
Southall, Turner, 17
Speake, James (Joseph), 152
Speake, Joseph, 159
Speedwell, 160, 161, 163
Spencer, Joseph, 16
Spencer, William, 58
Spiller, Benjamin C., 112
Spiller, William, 125
Spotswood, Alexander, 8, 9, 34, 35, 90, 110, 134, 135
Spotswood, John, 50, 51, 62
Springer, Uriah, 54, 61, 69, 130

Sprowle, Andrew, 151
Stadler, John, 114
Starr, James, 169
Stedman, John, 142
Steed, John, 44, 56, 91
Steele, David, 69
Steele, William, 162
Stephen, Adam, 41, 42, 140
Stephen Lacosté, Brumfield, and Company, 168
Stephenson, Daniel, 14
Stephenson, David, 30, 33, 45, 50, 55, 66, 179
Stephenson, Hugh, 86-88
Steuben, Friedrich Wilhelm Ludolf Gerhard Augustin, baron von, 5-6, 86, 92, 126
Stevens, ———, 13
Stevens, Edward, 16, 61, 89, 142, 145, 177
Stevens, John, 157
Stevens, Richard, 18, 50, 62
Stevenson, John, 55
Stevenson, Thomas, 130
Stevenson, William, 181
Stewart, John, 141
Stewart, Ralph, 139
Stirk, John, 83, 85
Stirling, Lord, 77
Stith, John, 34, 37, 43, 44, 179
Stockdale, Alexander, 165
Stockley, Thomas, 131
Stokes, John, 37, 50, 180
Stratton, Henry, 155, 168
Street, Joseph, 120
Stribling, Sigismund, 58
Strother, John, 119
Strother, William D., 184
Sturdivant, Joel, 155, 158
Stubblefield, Beverley, 37
Stubblefield, George, 15, 45, 70
Sullivan, ———, 145
Sullivan, James, 69
Susannah, 163
Sutherland, Fendall, 158
Swallow, Thomas, 157
Swan, John, 101, 104, 106, 131
Swearingen, Joseph, 57, 58
Swearingen, Van, 76, 89
Swift, The, 171
Symmes, John (Jonathan), 62, 63

T

Tabb, Augustine, 112
Tabb, William, 19
Taliaferro, Benjamin, 37, 89, 179

Index

Taliaferro, Francis, 15, 25
Taliaferro, John, 15, 25, 36
Taliaferro, Lawrence, 16
Taliaferro, Philip, 18, 36
Taliaferro, William, 16, 18, 36, 38, 42
Taming, 171
Tannehill, Adamson, 77
Tarleton, Banastre, 66, 180
Tartar, 162, 171
Tate, James, 145
Tate, Nathaniel, 143
Taylor, Francis, 36, 72, 117, 118, 121
Taylor, Henry, 23
Taylor, Isaac, 129
Taylor, John, 15, 19, 22, 31, 82, 134
Taylor, Reuben, 82
Taylor, Richard, 31, 35, 60, 68, 160, 162
Taylor, William, 36, 37, 60
Teabaugh, ———, 140
Teackle, Severn, 48
Tebbs, Thomas, 36
Temple, Benjamin, 18, 101, 102, 103
Tempest, 162, 173
Ternant, Jean Baptiste, 93
Terrill, Henry, 46
Terry, Nathaniel, 63, 92
Thackston, Benjamin, 24
Thetis, 162
Thomas, ———, 174
Thomas, John, 158
Thomas, Lewis, 54
Thomas, Mark, 130
Thomas, William, 171
Thomas Shore, McConnico, and Company, 164
Thompson, James, 140
Thompson, Laurence, 132
Thompson, Roger, 14, 25
Thompson, William, 125, 164
Thornton, John, 39, 40, 74, 75
Thornton, Peter Presley, 19, 105
Thoroughgood, 171
Three Friends, 166
Throckmorton, Mordecai, 18
Thurston, Charles Mynn, 75-77
Thruston, John, 18, 76, 131
Thurmond, Philip, 120
Thweatt, Thomas, 71, 92
Timberlake, Benjamin, 118, 119, 120
Timson, Samuel, 125
Tipton, Abraham, 120, 134
Todd, Levi, 128
Todd, Robert, 129
Tomkies, Charles, 52
Tompkins, Christopher, 157

Tompkins, Robert, 157
Torrey, Joseph, 82
Towles, Oliver, 15, 33, 48, 49
Towles, Samuel, 159
Towles, Thomas, 15
Travis, Champion, 17, 150
Travis, Edward, 155
Trenson, ——— de, 94
Trigg, John, 125
Trigg, William, 139
Triplett, Francis, 16, 145
Triplett, Simon, 22
Triplett, Thomas, 74
Trippe, Levin, 171
Tuffin, Charles Armand (marquis de la Rouerie), 79, 93-95, 181, 183
Turberville, George Lee, 72
Turn of the Times, 171
Turner, James, 20, 24
Turner, Philip, 167
Turpin, William, 13
Two Brothers, 171
Tyler, John, 17

U

Underhill, William, 156
Unger, Louis de, 119
Upshaw, James, 36
Upshaw, Thomas, 122

V

Valentine, Edward, 125
Valentine, Jacob, 111, 113, 154
Vanbeaver, John, 139
Vance, Robert, 54, 61, 69, 130
Vanmeter, Jacob, 133
Vartreese, John, 133
Vaudore, chevalier de, 94
Vaughan, John, 123
Vause, William, 57, 68
Venus, 172
Victory, 173
Virginia, 162, 163, 172
Vogluson, Martin Armand, 127, 136
Vowles, Walter, 15, 25

W

Waggener, Andrew, 67
Waggoner, Andrew, 57, 63
Walker, Edward, 23
Walker, Jacob, 100
Walker, John, 17
Walker, Thomas, 59, 166
Walker, Thomas Reynolds, 21
Wallace, Adam, 47, 52, 180

Wallace, Andrew, 57, 68, 180
Wallace, Gustavus Brown, 35, 39, 66, 71, 178, 180
Wallace, William B., 181
Waller, Edmund, 122
Walley, Zedekiah, 176
Walls, George, 43, 129, 133
Walton, Jesse Hughes, 84
Walton, Robert, 84
Ward, James, 141
Ward, Robert, 84
Ware, John, 14
Waring, Henry, 47
Warman, Thomas, 41, 77, 91
Warnecke, Frederick, 114
Washington, Charles, 15
Washington, George, 4, 7, 9, 10, 11, 27, 39, 77, 80, 93, 105, 183
Washington, John, 21, 43
Washington, William, 39, 40, 104, 105, 181
Washington, William Augustine, 19
Washington, 153, 159, 162
Waters, William, 99
Watkins, John, Jr., 43
Watlington, John, 125
Watson, Johannes, 157
Watts, John, 103
Watts, William, 103
Waugh, Richard, 90
Wayne, Anthony, 90, 91, 184
Webb, ———, 167
Webb, George, 150
Webb, Isaac, 48
Webb, John, 46, 47, 51
Weedon, George, 8, 9, 38, 62, 126, 184
Welch, Nathaniel, 113
Wells, John S., 166
Wells, Thomas, 66
West, Charles, 22, 39, 177
West, Thomas, 50, 62, 65, 87
Westcott, Wright, 157, 158, 163, 174
Westfall, Abel, 55
Whitaker, Aquilla, 133
White, Anthony Walton, 101, 103
White, John, 85
White, Richard P., 119
White, Robert, 121
White, Tarpley, 47, 181
White, William, 47, 58
Whiting, Thomas, 150
Wilkes, 172, 174
Willett, John, 168
William Pennock and Company, 169
Williams, James, 50, 143
Williams, John, 16, 125, 128, 129, 160
Williams, Otho Holland, 86

Williams, Thomas, 172, 174
Williams, William, 86
Williamson, David, 146, 147
Williamson, George, 145
Willing Lass, 172, 174
Willis, Francis, 74
Willis, John, 8, 9, 36, 47, 74
Willis, Lewis, 15, 62
Willis, Thomas, 72
Willis, Cowper, and Company, 167, 172
Willoughby, William, 144
Wills, F. W., 10
Wills, Willis, 21
Wilson, George, 133
Wilson, John, 139
Wilson, Samuel, 141
Wilson, Willis, 154, 157, 174, 181
Winfrey, J., 84
Winfrey, John, 24
Winn, James, 145
Winston, John, 19, 24, 32, 64, 71
Winston, Joseph, 143
Woelper, John D., 86
Wolf, 172
Woneycutt, Edward, 155, 160, 161, 174
Wood, James, 29, 33, 34, 57, 67, 117, 119, 121
Wood, John, 132
Wood, William, 10
Wooder, W., 171
Woodford, William, 9, 15, 30, 32, 34, 36, 37, 39, 41, 47, 179
Woodrup, David, 118
Woodson, Frederick, 111, 136
Woodson, Hughes, 50
Woodson, Robert, 34, 47, 48, 180
Woodson, Samuel, 59
Woodson, Tarleton, 62, 63, 82
Wootton, William, 167
Worthington, Edward, 128, 130
Wright, ———, 21
Wright, James, 33, 41, 53, 179
Wright, Patrick, 125
Wynn, John, 145

Y

Yancey, Robert, 181
York, 172, 173
Young, Henry, 33, 47, 48, 52
Young, John, 153, 155, 167
Young, Thomas, 120, 134
Younghusband, Isaac, 154

Z

Zane, Jonathan, 146
Zane, Silas, 69